Reinventing the IT Department

Reinventing the IT Department

Terry White

OXFORD AUCKLAND BOSTON JOHANNESBURG MELBOURNE NEW DELHI

Butterworth-Heinemann
Linacre House, Jordan Hill, Oxford OX2 8DP
225 Wildwood Avenue, Woburn, MA 01801–2041
A division of Reed Educational and Professional Publishing Ltd

A member of the Reed Elsevier plc group

First published 2001

British Library Cataloguing in Publication Data
A catalogue record for this book is available from the British Library

ISBN 0 7506 48627

FOR EVERY TITLE THAT WE PUBLISH, BUTTERWORTH-HEINEMANN
WILL PAY FOR BTCV TO PLANT AND CARE FOR A TREE.

Composition by Genesis Typesetting, Rochester, Kent
Printed and bound in Great Britain

Contents

Computer Weekly **Professional Series**   **xi**

Preface   **xiii**

Acknowledgements   **xvii**

1   Introduction – days of wine and roses   **1**

1.1 Mirror, mirror ... 'outside' perceptions of the in-house IT
     function   1
1.2 What is an in-house IT function?   3
1.3 Research   3
1.4 Inside perceptions of IT   4
1.5 On all sides – threats to the in-house function   14
1.6 If it's so bad why bother? – do companies need an in-house
     function?   30
1.7 No way back – why 'back to basics' cannot work   33
1.8 Seeds of the new IT – a new mindset   37

**2   I'm glad the hole is at their end of the boat –
     business in the new world**   **47**

2.1 Introduction   47
2.2 Unguided missiles – the future world economy   48
2.3 New reasons to exist – the changing role of business   53
2.4 Technology   60
2.5 People   76

3   Radicals and revolutions – anarchists in our midst   95

3.1   The revolution within a revolution   95
3.2   Complex adaptive systems   98

4   Stop the revolution – IT wants to get on board   107

4.1   Do we even understand the information revolution?   107
4.2   The business 'Bill of IT Rights'   110
4.3   Bill of Responsibilities   113
4.4   Ask the winners – successful new approaches to business   113

5   Play up, play up, and play the game   127

5.1   Before you play, find out which game you're playing   127
5.2   What does IT do – really?   128
5.3   Four-leafed clovers – lucky for some, but luck favours the astute   145

6   If we're so clever, why can't we think? – new way of thinking for IT   151

6.1   If you find yourself in a hole, it's probably a good idea to stop digging   152
6.2   Five ways to be wrong and four ways to be right   155
6.3   Active and passive thinking styles – the road to responsibility   163
6.4   Thinking and the new IT mindset   165
6.5   Thinking about IT – some ideas to play with   167
6.6   Why not? – Thinking like a renegade   174

7 The soft stuff is hard – the new business/IT relationship   177

7.1 Organisational relationships   178
7.2 Partnerships   181
7.3 Why there's no such thing as an internal customer   185
7.4 People as partners – a fundamental mindset shift   191
7.5 The new IT relationship   193

8 Building on quicksand? – the IT cornerstone – architecture   201

8.1 What is an architecture? – a non-technical position   203
8.2 Why architect?   206
8.3 Objectives of architecting   207
8.4 Managing IT architecture processes   210
8.5 Communicating your architecture   212

9 The 'Canute' effect – bringing new technologies in   221

9.1 Dealing with undercover technologies   224
9.2 A new technologies integration process   224
9.3 Last words on implementing new technologies   233

10 Rules about rules – standards, methods, tools   237

10.1 What is a standard?   238
10.2 Setting, applying and monitoring standards   242
10.3 Perspectives on standards   243
10.4 Trade-offs and education   247

11 Running the race – providing business solutions from IT 251

11.1 Delivery of solutions and outcomes 252
11.2 Intersecting with the business 'bill of rights' 254
11.3 The Russians are coming – the new solution providers 257
11.4 No projects 260
11.5 Providing solutions when the goal-posts keep changing 263
11.6 No development methodology 265

12 The home fires – core production 267

12.1 The core IT production domain 269
12.2 No Service Level Agreements – internally we work together 278
12.3 Intentional tension – driving core-production 282
12.4 Running the CIP factory 283
12.5 In-house or out-house? 288
12.6 Creating a self-organising core IT production facility 292

13 Thinking ahead – new strategy processes 297

13.1 Information management scenarios 299
13.2 Compiling the IT strategy 302
13.3 Strategy as a complex adaptive system 307
13.4 Implementation 308

14 The new IT people 313

14.1 The new psychological contract 314
14.2 What motivates IT people 316
14.3 Remunerating IT people 318

14.4 Treating employees as people   322
14.5 The job of managers   325
14.6 The hourglass organisation   326
14.7 Work in IT   330
14.8 Self-managed teams   332

15 Last round please – final observations   343

15.1 There is another way of doing this   343
15.2 So you want to be on the board?   343
15.3 Complex adaptive systems and IT   345
15.4 The business bill of rights and the new IT function 347
15.5 Endroduction   350

Index   351

Computer Weekly **Professional Series**

There are few professions which require as much continuous updating as that of the IS executive. Not only does the hardware and software scene change relentlessly, but also ideas about the actual management of the IS function are being continuously modified, updated and changed. Thus keeping abreast of what is going on is really a major task.

The Butterworth-Heinemann/*Computer Weekly* Professional Series has been created to assist IS executives keep up-to-date with the management ideas and issues of which they need to be aware.

One of the key objectives of the series is to reduce the time it takes for leading edge management ideas to move from academic and consulting environments into the hands of the IT practitioner. Thus this series employs appropriate technology to speed up the publishing process. Where appropriate some books are supported by CD-ROM or by additional information or templates located on the Web.

This series provides IT professionals with an opportunity to build up a bookcase of easily accessible but detailed information on the important issues that they need to be aware of to successfully perform their jobs as they move into the new millennium.

Aspiring or already established authors are invited to get in touch with me if they would like to be published in this series.

Dr Dan Remenyi, Series Editor
Dan.remenyi@mcil.co.uk

Series Editor

Dan Remenyi, MCIL

Advisory Board

Frank Bannister, Trinity College Dublin
Ross Bentley, Management Editor, *Computer Weekly*
Egon Berghout, Technical University of Delft
Ann Brown, City University Business School
Roger Clark, The Australian National University
Reet Cronk, University of Southern Queensland
Arthur Money, Henley Management College
Sue Nugus, MCIL
David Taylor, CERTUS
Terry White, Bentley West, Johannesburg

Other titles in the Series

IT investment – Making a business case
The effective measurement and management of IT costs and benefits
Stop IT project failures through risk management
Understanding the Internet
Prince 2: A practical handbook
Considering computer contracting?
David Taylor's Inside Track
A hacker's guide to project mangement
Corporate politics for IT managers: how to get streetwise
Subnet design for efficient networks
Information warfare: corporate attack and defence in a digital world

Preface

I wrote this book to challenge. I challenge the accepted ideas about information technology (IT) functions.

I ask whether there should be methodologies, projects, standards, service level agreements and IT strategies. I ask these questions because although we've had these IT tools for years, even decades, they seem not to be doing anything for in-house information technology functions. I challenge why there is so little architecture, relationship building and user-friendly communications in IT.

I wonder why IT people are so separate from the business? If fault is to be found it must be with the IT function itself. Why do we believe our job is 'development and support' when business people see this as the ground floor of IT's relationship with them?

This is not a text book – if you want completeness you aren't going to get it. I have tried to approach in-house IT from a management perspective, and from a business perspective. I can't tell you how to develop systems, run applications, and design architectures but I can offer pointers on how to manage this environment.

This book represents my opinions. In the chapter on 'Thinking in IT' I ask why ideas are so threatening to people. If your opinions differ from mine, that is good, because this is your chance to test ideas and think things through. But the book is scattered with challenges to convention, and I hope you won't disregard these opinions without giving them due thought.

Over the years I have developed a number of models and ideas which I offer to you now. I have based many of these models on sound research, but equally many of these models just feel right to me – you won't find scientific proofs. But if they feel right to you, please use them – they are just ideas after all. One early reader of the manuscript felt that things didn't flow in the book as well as they could. For instance, I put the chapter on strategy near the end. This is because of a deep-seated belief that life doesn't flow as well as it could. Life and your job are chaotic, and while I have worked hard to build a progressive flow into the book, I may not always have succeeded. The first six chapters of the book deal with the world and IT's relationship to it. Then we get into detail where each subsequent chapter tackles a subject specific to IT.

In the book I bemoan the fact that the business is 'them' and IT is 'us' and vice versa. I then spend chapters talking about the business with a 'them' view, and talk about IT in 'us' and 'we' terms. This apparent division between 'us' and 'them' is there to illustrate a point. I really believe that there is no divide between the parties: IT merely approaches business from an IT perspective.

Some of the ideas I promote seem to contradict each other. That's because some of the ideas I have, do contradict each other. That is the nature of paradox. But all of these ideas mesh well with my world-view. I believe that business is complex and chaotic, and filled with contradictions and paradoxes. If ideas contradict each other, simply choose the one that suits the circumstances, and don't become too obsessed with the right-ness and wrongness of the idea. If it works, use it.

I use the term 'CIO' throughout the text to describe the Chief Information Officer, as well as the IT Manager, Director or whatever the head of the in-house IT function is called. 'CIO' does not imply a member of the executive or board, merely the head of IT.

This book is primarily written for IT people, but business people should be able to get significant benefits from the ideas presented here. They can be applied with little or no modification to the wider world of business. Please feel free to do so.

Finally, I have enjoyed writing the book. It constantly presented me with challenges. I hope it does the same for you.

Terry White
TWReinvent@netscape.net

Acknowledgements

Thank you, book. You taught me about challenge, patience, completeness, and systems. At four in the morning you were there for me (alas). But through all the difficulties we faced, you remained my friend.

Thanks to Prof. Dan Remenyi, who cajoled me into putting my ideas down. His final threat: 'If you don't write the book, I will!' galvanised me into action.

Thanks to Les Crickmay, my architect of years gone by. Many of the ideas in this book are his through osmosis. Les kindly let me use his ideas without thought for recognition or reward.

Thanks to Nicki Kear of Butterworth-Heinneman. She was there at the end of the e-mail line to answer questions and help me in the task of constructing a book.

Finally, more than thanks – love – to my wife Sue, whose quiet confidence in me often surpassed my own confidence in myself.

$\boxed{1}$ Introduction – days of wine and roses

1.1 Mirror, mirror . . .'outside' perceptions of the in-house IT function

> There is a danger that far from being the leader in the transformation process, the IT function runs the risk of becoming an inhibitor to change and therefore irrelevant.
>
> (Ralph, 1990)

I'm driving back from a very successful workshop, in which I have helped a large bank refocus itself on the customer, and set a vision for their future service. This will revolutionise their bank/customer relationship. They are planning Internet access to any banking service, internet café's in bank branches, an Intranet which is directed solely at customer and sales support, data-mining operations aimed at life-long customer service, smart cards and more! There is one dark cloud, however: the bank doesn't think their in-house IT function is up to it. Oh sure, they might be able to handle the technology, but in the last session of a five-day workshop, I took the team through a 'show-stoppers' exercise. At the top of the list of show-stoppers, by a long way, came, 'the capacity of our IT function to handle the new mind-set'. Not the technology, the mind-set.

This is one of many examples. I have experienced this let-down at almost every one of the workshops that I have facilitated. One executive described his company's IT function as, 'the abominable no-men'. The complaints generally revolved around being powerless in the face of the IT boffins, of having to wage a battle to secure IT resources, of having to fight for priority, and of the IT function turning a simple concept into a multi-staged, multi-million, multi-year project. And yes, heaven help the sorry soul who buys their own technology and gets it working. Mostly business people complain that their IT people are not the enablers of business change that they hold themselves out to be. If anything they are 'disablers' of change.

It is of course an indicator of a troubled business/IT relationship when there are no IT people at these strategic workshops. I asked a senior executive why there was no IT representative, expecting the answer, 'oh, we'll fill them in afterwards.' His reply surprised me; 'we did ask them, but they were unable to send someone. Secretly I'm pleased, they only hold back our thinking.'

I'm struck by the amount of 'them' phrases that I still hear these days.

There are of course many valuable and successful IT functions, much appreciated by their business. Every year I preside over the selection of the 'IT Manager of the Year' award. We get a number of nominations which hold enormous praise for their IT manager, and by implication, their IT function as a whole. Well done! But as a total percentage of businesses, those that feel good about their IT functions are small.

Here's a quote from Kit Grindley[1], who studied what CEOs thought of their IT functions. One of the CEOs responded:

> Like other chief executives, I feel I'm being blackmailed. Not just by the suppliers, I expect that. But by my own IT staff who never stop telling me what the competition are spending.

1.2 What is an in-house IT function?

In discussions with various business and IT people about this book the question of what an 'in-house IT function' is, has been asked. As you will see later, I redefine the traditional in-house IT function, but for now, we're talking about any company which deems it necessary to have an IT Manager, director or whatever, or has an IT department, which goes by any of an assortment of names. Size isn't important – we could be talking about a three-person operation, up to the multiple-thousand staff establishment. What we're not talking about is the outsource operations, or the independent software houses, although this book will be of interest to them, even if to give them competitive ideas.

I also use the term 'Chief Information Officer' (CIO) in its original sense which was to *describe* the position of the IT Manager, Director, or Department Head, rather than to *name* the position. In this book the term 'CIO' describes the person who heads up the IT function whatever their title may be.

1.3 Research

There is a general crisis for the internal IT function. Research suggests that there is a wide dissatisfaction with the quality of in-house IT.

1.3.1 Time, cost, relationship, quality

It seems that business in general has a problem with the time taken and the cost of developing information systems solutions[2]. Moreover the process of solutions development is seen as inflexible and cumbersome[3].

Business executives are unable to assess whether they are getting value for money from their IT dollars[4,5]. They know that they need IT (if so many gurus keep on and on about it, they must need it surely?), but they have a sneaky suspicion that things were better before the advent of these so-called miracle machines. They're wrong of course, IT is probably *the* competitive tool of the era, but not the way their in-house IT people are delivering it.

IT processes do not seem to be tuned into business cycles, cycles which are dictated by the need to respond quickly to the market[6]. And the rules have changed: quality and price are basic pre-requisites. What matters now is the speed of implementation of new ideas which now defines the competitive edge[7,8].

The traditional information systems development process requires accurate specification of business requirements, sign-off on specification documents, and (some time later, perhaps six months, one year, two years or worse), user acceptance testing. Research suggests that businesses frequently do not know exactly what they want, change their minds, and are more concerned with results and outcomes than with the production of a system[9]. And this systems development method has been far from successful.

1.3.2 The trigger point – IT supply exceeds demand

There's another factor to consider: David Birchall and Laurance Lyons[10] talk about the IT 'trip-wire, or "trigger-point" in the relationship between the needs of business and the inability of IT to meet them (see Figure 1.1). What they suggest is that before about the mid-1980s, businesses needed more from IT than was available. IT people held the upper hand – they were in demand. If you remember, the PC was still a hobby novelty in the late 1970s. It took until the mid-1980s for PCs to become standard business tools, with enough software to meet business and personal needs, and with hardware that was getting cheaper by the day. From the day that the average businessman had more computing power in his study at home, compared to that which

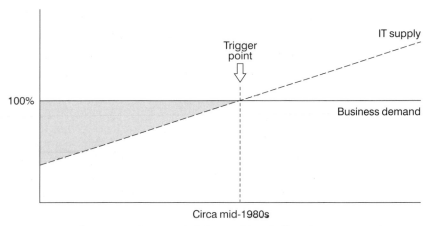

Figure 1.1 When IT supply exceeded demand (Birchall and Lyons, 1994)

his in-house IT function was able to give him, the writing was on the wall for traditional IT methods, organisations and people. It is a logical conclusion that because the average business person's needs are being met in a different way, in-house IT functions must provide services in a totally different way. That's what this book is about. Of course you can choose not to change, or to make token or incremental changes to the way you work in IT, but my bet is that within a few short years, you and everything you hold dear in traditional IT, will be irrelevant.

1.3.3 Automating, informating, and transformating

In 1988 Zuboff[11] suggested that we could label IT in the following ways: 'Automating' referred to 'the application of technology that increases the self-acting, self regulating, and self-correcting capacities of systems,' while 'informating' describes 'the application of technology that translates objects, events, and processes into data, and displays that data'. These contrasting capacities of IT can coexist in the same system, indeed informating capacity evolves from automation. My spellchecker revolts at these cumbersome words, but they carry in them the basis of fundamental attitude differences between IT people and business people. This is because business people reckon that 'automating' and 'informating' are just 'hygiene' factors – those things that IT people must get right, simply because it's their job. What really interests business people is the 'transformating' role of IT. Your average businessman or woman wants to do business, not IT, and they reckon (rightly or wrongly) that you can buy the 'automating' and 'informating' capacity off the shelf at the nearest PC store. What they really need are the breakthrough ideas and technologies that will change the competitive equation, that will put their business in front and keep it there. And IT people who get in the way, or are stuck in the 'automating/informating' job profile are not really adding value. Now here's the difficult part. There's no way you can get to the transformating stage unless you can handle the other two elements with one hand tied behind your back. You're not paid to make a meal of it, just to do it.

1.4 Inside perceptions of IT

It's not all bad: In most internal surveys which assess the effectiveness of the IT function, the IT people are harder on themselves than the business is. A cynic would perhaps suggest that business people don't know enough to be too critical, and there's some truth in that. There's also some truth in the fact that IT people seem to suffer from low corporate self-esteem. And there's a vicious cycle here: because IT people are subject to unreasonable demands, which require enormous courage and self-confidence to provide realistic costs and time estimates for. So they shave a bit here and there, knowing that once the project is underway the funds will come, albeit painfully. Of course they don't deliver on time and budget, but they knew that would happen.

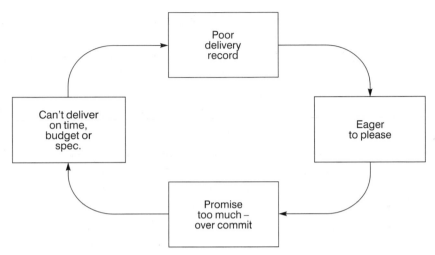

Figure 1.2 The vicious cycle of IT esteem

However something unhealthy is happening here, which is not good for either party in this sad cycle: business people are learning not to trust IT people, and IT people are setting themselves up to fail. A little later I will discuss the reasonable complaint of IT people, that business people place impossible demands on them. But for now, I just wonder how much time and energy, pain and stress, and how much damage is being done to the business/IT relationship by this cycle. There is no easy answer to the cycle either. The only way to resolve it, is not to play the game, not to provide traditional IT services because traditional IT methods cannot deliver in today's business environment! We have to discover a new way of automating, informating and transformating the business environment. The trouble with a new way is that it is a new way, and that always raises doubts and concerns from the traditionalists and Luddites.

1.4.1 Some standard grievances from IT

'Grievance' may be a harsh word, but let's look at its dictionary definition, and judge then whether it's appropriate or not: a grievance is, 'indignation or resentment stemming from a feeling of having been wronged[12].' I think the shoe may fit. I have no doubt that IT people *have* been wronged. And they have a right to be indignant and resentful. But only from within an IT frame of reference. Trouble is that business no longer lends too much credence to the IT frame of reference, if it ever did. Charles Handy[13] has this to say about your frame of reference:

> If the new way of things is going to be different from the old, not just an improvement on it, then we shall need to look at everything in a new way.

> In the long perspective of history it may seem that the really influential people in the last 100 years were not Hitler or Churchill, Stalin or Gorbachev, but Freud, Marx and Einstein, men who changed nothing except the way we think, but that changed everything.

> (Handy, 1989)

So the challenge is to look at the same thing that everyone else sees, and to see differently. To think differently. And to act on those thoughts.

It seems to me that if we choose a different thought pattern, a different pattern to the same old tired 'grievances' that we've all heard, probably even muttered ourselves, then we are on the road to a new way of doing in-house IT. Gary Hamel and C.K. Prahalad[14] suggest that true leaders are those who can 'reframe' the same picture that everyone sees in such a way that it presents opportunities and excitement in business. They believe that traditional thinking can be a millstone which holds progress back:

> When environment changes rapidly and radically, these (traditional) beliefs become a threat to survival.

> (Hamel and Prahalad, 1994)

So let's have a little fun here and look at the standard IT people's gripes and attempt to 'reframe' them to unlock the opportunities that are available if we just choose to think differently.

Here are some of the standard gripes that I hear from IT people, and my reframed view: read through the following section, then later, once you've finished the book, test the reframing thoughts against the ideas I offer.

1.4.2 'Business people refuse to learn IT. They don't know enough to use us properly'

Often IT people complain (as does a significant amount of academic research), that business people cannot continue to remain ignorant of IT realities, and that they should learn a little about how IT works before being so quick to demand and complain.

Let's try that from another angle. Why *should* the business learn about IT? In a discipline in which half of everything you know is redundant in three years, how much training is needed before we will be satisfied that business people know enough. Surely IT people are being unrealistic in demanding that others learn their discipline before they can talk to them? Is there another way? Can we make IT so accessible that business people don't need to learn? Or perhaps they want to learn because it's so interesting.

The challenge is for IT people to talk the same language as business. And if you have to describe your network in terms of hose-pipes, storage tanks and sprinklers (as I have done), then so be it.

Here's a thought – try your average home PC owner: how many hours does he or she spend, just messing about learning? I wonder if it's more to do with accessibility than with technophobia? Can we focus the business on the transformation abilities of IT and leave the 'hygiene' factors to the experts?

So here's the reframe: Business people don't need to learn IT. IT can be presented in accessible and meaningful terms. Alternatively, learning IT is so attractive and easy that businesses learn without any effort.

1.4.3 'We're misunderstood – we want to help but they won't let us'

Many IT people complain that they aren't invited to the strategy workshops, the 'centre circle,' the think-tanks. And if they aren't invited how can they possible play a strategic role in the company's future?

It is true that over half of the Chief Information Officers (CIOs) are not represented at board level[15]. The re-framing question would be: why not? Are executives that stupid that they don't see an essential and strategic resource?

Reframe: inclusion is earned. You need to make yourselves indispensable when it comes to corporate thinking. What's your action plan to be invited to the party? If you don't have one, do you deserve to be there? Don't believe poet John Milton who wrote:

> They also serve who only stand and wait.

They serve those who earn the right to be served. Have you earned the right? And if not, what is your plan to earn that right? (If your plan is in the automate/informate mind-set, you're not going to make it.) Transform the way your business operates before you ever think of board-room rights.

1.4.4 'The business has unrealistic expectations of us'

Yes that's true. Often the average business person's perception of what can be done far exceeds your, or anyone else's abilities. I call this 'magazine' management. Usually an executive has read a magazine, or sat next to a salesman on an aeroplane, and then wanders over to your desk and says something like, 'can you give me a fully on-line call-centre, linked to our sales and service database, which guides the operator through the optimum customer solution, based on all the learning in the company? . . . By next Tuesday?' It requires enormous courage to say no, when you cannot do the job.

I prefer to say yes. This isn't a silver bullet solution, but I tend to guide the requestor through a menu of high level options, in which they make the choices on what to include and what to leave out in the solution. So the answer would go something like this, 'yes, I can give you a prototype call-centre by next Tuesday.' (Then just wander down to the local PC store and pick one off the shelf.) The rest of the project will be about how to use the tool, how to link it to your databases and to other applications, or do you need to build your own? What additional options are needed, etc. Probably the most important part of the project will be about business readiness and processes, not about the technology. This, of course, makes you and your technology an enabler of the idea. Alternatively, ask your business partner where they got this fantastic idea, call the sales people of the product concerned and get them to come in with their total solution. That way you're in control, and are not saying no all the time – let someone else say no.

Now I've been deliberately trite here. I know that the demands placed by the business on you are more complex and politically more sensitive than can be resolved with a PC package, but the emphasis here is in this reframe: respond to unrealistic expectations with an open mind, and a genuine desire to meet them. Most of the time IT people get into trouble because of their attitude to new and wacky ideas. Just remember that nearly every world-beating idea started out as an unrealistic expectation. If you want to be an enabler in your business, your attitude to unrealistic expectations will have to be upbeat and can-do. As George Bernard Shaw said:

> The reasonable man adapts himself to the world; the unreasonable one persists in trying to adapt the world to himself. Therefore, all progress depends on the unreasonable man[16].

> (Shaw, 1903)

1.4.5 'We are doing a good job – what is this nonsense?'

I've heard this one as well, 'we know we're doing a good job. You are just trying to stir up trouble by suggesting that our days are numbered.'

If you are doing a good job now, well done! But 'now' does not mean tomorrow. Perhaps you need to pay attention to some reframe thoughts:

1 The number one predictor of failure, is success. The more successful you are the more you have to work at changing the rules that made you successful. Success can deaden your response to changing circumstances, can make you complacent, and when you wake up, you're gone. Everyone else is working to bring about your company's downfall, why shouldn't you? Actively set about replacing your winning formulas with other winning formulas. So, if it's not broken, break it.

2 Who says you're doing a good job? If you say so, the alarm bells should be ringing. If your business partners say so, perhaps you have some cause for celebration – but see point 1. However, how do you know if your business partner's good opinion of you is justified? Perhaps they have very low expectations, or are simply resigned to average performance. The only way of really knowing if you and your in-house IT function is performing well is through benchmarking yourselves with the real world. There are many external benchmarking services. Avail yourself of one. However they will mostly be able to tell you about your 'hygiene' factors. Few

deal with strategic alignment and IT leadership. And even if you are performing well by automate/informate standards, see paragraph 1.

Remember who pays the bills. Also remember that in general, IT performance has not matched senior executive's expectations or expenditure:

> General Managers are tired of being told that information technology (IT) can create competitive advantage and enable business transformation. What they observe and experience are IS project failures, unrelenting hype about IT, and rising information processing costs.[17]

Ultimately, it comes down to this: what is good IT performance? It is how well you develop and support systems? Or is it, how much of an edge that you give the organisation? If you think the latter may be the case, you're on your way to reframing the role of your in-house IT function.

1.4.6 'Never mind the ball, get on with the game'

Too many in-house IT functions and CIOs are playing a different game to the rest of their organisation. They think that development and support of systems is what they do.

Nicholas Imparato, and Oren Harari[18] offer an intriguing new definition for performance: they suggest that the old definition of: $P = A \times M$ or Performance = Ability × Motivation is seriously flawed. Ability breeds habit, habit breeds resistance to change, and resistance to change is the kiss of death for new ideas. They describe a franchised computer retail store who did some internal research and were puzzled to find that the more successful sales people were those who had less experience in the store. It seems that inexperienced people listened attentively to customers and did their best to accommodate their sometimes difficult requirements. The more experience they acquired, the less they listened, and the more they sold their *own* solutions to their customers. I sometimes wonder if business is not a result of the good abilities of IT people. Are they so good that they have stopped listening?

Looking at the motivation side of the equation, Imparato and Harari suggest that motivated people are failing all the time. It seems that working hard is no longer a recipe for success. Because no matter how hard you play the game, if it's the wrong game, you're of no use to your organisation. What they imply is that motivation on its own is not good enough, neither is ability on its own. Nor is the combination of the two. They propose that 'accuracy of role perception' is the missing ingredient. What is the role of in-house IT? Development and support are background or even outsourceable activities. What really matters is the strategic and competitive role that you and the in-house function play. If you don't make a difference, you don't matter. It's that simple. So stop playing the IT game, and start playing the business game.

1.5 On all sides – threats to the in-house function

In-house IT functions feel threatened. They're not threats so much as alternatives, and if you choose to think this way, they are an opportunity to clear your desk of all the menial IT work that holds you back from taking centre stage in making a difference to your organisation. Other 'threats' are opportunities to create strong allies within the business, and to educate and create relationships within your organisation.

1.5.1 What are the threats to in-house IT?

In-house IT functions are indeed threatened. Business dissatisfaction is growing[19]: In a recent study it was found that in general, expenditure on Information Technology represented the worst return on investment of any form of capital expenditure. Put it another way – CEOs could have spent their money on any other form of capital, and done better than they did with IT. Sobering stuff.

Where are the threats then? They come from outsourcing, solutions providers, in-sourcing, consulting, 'satelliting' and ignoring. We'll go through them briefly:

Outsourcing

Outsourcing involves having your work done by someone else. Usually this involves a long-term contract for the provision of a service.

Outsourcing used to be called 'bureaux' in the late 1970s and early 1980s. This serves to illustrate that 'outsourcing' is not a new concept. It is an old concept which fell from favour. The reasons it fell from favour are still valid in the outsourcing environment:

- insufficient management from the principal;
- poor service from the outsourcer – usually as a result of over-commitment;
- outsourcers (bureaux) holding principals to ransom;
- poor contract set-up;
- core competencies outsourced.

Complacent IT people can point to these disasters and suggest that outsourcing is just a cycle, and the work will come back in due course. This time things are different, and I wouldn't hold my breath while waiting.

In-house IT should outsource as much as it can, keeping in mind that you still have to manage the outsourced areas.

Solutions providers

The real threat to in-house IT functions comes from 'solutions providers.' These are companies who offer business IT solutions, be it data warehouses, or intranets, or integrated business systems. They target business people, not IT people. They offer the whole deal – fully customised and installed products, with training and support. They don't care about your legacy systems or your architecture – they do care about providing the business with useful and useable IT tools. I have a friend who sells such products and his standard answer to a business person who asks whether he should include his IT people in this solution is, 'will they add to, or take away from, your efforts.' Invariably the business doesn't reflect long before leaving the IT function out until it's too late – like after the board meeting decision, at which IT is not represented.

In-sourcing

This involves doing your own work, but having to compete on a commercial basis. Your organisation retains the (often implicit) right to get their IT services from other suppliers. You are expected to operate as a profit centre. I've dealt with many such units, and they struggle to offer viable services to their organisation, and are often forced to take on outside work to make ends meet.

Also difficult for the newly in-sourced function, is re-educating the business into paying for services that have previously been 'invisible.' Like that technician who is always on call to the executive team. Or the after-hours installations. Or just the general visits and chats about things that concern the business. I've yet to come across a unit that successfully charges for attendance at interminable meetings, but I'm sure there are some. This brings about a side-effect. If you charge for all your services, including attending meetings and workshops, don't expect to be included in too much strategising or thinking. There is an 'up' side to all this accounting for your efforts – you focus on essential work, and very quickly discard that work which does not pay.

There are also a number of other dangers in having every element of IT operate on a profit basis. Research, training, relationship-building and many other areas require a net input, in order to have a net output elsewhere.

'Satelliting'

More companies are choosing not to downsize, but to 'satellite.' This is really about outsourcing to a previously in-house unit setting them up as a satellite to the central business endeavour. Usually the main business will undertake to provide 80% of their business to the satellite for the first year, 60% the next, and so on. This is a soft landing for the satellite unit, but they are expected to be economically viable in a short period of time.

While satelliting represents a humane way of downsizing, its causes and effects are the same – the company can't afford you, and very soon you will be on your own. It behoves you to start developing some entrepreneurial spirit, and fast.

Ignoring

This is probably the most common threat to in-house IT. In some research I did recently into how companies integrate new technologies into their existing environments, I found that one of the major problems was what I call 'undercover' technology. Where someone in IT receives a phone call to support a little PC package that was installed three years ago, but now needs integrating with the corporate systems, or needs upgrading. Someone's pet has just been discovered, alive and well, and living in the basement.

What do you ignore? Normally you ignore those things that annoy, or provoke you. You ignore fine distinctions – over meticulousness and pedantism. You can ignore your obligations and responsibilities. And IT people may represent all of the above to the average business person. Finally, ignorance and ignoring are related behaviours. You ignore something because you don't know better.

The net effect of being ignored, other than frustration, is that IT has to deal with undercover technologies. Also the value of IT is brought into question, 'if we can afford to ignore the IT function, why do we need them at all?' A mixture of in-sourcing and ignoring, is when another unit is tasked with work that should be being done by you.

1.5.2 What areas in the in-house IT function are threatened?

So what's threatened by all these outside forces? Traditional in-house Information Technology functions were responsible for the development and support of their organisation's computer systems. The emergence of the independent software vendor in the mid-to late-1980s[20], and the rise of outsourcing service providers in the early 1990s, has changed the landscape for internal providers of computing services.

1.5.3 Traditional IT organisation

Essentially there are a number of traditional functions or departments within the stereotyped IT department: development, maintenance, and facilities or operations[21]. Other functional elements such as PC support, training, end-user liaison, change management, decision support services, installations, etc., can be found as well. I'll deal with in-house processes and the suggested functions which might address these processes in Chapter 3.

All traditional in-house IT functions are replaceable or outsourceable in some form or other. The key decisions will be less about whether they *can* be replaced, but rather whether they *should* be replaced. As Charles Handy puts it:

> Too often organisations drift into this decision, gradually hiving off functions until they are left with what is inconceivable or too inconvenient to give to others[22].

(Handy, 1989)

All traditional IT activities are 'threatened.' The trick is to build a rational and strategically sound plan for outsourcing, replacing or satelliting many of the traditional IT functions, and keeping those which truly add value, and make a strategic difference to the organisation. (It might be worth remembering that 'strategic' means 'important or essential in relation to a plan of action.' Whose plan, what action?)

I once took an IT function through this logic, to the enthusiastic nods of all present. It was settled, they would reduce their department from 200 staff to less than 30. But the crunch came when I asked who amongst them saw themselves in the remaining 30 – they all did. From this and many other such experiences, I have come to believe that IT people behave according to a deep seated assumption:

> Change is all right only if we do it to someone else

or:

> I don't mind change, as long as I don't have to do anything different.

I don't underestimate the resistance to change that IT people say they don't have

I'm not calling for universal downsizing, or as it has lately been called: 'dumbsizing' or even 'brightsizing[23], (when all your bright people leave). There are many studies which show that on average 70% of downsizing efforts fail[24]:

Downsizing is usually an act of desperation – throwing people overboard to lighten the financial load.

Downsizing is absolutely useless if the survivors end up doing the same things, only more so[25]. It leads to burnout, stress, resentment, and in the vast majority of cases, failure. The final word on downsizing must go to Gary Hamel and C.K. Prahalad[26]:

> Downsizing, the equivalent of corporate anorexia, can make a company thinner; it doesn't necessarily make it healthier.
>
> (Hamel and Prahalad, 1994)

What's needed in in-house IT is a total rethink about the function and effectiveness of the traditional activities that we have held dear for the last 20 or 30 years.

The systems development life cycle (SDLC)

How we love those acronyms! But I'll stick with 'SDLC' because it does shorten this paragraph, and I presume I'm speaking to IT people.

Pick up any pre- to mid-1980s textbook on IT, and it will give you loving descriptions of the Development Life Cycle, with comparisons between different methodologies and lucid arguments on whether 'Maintenance' should be included in, or excluded from, the SDLC. Even Rapid Application Development gets the same treatment.

For completeness, here's a typical SDLC:

Step 1: the Need: the business expresses a need for a systems solution, or there is a strategic plan which dictates the use of IT. (Recent research has shown that only 34% of companies actually *have* a corporate IT strategy[27].)

Step 2: the requirements: the business details their need in such a way that the IT function can translate it into a system (or a proto-type). Usually this takes the form of a specification document. (Both a business specification document and a technical design specification.)

Here's the rub. There are four things about a specification document (spec.) that I have a problem with:

1 A spec. assumes that the business knows what it wants – in detail. Often they don't, and why should they? So, they read something in a magazine or some guru's management breakthrough book, and they want some of that. But what exactly, they're not sure. And a lot of their wishes *are* pie in the sky. Yes, it is a wish list. What IT people have to do is to accommodate the 'I'll believe it when I see it' mindset.

2 A spec. requires that the business predict business conditions 12, 18, 60 months in advance. In detail. (The time is determined by IT's ability to deliver, nothing else.) So tell me where a company like Microsoft will be two years from now? Because that's what we're asking of the business.

3 Once the spec. is written, IT needs the business to 'freeze' their requirements. And boy are we grouchy when 'they' want to change the spec. We have 'variation orders', and change control and all manner of hurdles to put in the way of change. Here's another thing: have you ever seen the look of complete bafflement on the faces of business people when IT people require them to go through a walkthrough of the design documentation. (Of course you've seen the look, but have you taken any notice of that look.) What IT people do is educate business people on how to read specs, design documents, and screen layouts. I've even seen business people working late into the night, poring over these documents with all the earnestness of engineers verifying a space shuttle mission. Little did they know that the system would never be delivered:

> Of all software projects incorporating over 64,000 lines of code, 25% failed to deliver anything; 60% were over budget and behind schedule, and only 1% met requirements on time and on budget.
>
> (Beam, 1994).[28]

4 Finally, who actually reads these things? My experience is that most specs. are read during the testing stage, in an attempt to convince the business that this is really what they wanted – because it says so in the spec. I've often heard a harassed business person saying, 'but, that's not what I meant!' Poor soul. His signature is at the bottom of the spec. so it must be what he wanted. Many spec. documents unfortunately turn into blackmail letters. After all, millions have been spent on what 'they' signed off. What is it with a 'user sign-off'? Does the finance department ask the business to sign-off on the budget? Or human resources ask for sign-off on the personnel manual? (Some do, but that's another story!)

There are significant flaws in the specification process. I was involved with the writing of a book the working title of which was *Managing IT while the Goal-Posts Keep Changing*[29]. In it we argue that a 'specification document' has to be short, clear, and *constantly* revised. A very different approach.

Step 3: Construction: IT people go away and develop the system

I refer you back to the quote in point 3 by Beam, 1994 IT people do not have a good record of delivery. Many books and papers have been written on the subject, but none deals with the human elements of managing complex software projects better than the classic *The Mythical Man-Month: Essays on Software Engineering* written by Frederick Brooks[30] in 1975. While the book is over 20 years old, it is disappointingly instructive to note that the book is still relevant: we haven't been able to solve the problems of non-linear economies of scale in collaborative work – in other words, adding more people to a complex project will slow it down, not speed it up. Brooks has issued a new '20th Anniversary' edition which contains four new chapters, including one entitled *No Silver Bullet*. Get the book, if just for that chapter.

I am not a development expert. But two things strike me about the process of software development:

1 If you find yourself in a hole, stop digging. (Unfortunately, IT people seem to equate activity with achievement. Digging is good. Ask the 'project widows' and widowers.)

2 All projects reach a point of no return, and that this point is ludicrously close to the inception of the project, often after the idea has been accepted by the executive.

After that point, we don't seem to build in any elegant withdrawal strategies – procedures that will allow us to back away from the project, or to try a different tack, while keeping the egos of all concerned intact. The emotional and personal cost of stopping a project far outweighs the financial cost – but you never see allowance made for personal pride and face-saving. Someone once said that a truly strong organisation is not the one which succeeds, but the one which can fail, quickly, and without over-commitment of resources. 'Fail quickly' and succeed in the long run.

One of the most difficult parts of a development project is to convince everybody that the pilot project is just that, and not 'Implementation – Phase One.' And that a 'go/no-go' decision means that we may decide to scrap everything we've done so far. Certainly when you look at the net cost of a project over time (Figure 1.3), you can easily pick up the trend of creeping financial commitment. So stop early, before the thing gets out of hand. Indeed, how about having a project that consists of short-term goals and objectives, strung together in a coherent way,

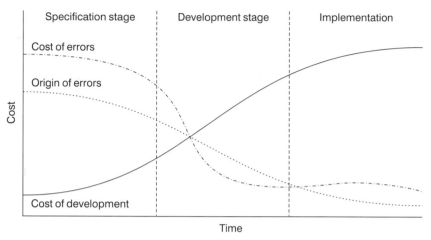

Figure 1.3 Actual costs are low, but most latent costs are incurred during specification. After Friedman[31]

each of which has a 'go – no-go' decision before progress can continue? Supporting this argument is research done by DeMarco[32] who found that while nearly 60% of software errors originate during the specification stage, and more importantly, *82% of the cost of fixing errors is incurred in fixing specification errors.* So why do we continue with methods which have proven delayed costs? DeMarco did this research in 1978. And we haven't changed the SDLC, so these inherent faults are probably still as relevant today as they were then.

Secondly, software development projects are more about people, communication, some simple planning and scheduling, people, and communication. Yes, I've repeated people and communication because I firmly believe that technical project approaches don't work if you don't have the necessary people skills. But a people-centred approach has a better chance of success, even with very basic technical skills in the project management team. Some of the problem seems to be that when asked for technical advice, our project managers roll up their sleeves and help out but they lose sight of two things: the overview of the project, and what the business needs from the project in the first place. I was once dumped into the late stages of a payroll project, and asked to manage the latter development stage, the testing, and the implementation. I asked what I thought was a very sensible question, 'where's the flowchart thingy?' 'You mean the Gantt Chart?' they said. 'We haven't actually had time to put one together,' and they pointed me at the initial project specification document, which of course had no relevance to what was happening now. So after a few interviews of the project team members and the affected business people, I put together a very simple flow chart – I couldn't do Gantt or PERT charts then. This one page document became the chief reference document around which I managed the people on the project.

Sometimes we overcomplicate the job of managing and developing software projects. Mind you, what are you doing developing in the first place? Buy a package. And then concentrate on managing the people, using simple tools and aids.

Step 4: Testing: Programme, System, and User Acceptance – the system is tested

Testing, negotiating and arm-twisting is more like it. This is when the business people say things like, 'but it doesn't work,' and IT people say things like, 'it's not in the spec.' or 'we'll put that in later.'

It also seems illogical that the testing phase of any project is the most time-compressible. As the project slips, the implementation date remains constant. We justify this compression of all testing into one frantic week or month by saying, 'we padded the timetable here anyway,' never realising that more slippage equals more testing. And why has the project slipped anyway?

Normally projects slip because of poor specification, poor planning, poor estimation of resources required (remembering that time is a resource), inadequate assignment of authority, and inadequate business involvement[33]. Funny that all of these reasons concern the specification and construction phase of the project. It seems that very few projects fail as a result of poor technology. Most project failures seem to be related to how we choose to run the project rather than what solutions we provide.

Step 5: Implementation

Sometimes we IT people call this 'conversion.' I'm not sure if we're talking about a 'road to Damascus' experience here, or that we are converting user expectations downward, or that we're converting a whole bunch of tricky coding into equally tricky operating procedures.

This, if anything, is one of the central roles of the modern in-house IT function. They must concentrate on change management, transformation governance structures, flexible planning schedules and 'can do' problem solving. Relationship management is central to the new IT function. I deal with this at length in Chapters 4 and 5.

There are several major influencing factors which affect the success of the implementation of a software technology[34] into organisations, and they are not technological in nature:

- the relationship between the IT function and the business is one of the prime determinants of success in implementing new technologies;

- the behaviour, professionalism and maturity of participants in the implementation process affect its success;

- the physical nature of the company: is it centralised or dispersed? (This is important because it affects ease of communication and logistics.) Is its culture authoritarian or empowered? – these factors affect the difficulty or ease of implementation;

- only 25% of companies studied regarded the technology as an issue in the implementation;

- as you can see, implementation is about people and communication, not about technology.

Development

I have already pointed to what I see as fatal flaws in the Systems Development Life Cycle, the SDLC. But I am often faced with sceptics who ask how they should develop if they do not follow the SDLC. I have a simple, and intentionally simplistic response, 'don't develop.' Then of course, I get the rejoinder, 'but we have to. Our business is sufficiently different that no packages suit its requirements.' There's an 80/20 rule here: 80% of the time, both the business and IT are less than honest with themselves. And maybe 20% of the time, there is a real need to be different. But left to themselves, IT people *like* developing things. So they don't argue too arduously when faced with the 'we are different' question. There is a need to develop, but nothing like we IT people would have business people believe – 20% one fifth, that's all. When you passed your exams with 80% you were ecstatic! Why can't we be that pleased about avoiding 80% of development?

Rather we should really be examining this question of 'difference.' And is that difference worth the *real* cost of running an in-house development factory? And is it worth all the maintenance (that developers *hate* to do) that will be necessary over the life of the system?

Production

It's strange: we call it 'Operations,' or 'Facilities,' or 'Production,' but we don't follow factory-based procedures which have been developed and refined since the turn of the century. I personally found the concept of the 'Bathtub Curve[35],' particularly relevant to systems that I was responsible for operating and maintaining. The Bathtub curve is used in appliance and hardware quality assurance to describe the high rate of failures at the beginning of a product life-cycle, a 'flat' period, followed by a rising failure rate toward the end of the product's life-cycle. The plot of failures looks like a cross section of a bathtub. But I have yet to find a 'Facilities' person using it, or singing its praises. Other factory measures, like operator efficiency, throughput, statistical process control, acceptance sampling, and life-cycle management are used less than diligently.

Stability has a cost. I had a client who valued stability and control to such a degree that they did everything manually as well as by computer, and then they compared the results. They trusted their manual process more than their computers. Of course they were carrying 200% more staff than they needed, with all this checking and crosschecking. (This is true, and this was a bank! The good news is that there was only one way to go, and that was up.) But in less extreme cases we need to be aware that the 'Facilities' department sees their main purpose as keeping systems stable. Of course development and their users are determined to change everything.

I was asked to set up a million-dollar-budget training programme for a client. I phoned a number of facilities which had country-wide training sites. My business did not go to the company's representative who told me that their facilities manager would *never* allow me to load someone else's software on their machines. Say goodbye to a few million, in the interests of stability!

'Production Facilities' seem to lose sight of the essential paradox of computing: the more stable things are, the less they meet changing business needs. So the answer lies in the production facility acceptance of constant change among constant stability. How do we get production to say, 'please change – we can handle it?'

Information

The rules of information flow in organisations are being understood with greater clarity[36], and we're starting to see that:

> Organisations are information systems. They are communication systems. And they are decision-making systems[37].
>
> (Morgan, 1997)

Information flow is starting to be understood as a networked phenomenon, rather than our traditional Anthony's Triangle[38] that divides business activities into Operations, Management and Strategy. More and more authors now believe that everyone strategises, and with the increasing number of self-managed teams, everyone manages as well. So the traditional information hierarchy becomes a limitation to decision-making. So if your information flow does not match your organisation structure or preferably lead it, then look to your CV, you may soon be needing it.

Another trend in information is the concept of knowledge assets[39]. While many companies solemnly declare that, 'our people are our greatest assets,' very few behave as if they believe it. It is the role of IT to provide not only the medium for allowing people within organisations access to information, but also to provide the organisation with ways of accounting for their intellectual capital. Until organisations can rigorously account for their knowledge, they will continue to treat people, and the knowledge they hold, as expenses not assets.

It is time for IT professionals to stop acting like librarians. I am being unfair to librarians here, but the analogy was first put to me by a CEO who said that his IT people were happy to keep, codify and file the books, but not to actually read them. He was telling me this by way of explanation why he believed that so

30 | **1 Introduction – days of wine and roses**

1.6 If it's so bad why bother? – do companies need an in-house function?

few IT people made it to the top of organisations. They never seemed to get *involved* with the real business. Here's a reframe: what if every report produced by IT was read by IT? And acted on appropriately. The sceptic might say that then IT people would get so involved in business, that they wouldn't have time for IT. Exactly! IT people should *manage* the IT side of the business, not do it.

1.6 If it's so bad why bother? – do companies need an in-house function?

Yes they do.

But not the in-house functions that many of them now have. In the same way that we do not expect our factory manager to know the details of how every piece of machinery on his or her shop floor works, or indeed to design and manufacture that equipment, we should not expect the same of our IT people. IT should manage the provision of IT services to the organisation. They should manage the relationship between IT and the business, and they should read the reports and get involved.

IT people come in two flavours: those that work for IT companies, and those that work for organisations whose business is not IT. And there lies a great divide. Certainly get into Development, and Maintenance, and Production if you provide those services to other companies. But stay away from them if your company sells something else.

Organisations need IT people. Not to do the IT work. There's plenty of choice amongst the IT service providers. But they need IT people to forge the link between IT and the business. To manage those links. To be involved in their business. And most of all, to help them change faster than their competition.

1 Introduction – days of wine and roses

1.6 If it's so bad why bother? – do companies need an in-house function?

31

1.6.1 Of course it's not all bad – some hero tales

Successful in-house IT functions

There are numerous examples of successful in-house IT functions. Federal Express with their central hub at Memphis, bar-codes, scanners and their SuperTrackers system which can pinpoint any package in their system at any time. American Airlines who provided travel agents with terminals and redefined timetable and reservation systems, and by the way, pushed their non-flight revenue above their flight revenue. American Hospital Supplies, who gave their customers access to their databases and directly connected demand to supply. Otis Elevators, whose preventative maintenance system allows them to promise unprecedented service levels. Amazon.com who created a virtual bookstore. The list goes on.

A friend of mine once asked me the question, 'what is the height of buildings on Manhattan Island?' Because I knew this had to be a trick question, I vastly downgraded my reply to, 'fifteen floors.' His reply surprised me, 'two floors,' he said. Now I've tried to check whether this is a correct answer, but I haven't been able to do so. The next time I was in New York, I did check out the lie of the land, and except for the financial district with its 200-odd skyscrapers, the rest is a lot lower than I had thought. Taking Central Park, the streets, and all the lower buildings into account, I suppose the new number of floors divided by the area might equal two. It doesn't really matter. The point of the story is that the tall buildings took my attention away from the short- and medium-sized buildings. And so do the stories of Information Technology triumphs take our attention away from two things: firstly, this is not normal for IT functions, and secondly, there are a whole bunch of things being done by the companies which successfully use IT.

32

1 Introduction – days of wine and roses

1.6 If it's so bad why bother? – do companies need an in-house function?

What are successful in-house functions doing right?

Firstly, they deliver. But in the case of American Airlines, it was not all at once. Max Hopper didn't roll out a complete system. He tied the operational elements of the business together using IT, before he made a few old terminals available to selected travel agents using existing and available systems. Only when that concept had proved itself was he able to expand the reach of IT. The successful IT function establishes credibility through small initiatives.

Secondly, the IT focuses on the external customer. The first winner of our 'IT Manager of the Year Award' was the CIO of a very successful bank. I asked him how much time he spent with customers. He told me that he spent upwards of 30% of his time with customers, because the bank's product was its systems. He wasn't a back-room boy.

Third, the IT function is part of a whole. The systems are useless unless the company culture supports them, and people are well qualified to use them. People are probably more important than the system. Relationships are important. The CIO spends a considerable amount of his or her time selling, explaining, being there for the business, and generally *not* managing IT.

Even if it's a disaster, what happens to the internal IT function?

Even if IT is a total disaster, and the business turns its back on the in-house function or even fires it, the IT does not go away. It dissolves but the essential IT work gets done, or the company hits a brick wall. This is what I meant when I said that 'ignoring' was the greatest threat to IT. Information Technology is an integral part of modern business, and if the in-house IT function cannot perform, then it will be replaced.

1.7 No way back – why 'back to basics' cannot work

When I talk to IT people about the need to radically change the way we do in-house IT, the most common response is that I'm being too critical. That yes, there may be problems with delivery and the way IT operates in the business, but that's because we didn't know what we know now. We just need more and better tools, more understanding from the business, and to work smart, not hard. In other words, if we get the basics right, things will be better. The bad news is that the basics are wrong. So going back to them will make things worse, not better.

Herman Maynard and Sue Merhtens[40] describe the process of 'implosion' that occurs as companies fail:

> Implosion is the process of liquidating assets, business units, manufacturing capability, technologies, research efforts, market development programs, and people to improve short-term earnings and cash performance.
>
> (Maynard and Merhtens, 1993)

And the one thing that accelerates this implosion is the 'back to basics' movement. Back to basics is bad news. As Land and Jarman[41] put it:

> This backlash against change is rooted in fear, which limits an executive's perception of reality and leads him or her to repeat fruitless, non-productive activities.
>
> (Land and Jarman, 1992)

Someone once said that the definition of an insane person is someone who does the same thing again and again and expects different results. But this seems to be many executives' responses to a changing environment. The rules of IT have changed. Doing the old IT faster, slicker and better, is still doing the old IT. We need a new IT.

1.7.1 The rules have changed – irrevocably

Business rules have changed. I devote Chapter 2 to discussing these changes in some depth, because if IT is to be an indivisible part of business, it must undergo the same changes.

Briefly however, there have been five major shifts in the economic landscape:

The world economy has changed, basic definitions of business components are changing, time, size and distance are being compressed, the way companies relate to employees is changing, and the ability to change has become the prime determinant of success.

New definitions

Time, size and distance compression

In the 1970s there were a number of books and many articles published which tried to tackle the question of what managers were going to do with their time, now that computers had freed them up from the mundane and tedious data collection, collation and reporting. Most predicted a reduction in the management class, and an increase in thinking and leisure time. Ask any manager – this hasn't happened. If anything they have less time to get things done. Time and distance are compressed by e-mail and the Internet. I find myself being aware of time zones around the world as never before, as I converse with business associates.

Products are moving from being standardised 'one size fits all' to being customised to fit the requirements of individual customers. Distribution is easy and world-wide and marketplaces are global. Automation has allowed a significant shrinking of both the timing and sizing of production runs.

If the IT function is not seen as an enabler and leader of technological change, they are unlikely to have a significant role in the future of their organisation.

The way organisations relate to their people

There is an irreversible shift in power in organisations. For reasons explained in Chapter 2, customers have gained the power. They now vote with their wallets. Their sense of quality and service is constantly being revised upwards. They want what they want, not what you are prepared to supply. This shift to customer power then leads to needing to have resourceful and innovative customer service staff, to being able to change the way you operate, quickly enough to respond to new customer demands. Needing better people shifts power within the organisation outwards to the customer interface, as against the traditional management and long service employees. The socio-psycho contract between employer and employee is irrevocably changing. How companies motivate and align employees, set goals, manage work, measure performance and reward people is changing. Old management styles are becoming inappropriate or even becoming a threat to survival.

Change defines progress

One of the more difficult elements of the new way of doing business is the need to constantly change. Many people believe that business change is like a river, with rapids to be negotiated and quiet stretches and pools in which you will have time to consolidate. Unfortunately it no longer works that way. The ability to change quickly and constantly without the need for quiet consolidation has become one of the key factors in enduring business success. This has deep implications for IT. They need to redefine their concepts of standards, stability and platforms. They need to change their attitude to changing business needs and requirements and above all, they need to deliver stable technology in continually shifting environments.

1.7.2 What 'back to basics' really means

It is perfectly natural to want to revert to an old, better way of doing things. But the problem in IT is that there is no old and better way. The old ways no longer fit the new business environment.

I was doing some work for a large conservative company, and after a particularly difficult steering committee meeting, my client commented, 'every morning the Managing Director wakes up, looks at the calendar and groans, because it's not 1972 again. IT is not just a bad dream.' We in IT need to be aware of our own thinking: do we wish it was 1980, when programming was programming, mainframes were mainframes, and chickens could cross roads without bad jokes being made about them? Those days won't be back. We'll never go back to when users kept their hands off the systems, and said, 'I'm sure you people know what you're doing, just keep me informed.' We need to be aware that often 'back to basics' thinking is rooted in the 'if only it was 1972' mindset.

Looking forward is a hard choice to take. We are much more certain of past events, tools and techniques. It is easier to call on experience or history than to invent a new approach. Firstly you have to do the thinking, and as Henry Ford said:

> Thinking is difficult, that's why so few people do it.

Then you have to defend your new idea or technique, or plan against an often uninformed attack.

Finally, having justified your new idea, you have to implement it. And there's a good chance that things will go wrong, and in come the 'I told you so' brigade. New ideas take enormous effort and there are struggles against significant resistance.

It appears to be much easier and safer to use tried and trusted approaches to problems. Which is why 'back to basics' has such an alluring ring to it.

1.8 Seeds of the new IT – a new mindset

The first challenge to developing a new IT mindset is to be able to really see what's happening. Once you have found a new freedom in which you are not constrained by old attitudes, you can look to business for some answers. Business provides many models and ideas for IT people to try and to adopt.

1.8.1 Look – really

Change is happening all about us but we may be applying selective filters. Jennifer James[42], a consultant and author in creativity suggests that one of the first steps in problem-solving is problem-finding. And finding problems within one's own domain is often very difficult. She suggests that 'what you see is where you stand,' meaning that your position and perspective on a problem are all coloured by your history, organisational role, experience and beliefs. Therefore a good source in problem-finding is outside of your immediate circle. Business people, staff, other IT professionals all offer perspectives on your problems. The difficulty will come in really listening without riding to the defence of your dearly held ideas. I'll deal with problem finding in more detail in Chapter 3.

1.8.2 The hidden curse of realism

'Be realistic!' That cry has probably killed more new business ideas than any other. It is often a disguised way of really saying, 'be pessimistic!' Most people prefer the comfort of the known than the discomfort of uncertainty. Often people's own filters do not allow them to see the positive aspects of new ideas. Whatever the case, 'be realistic' is never good for new ideas. Besides which, how often have you met a critic who tried to make things better? The exception to this rule is when 'realistic' thinking is brought to bear as part of a structured problem-solving method such as Edward de Bono's 'Six Hat Thinking'[43] model.

At this early stage of thinking about a new way of supplying in-house IT services, you should allow yourself to play with optimistic ideas. About 80% of all our business conversation and thinking is rooted in past events.[44] Give yourself freedom to think into the future, to ask yourself the 'what if' questions, and to explore the implications of the answers you come up with. They are just thoughts after all. No money has been spent. Being realistic often stops our thinking process even before we get started. Allow yourself to think without this restriction – you will be surprised with the answers.

Charles Handy[45] suggests that when things are going really well, you should be thinking of the next wave of change. He suggests that there are four stages of thinking about these new ideas: idea creation, testing the idea, implementation, operationalisation. The most important point is that the first two stages require little capital outlay[13]. So you can have and test many ideas without needing to justify any significant expense.

1.8.3 Business shows the way – follow their example

When you read Chapter 2, constantly apply the ideas presented there to yourself, your department and your business. Remember you have given yourself permission to have future thoughts without having to be realistic or to justify your ideas. Ask yourself how the many business trends apply to IT as well as how you can become an enabler of these trends for business.

How IT can become the heroes of the new wave of change? Don't be afraid to go out on a limb – that's where the fruit is.

1.8.4 Here be dragons

If you've ever seen an ancient map of the world, you might remember that in the unexplored corners of the map, the map-maker would inscribe, '**Here be dragons**', or something like that. When there is no information available, people tend to make up their own. 'Here be dragons' was the map-maker's way of saying, 'we don't know anything about this area, please proceed with caution.' There were no dragons of course. But many mariners believed the map. Many people would rather believe the negative side of any story – it seems to be the way most people are. As Joe Flower[46], a change management specialist says: 'call me Cleopatra – Da queen of denial.' But before you believe the old map-makers of IT, and before you adopt the Cleopatra moniker mark the following words:

> Time has run out for IT managers who act like a protected species. Their three-fold failure to understand the business they are supposed to be part of, to communicate with their business colleagues, and to deliver cost effective systems has led to a collapse of faith in the IT department itself, and a determination by business managers to find alternative solutions to their computing needs.
>
> (Computer Weekly, 1991)[47]

Implementation ideas

Here are some ideas and suggestions to help you move from thought to action. This 'implementation ideas' section will occur at the end of every chapter to give you tips, exercises and projects to initiate as a result of the material in that chapter. Feel free to add your own action ideas. You may wish to do these exercises on your own, or more beneficially, you may wish to include them in a creative workshop (include people from outside your own sphere for really challenging results).

Warning: this is not a thought-free zone

1 There are two realities: the objective reality, which includes the things you see, the data, etc. And the subjective reality, which is your interpretation of what you see. Most conflict happens around subjective realities. So here's the challenge: compile a list of objective and observable facts about the in-house IT function. Now draw up two columns. In the first, give your interpretation of the data. In the second, give another totally different interpretation. This will help you in dealing with business criticism of the IT function.

2 Write a list of your grievances about how the business treats its IT function. Now write a 'reframe', an alternative, even opposite way of looking at the gripe. Do these reframes give you any ideas for immediate action? Prepare an action list.

3 Use the following template to identify threats and opportunities to IT in your company.

Driver of change	1	2	3	4	5

Firstly, instead of treating things as 'threats or opportunities' see them as drivers of change in the IT function. Draw up the list of drivers first. (When I run this exercise in workshops drivers such as, 'business support', 'system instability', 'constant change', Fred Smith (who may be pro or con), etc. come up.)

Secondly assign a value to the driver, with 1 being a negative force, 3 being neutral, and 5 being a positive force.

Now draw up an action list based on how you will harness the positive forces, track the neutral forces (or turn them positive), and neutralise the negative forces.

4 Draw up a list of the things that IT delivers to the business. How can you package and market this delivery better?

5 Allow yourself to play with ideas. Take a full half-hour to *draw* the IT function of the future. You may not use words, only use drawings to depict concepts. A way of thinking about the future is what I call 'future-past-tense thinking': allow yourself to travel two years ahead and identify what you *did* to be in the enviable position you find yourself in then. By using both pictures and the future-past tense you start the subliminal process of change in your own mind. That's all you want to do at this stage.

References

1. Grindley, K. (1991) *Managing IT at Board Level*. Pitman Publishing
2. Earl, M.J. (1992) Putting IT in its place; a polemic for the nineties. *Journal of Information Technology*, Vol. 7
3. Economist (1991) Too many computers spoil the broth. *Economist* p. 30, 24 August
4. Remenyi, D.S.J., Money, A. and Twite, A. (1995) *Effective Measurement and Management of IT Costs and Benefits*. Butterworth Heinemann; Oxford, UK

5. Le Roux, D.C. (1997) *A Model to guide management questions on the value of Information Technology.* Unpublished Doctoral research proposal, University of Pretoria

6. Stalk, G. and Hout, T. (1990) *Competing against time.* The Free Press, New York

7. Treacy M. and Wiersema, F. (1993) Customer Intimacy and Other Value Disciplines. *Harvard Business Review*; p84–93, Jan-Feb

8. Pritchett, P. (1994) *New Work Habits for a Radically Changing World.* Pritchett & Assoc., Dallas, Texas, p.10

9. Earl, M.J. and Feeny, D.F. (1994) *Is Your CIO adding Value?*, Management Review, Vol. 35, No. 3

10. Birchall, D. and Lyons, L. (1995) *Creating Tomorrow's Organization.* Pitman Publishing; London

11. Zuboff, S. (1988) *In the Age of the Smart Machine: The Future of Work and Power.* Basic Books, New York

12. *The American Heritage® Dictionary of the English Language* (1992) *Third Edition copyright.* Houghton Mifflin Company

13. Handy, C. (1989) *Age of Unreason.* Random House; London

14. Hamel, G. and Prahalad, C.K. (1994) *Competing for the Future.* Harvard Business School Press

15. Boynton, A.C., Jacobs, G.C. and Zmud, R.W. (1992) Whose Responsibility is IT Management? *Sloan Management Review,* Summer

16. Shaw, G.B. (1903) *Man and Superman,* 'Maxims for Revolutionists: Reason'

17. Earl, M.J. and Feeny, D.F. (1994) Is Your CIO Adding Value? *Management Review,* Vol. 35, No. 3

18. Imparato, N. and Harari, O. (1994) *Jumping the Curve.* Jossey-Bass

19. Remenyi, D.S.J., Money, A. and Twite, A. (1995) *Effective Measurement and Management of IT Costs and Benefits.* Butterworth-Heinemann, Oxford

20. Salzman, H. and Rosenthal, S.R. (1994) *Software by Design.* Oxford University Press, Oxford

21. Ahituv, N. and Neumann, S., (1982) *Principles of Information Systems Management*. WC Brown Publishers; Dubuque, Iowa

22. Handy, C. (1989) *Age of Unreason*. Random House, London

23. Weiss, A. (1995) *Our Emperors Have No Clothes*. Career Press; New Jersey

24. Hammer, M. and Stanton, S.A. (1995) The Reengineering Revolution. HarperCollins, London

25. Koch, R. and Godden, R. (1996) *Managing without management*. Nicholas Brealey Publishing, London

26. Hamel, G. and Prahalad, C.K. (1994) *Competing for the Future*. Harvard Business School Press

27. Remenyi, D.S.J., Money, A. and Twite, A. (1993) A Guide to Measuring and Managing IT Benefits. NCC Blackwell; Manchester

28. Beam, K. (Ed.) (1994) Software Engineering Productivity and Quality, *IS Analyser*, Vol. 32, No. 2

29. Remenyi, D.S.J., Sherwood-Smith, M.J. and White, T. (1997) *Maximising IT Benefits: A Process Approach*. Wiley

30. Brooks, F.P., Jr. (1995) *The Mythical Man Month: Essays on Software Engineering*. Addison-Wesley Publishing

31. Friedman, A.L. *Computer Systems Development: History, Organization and Implementation*. John Wiley & Sons, Chichester

32. DeMarco, T. (1978) *Structured Analysis and System Specification*. Yourdon Press; New York

33. Villegas, A., (1999) *Project Management Web Page*, http://www.usfca.edu/~villegas/classes/

34. White, T. (1995) Towards a Model for the Integration of New Technologies into Organizations. *Unpublished Master's Thesis*; University of the Witwatersrand

35. Pycraft, M. *et. al.* (1997) *Operations Management*. Pitman Publishing, London

36. Senge, P.M. (1990) *The Fifth Discipline*. Doubleday

37. Morgan, G. (1997) *Images of Organization*. Sage Publications; CA

38. Anthony, R.N. (1965) *Planning and Control Systems: A Framework for Analysis*. Harvard University Press, Boston, MA

39. Viegde, C. (1997) Knowledge Management: remaking organizations through learning. In: *Leveraging Knowledge for Business Performance*. Wits Business School, Johannesburg

40. Maynard, H.B. and Mehrtens, S.E. (1993) *The Fourth Wave: Business in the 21st Century*. Berrett-Koehler, San Francisco, CA

41. Land, G. and Jarman, B. (1992) *Breakpoint and Beyond: Mastering the Future Today*. HarperCollins, New York

42. James, J. (1996) *Thinking in the Future Tense*. Touchstone; New York

43. de Bono, E. (1993) *Serious Creativity*. Harper Collins Publishers

44. Krisco, K.H. (1997) *Leadership and the Art of Conversation*. Prima Publishing; California

45. Handy, C. (1994) *The Empty Raincoat*. Arrow Business Books; London

46. Flower, J. (1996) The root ideas in dealing with change. *The Change Project Website*; http://www.well.com/user/bbear/articles.html

47. *Computer Weekly* (1991) Does the IT Department have a future? July 25

2 | I'm glad the hole is at their end of the boat – business in the new world

2.1 Introduction

There is a cartoon that strikes me in which, at one end of a small boat, two people are bailing frantically as water pours in through a hole at their feet. At the other end of the boat two other people sit doing nothing, and one of them remarks to the other: 'I'm glad the hole is at their end of the boat'. It seems to me that this may be the attitude of too many people in business today, and dare I say, of IT people as well.

It is important for IT people to understand and get involved in the wider issues facing their company. It is no longer an acceptable survival strategy for IT people to say: 'the hole is at their end of the business'. A significant amount of the work I do at the moment relates to the business perception of the irrelevance of IT in the core business. Many of the business people I deal with see IT as 'box-droppers' and desktop techies.

In the real business, there are real problems, and technology is only ever part of them.

There are three types of organisation: those with their backs to the wall, those that can see a wall coming, and those who say:

'wouldn't this be a great place to build a wall?' Information technology correctly implemented will be the saviour of many businesses facing the wall.

So if IT people want to build their own walls (rather than being offered a cigarette and put up against one), then it would be a good idea to look at the significant changes which are occurring in the business environment.

2.1.1 Boiled frogs and Peruvian Indians – the nature of change

Before we move on, perhaps it would be an idea to remember what Charles Handy said about boiled frogs and Peruvian Indians.[1]

It seems that if you put a frog into hot water, it will immediately jump out. If however you put the frog into cold water, and slowly raise the temperature (and I've not tried this, I'll take it on trust thanks), the frog will not notice the incremental change, and will remain in the water only to be boiled to death. The moral of this tale is that we often don't recognise incremental changes, and allow ourselves to be overwhelmed by something that has grown slowly, often in full sight. Some examples that come to mind are PCs and the Internet that may seem to have been here forever but are having enormous influence on society and the world economy. Davidson and Rees-Mogg[2] would have it that these two technologies will bring down governments as we know them today, as power shifts irrevocably away from collective structures to lie in the hands of the individual.

Handy's other story about change strikes more of a chord with me. The Peruvian Indians saw the sails of the Spanish Conquistadors on the horizon. But because European sailing ships were entirely outside their experience, they put it down to a strange cloud formation and let the invaders in. IBM's initial response to the advent of personal computing demonstrates this response, with their assumption that mainframes would rule forever. To their credit, once the penny dropped, they set up two competing teams to develop the cheapest most stable PC and cornered the market for a while. (Of course they did still miss the mark by regarding their business as being hardware and by giving the job of developing the PC operating system to a certain Mr. Gates and his team.)

Now two types of change are depicted here: firstly, incremental change which we see but which we don't act on because after all: 'it's not so different from what we have come to accept as normal'. The second type of change is equally visible, but because it does not fit within our world view, we ignore it with potentially devastating results. Something like the proverbial ostrich putting its head in the sand. Here's a useless fact which might explain the ostrich's behaviour: did you know an ostrich's brain is smaller than its eye?

Someone once said: 'a mind is like a parachute, it works best when it's open'. So here's the challenge to you: read this chapter with your mind like a parachute: look for the 'frogs' (or invisible incremental changes) and 'sails' (or visible, but beyond our experience, changes) which will directly affect your future.

2.1.2 The race is on – major themes of business change

> The propensity to truck, barter and exchange one thing for another . . . is common to all men, and to be found in no other race of animals.
>
> (Adam Smith, 1993)[3]

Is the light at the end of the tunnel just an oncoming train? There are many futurists who will portentously tell you of revolutionary changes coming down the tunnel. I am not a futurist, nor can I carry off 'portentous' with any conviction. However, I would like to look at a number of major business changes that they predict, because these changes will materially affect both your work life and your personal life, often not necessarily for the better. I'll look at the future world economy and the role of business in that economy. I obviously want to examine how technology is changing the landscape, and finally I would like to spend some time examining how the people side of business is irrevocably changing.

2.2 Unguided missiles – the future world economy

> Practical men, who believe themselves to be quite exempt from any intellectual influence, are usually the slaves of some defunct economist.
>
> (John Maynard Keynes, 1936)[4]

The problem seems to be that we have a new world economy that affects everyone, through processes which are not wholly palatable, and no-one seems to know what to do about it.

2.2.1 Circles within circles – the nature of the new economy

Peter Drucker[5] observes that the term 'world economy' only came into common use in the mid 1970s. Before that it was 'international trade'. He adds:

> Twenty or thirty years ago, the economy outside the borders of a nation ... could be seen as different, as separate, as something that could be safely ignored in dealing with the domestic economy and in domestic economic policy. That, as the evidence makes unambiguously clear, is sheer delusion today.
>
> (Drucker, 1995)

Drucker goes on to split the new world economy in two parts: traditionally, 'international trade' consisted of foreign commerce and foreign investment. Trade was based on merchandise transactions. These days, trade and investment are merging into one transaction, and trade has transmuted into more of a relationship between producers, with transactions being book-entries in the ongoing alliance. But more important in this part of the world economy is the trade, not of merchandise, but of services. In the USA, services such as financial and retailing services, higher education, tourism, royalties on books, videos, and technology and professional services amount to two-thirds of the US merchandising budget. Drucker says this is a conservative estimate in a fast-growing trade area. Now here's the sail on the horizon: most of these services are impervious to traditional merchandising forces, and secondly, most of these services involve the import and export of knowledge. So we can't see it and we can't count it, and we can't apply our rules to it. Does that mean it doesn't exist?

The second part of the new world economy, according to Drucker, involves the flow of money and information. The flow of 'market money' exceeds by an order of magnitude the 'real money' in any day. People are trading money. David Korten, in his book: *When Corporations Rule the World*[6] has this to say about the money market, or the 'money game' as he calls it:

> For every $1 circulating in the productive world economy, $20 to $50 circulates in the economy of pure finance – though no-one knows the ratios for sure. In the international currency markets alone, some $800 billion to $1 trillion changes hands each day, far in excess of the $20 billion to $25 billion required to cover daily trade in goods and services . . . This money is unassociated with any real value.
>
> (Korten, 1995)

The worrying thing, apart from the inverted pyramidal nature of the money game, is the fact that most money trading 'decisions' are being made by computers on the basis of complex mathematical formulas. As Korten says:

> This is a long way from the invisible hand of the market Adam Smith had in mind when 'The Wealth of Nations' was published in 1776.
>
> (Korten, 1995)

This is significant, because money-flows were traditionally used as stabilisers in the world economy, restoring equilibrium where needed. Now, they have become de-stabilisers of national economies, for example forcing fast and alarming rises in interest rates.

People also trade information: software, e-mail, magazines, meetings, rock concerts, films, and many other forms of information are flowing across borders and around the globe. The fees, royalties and profit generated by this information flow are growing faster than any other category of transaction ever grew before in economic history[7]. Information-flows are more benign than money-flows, but they are a social phenomenon which is redefining the role of governments[8], businesses[9], and individuals, and the relationships between all of these. I'll examine these relationship changes in more detail later.

> The first lesson of the world economy is that the two most significant phenomena – money flows and information flows – do not fit into any theory or policy we have. They are not even 'transnational'; they are outside altogether, and 'non-national[10].'
>
> (Drucker, 1995)

The sail on the horizon is this: money and the world economy is for the first time behaving as a truly chaotic system, with rapid and excessive fluctuations which obey no traditional rules. How good is your chaos theory? It may be your key to understanding the future.

In short, Drucker is announcing a new world economy of which the greater portion is made up of money, information and services, none of which conform to traditional economic principles. The basis of this new economy is knowledge.

2.2.2 Growing pains or death throes? – growth and the new economy

> I saw a Western economy blissfully ignorant in the massive swings in the fortunes of nations... Most disturbingly, I saw that we ... have become the architects of the single greatest challenge to the survival of humanity: the consumer society[11].
>
> (Firmage, 1999)

In 1972 the Club of Rome published the results of a modelling study in which they predicted that within 100 years from then, the earth would reach the limits of growth in many renewable and non-renewable resources[12]. The book caused an uproar.

In 1993 three of the authors of this first book published a follow-up study[13], in which they concluded that we have already exceeded the limits to many of our resources. The question is now more about how we recover, if at all.

Scary stuff, but such studies do set us up to look at some 'frogs' which may become an opportunity or a threat in the near future. Firstly we need to recognise that the old adage of 'growth is good' needs some modification. Where and how will we grow if we can't sell our product or get the resources? For example: it is predicted that 20% of the motor vehicles manufactured in the USA in 2000 will never be sold[14]. So we need to change our thinking from 'big is better' to something else. And that something relates to quality. High quality, many featured, low cost vehicles will still sell. The production emphasis will switch from 'big is better' to 'better is better'.

Secondly Drucker and numerous other authors have already suggested that the world economy is switching from production and merchandise to knowledge. The question then becomes: 'how can we leverage our knowledge?' That leads us to finding new and acceptable ways to measure and account for knowledge[15]. Thomas Stewart[16] describes knowledge as a troublesome asset: it is 'non-subtractive' in that it can be used without being consumed; it exists independent of space, it hasn't a fixed location; it has multiple lives, because you can sell it to someone then sell it again; some forms are extremely sensitive to time and there is no correlation between knowledge input and knowledge output. All of these qualities will drive traditional accountants up the wall.

Because IT and the management of data, information and knowledge are so closely linked, I'll deal with the question of knowledge and its effects in much more detail as we go through this chapter.

Given a limited world and limited resources, and adding to it population growth and the vast disparity in wealth amongst that population, you don't have to be a rocket scientist to work out that we have an unstable system. Joe Firmage, who created a software company and made $24 million by the age of 21, says the following:

> Eventually, people are going to understand ... that the hectic, unbridled, unrestrained pace of economic activity – with no connection back to the resources from which it draws, namely the earth – is fundamentally unstable.[17]
>
> (Firmage, 1999)

Apart from the 'what can I possibly do about it?' reaction, we should give some thought to what new economic activities will emerge as a result of the challenge: there will be an increase in environmental economic activity – cleaning water, air and land will become big business, as will agricultural biology or improving agricultural practices and yields. Energy management will become important, as will the management of unwanted by-products of manufacturing activity. Did you know for instance, that batteries take about 50 times more energy to produce than they ultimately deliver, and that they represent a major pollution source?[18] Did you also know that a wind-up radio has been invented, and is being bought by governments all over the world – no batteries required. This sort of thing is where new economic activity will prosper.

Sustainability will become a measure of both a company's product value and of its worth. Many consumers are beginning to downsize their consumption activities[19] buying down on their houses and vehicles, and producing much of their food at home. 'Sufficient' has become their new watchword.

In some instances villages, towns and communities are providing their own services for themselves: doctors, carpenters, gardeners, plumbers and others are providing services to members of their community at no cost – rather they barter for other goods available within that community and this barter takes place on a local PC network within that community.

The new world economy may appear to be a gloomy picture. That we have to thoroughly rework old and unfit ideas about what's good for people in the long run, is beyond doubt. We are capable of astounding leaps of development and advance, and that more and more people are paying attention to the correct economic challenges. So I'll leave that for now, (the hole's on their side of the boat after all!), in the interests of moving on to business trends which affect, and are affected by, IT.

2.3 New reasons to exist – the changing role of business

In South Africa, after the newly elected democratic government came to power, they set up a Truth and Reconciliation Commission to examine the crimes and deeds committed during the Apartheid years. When South African business was called to the commission, and asked why they didn't do more, why they didn't get more involved in the lives and injustices of their employees, their answer can be paraphrased as: 'the business of business is business, not politics'. A similar situation to the boat cartoon I described earlier. Having said that, a number of South African businesses were major forces of change in that country.

But the role of business in the world economy and the lives of men and women is necessarily changing.

> Corporation: An ingenious device for obtaining individual profit without individual responsibility.
>
> (Ambrose Bierce, 1906)[20]

2.3.1 Profit or loss – why do businesses exist?

So what is a business for? In the 1960s the answer was not even debated:

> The purpose of business is to maximize medium-term earnings per share.
>
> (Handy, 1994)[21]

However, 40 years later, the leading businesses are redefining what 'success' means. They are looking at why they are in business in the first place, and what their purpose in the economy, society and the environment signifies. They are looking at who their important stakeholders are. They are redefining their boundaries – where their business starts and ends. They are looking at their definition of assets, and finding that traditional views of capital no longer fit the way they, and the stock markets, value themselves. They are re-evaluating information and its purpose in business.

These and other basic definitions of the 'business of business' will have a profound effect on the role of IT in the businesses who are asking these questions of themselves.

Drucker believes that business has a new purpose in the new economy:

Profit: yes this is important, and still the primary business imperative, but other factors are playing a role in why businesses exist.

Responsibility: Reich[22] and Drucker are of the view that most of the power in modern world terms lies not with governments or with individuals, but with companies. And with power comes responsibility. As Drucker asks, if not business, then:

Who will look after the common good?

Organisation: the task of organising effort around a common goal or vision remains a prime role of business. We need to gain economies, not necessarily of scale, but of flow and organisation.

Relationships: the business of negotiating and maintaining relationships between organisations, and between companies and 'employees' is an essential part of why companies exist.

Survival with purpose: Handy[23] believes that businesses exist to make a profit in order to continue to do things, or make things better and more abundantly. In doing so they improve the lot of all stakeholders in the business.

2.3.2 Who owes what to whom – business stakeholders

And who are the stakeholders in business? Handy believes that in quoted companies, the shareholder, traditionally the primary stakeholder, has changed from being an 'owner' of the business to more like being a 'punter' or gambler. His logic requires owners to take some responsibility in the behaviour and running of the company, which of course shareholders do not. Reich[24] agrees, and adds that the link between ownership and responsibility has been broken by the advent of the professional manager. Firmage[25] is a little more vociferous in his reading of the impact of Internet-based investing in shares:

> The public is now driving the equity markets . . . Never in the history of Wall Street have you had the ability of John Q. Citizen to . . . go directly with their own investment purchase decisions. The difference is that it's based far more on a Las Vegas mentality . . . How much of this investing is rooted in a solid knowledge-based decision making process? . . . Virtually none, I would guess.
>
> (Firmage, 1999)

So what's the problem? Well gamblers are in it for the quick buck. They move to where the return is greatest in the short term. And if that return is being generated by trashing the productive capacity, or the employee base, or the environment, of what interest is it to the shareholders? Again, a simple evaluation would suggest that this is an unsustainable system.

Therefore as many authors point out, responsible companies must look to a different set of stakeholders to define their performance criteria for them. Handy suggests that there are essentially six stakeholders in a company's activities: yes the shareholder is still there, but we must add: employees, customers, suppliers, the community and the environment to the list. And satisfying these stakeholders, or even serving them, is going to complicate business transactions enormously. Here's the frog: how can IT play a role between a company and all of its stakeholders?

2.3.3 Seeing things through different lenses – the new business focus

The focus of business attention is changing as well.

Intelligent businesses are concentrating more on what's happening outside their companies which, if they apply their learning correctly, helps them improve their internal processes. The customer, competitors, suppliers and market forces are important elements in business focus.

Business focus is changing in how it strategises, plans, executes and measures its activities. It used to be that senior staff could develop a five-year plan, and carry it out with some certainty. Those days are over. As Karl Albrecht[26] says:

> Hitting the exact targets of any plan you could write would be a sheer accident.
>
> (Albrecht, 1994)

Henry Mintzberg[27] has suggested that your planning could be deliberate, or 'emergent' in which you look back and see a pattern of responses which have meaning. This is a powerful technique. Look back on how things have panned out for your company. Did events follow the stated strategy? Or did they take their own course, independent of the strategy? Your emergent strategy tells you a lot about how your company really works.

Formative evaluation[28], on the other hand, is an idea where you define a broad outcome space, and then evaluate your progress at short intervals, and form new plans to reach your outcome from where you are. Some call this strategic intent, and the important process is to constantly check your progress and adjust your actions. Many companies are also developing scenarios[29] to help them respond to a range of future conditions.

Companies are starting to measure themselves differently too. Traditionally the market value of a company was derived from its tangible assets: its fixed assets, investments, current assets and the like. There is a growing recognition that companies need to measure their value and performance on a wider front. Kaplan and Norton's[30] 'Balanced Scorecard' measurement has gained significant acceptance as it links financial, customer, internal process, and innovation and development measures into a coherent whole. Many of the companies I have worked with have accepted the idea of a balanced scorecard, but are having difficulty implementing it. It comes down to two related things: firstly, we still think like accountants, and secondly, our systems are not geared to measure the softer elements of the scorecard. It is mostly a mindset problem though: There's the saying: 'nothing counts unless it can be counted'. So let's count the counters. Charles Handy[31], observed that there were 170,000 registered bean-counters in Britain in 1995, and only 7000 in Japan. These were members of accountancy bodies in each country. There were 20,000 in Germany and 4000 in France. And if you believe that: 'what you see depends on where you're standing', then in a measurement system which is largely dependent on non-financial measures, the bean counters are going to have difficulty seeing the value of those measurements. So IT has a significant role to play in the successful implementation of a wider and more inclusive measurement ethic in our companies.

2.3.4 If our people are our greatest asset, why do we treat them like liabilities?

I am unaware of any accepted accounting treatment of people who work for a company other than as a cost. Of course, costs are something you try to minimise.

But smart businesses are seeing their people in a different light: the focus is slowly shifting from treating people as 'work capable units', to understanding that they are complex and often unpredictable entities with the capacity to produce astounding results if their barriers to performance are removed.

These companies understand that in a knowledge economy, they must focus less on control of individuals and concentrate on the guidance and enabling of people to carry out increasingly complex tasks. And that's one of the reasons that the 'vision, mission and values' focus has swept the business world in recent years. You can't control people in the new economy: employees have access to too much information, too many alternative opportunities, and are required to think too much if you are to deliver the services required by your customers. Employees are starting to assert their human rights in often de-humanising working environments. To motivate and direct them requires their support for the organisation's goals and their judgement in solving your customer's problems.

How companies reward people is also changing. They are focusing more on outputs, deliverables and outcomes, rather than paying them an 'attendance' salary or wage. Some companies I know have re-contracted with their employees, with up to 70% of their 'salary' being at risk, dependent upon them reaching a goal or delivering an output. This is significantly changing the employment landscape.

Many businesses are down-scaling. A good friend of mine is an anthropologist, and he is not surprised by this trend to move from economies of scale, to human scale. He says that now that technology allows us to do so, it is possible to revert to our ancestral human units: a family consisted of between four and ten people, and so do work-teams. However, an extended family numbered up to 100 people, and so many departments are limiting themselves to this size. And a village consisted of between 1000 and 3000 people, and so do many business units.

And the workplace is shifting as well. In the industrial revo-lution, the trend was to move people close to the immovable capital, the production facility. Now with three trends occurring: the automation and miniaturisation of production; the move towards service provision; and the new mobility of computers and communication, it is possible to move the new critical asset, people, to where they will be most effective. This means more people are in the field, at customer premises, or at home, far from the source of production. And this in turn means that the old 'line-of-sight' command and control management style will come to an end.

2.4 Technology

Much has, and will be written about trends in technology. I can't hope to condense all of that into a section in a chapter. So I will compromise and only look at particular areas of technology. It seems though that once you adopt a systems approach, there is a certain inevitability in where these technologies will lead us. The technologies I have chosen are obviously not the only technologies which are going to affect our future. If you want to do some work of your own on technological scenarios, Peter Schwartz gives you a method to follow, in his book: *The Art of the Long View*[32].

Business and economic thinkers are announcing a new world economy, of which the greater portion is made up of money, information and services, none of which conform to traditional economic principles.

2.4.1 Why do technology?

There are many reasons people have chosen (or been forced) to use technology. In Chapter One I discussed Zuboff's analysis of technology as falling into the 'automation, information and transformation' role in the organisation.

Compression drives us to use technology – it allows us to compress time, dimensions, distance, costs and data.

Time has been compressed in product development times, production cycles, order fulfilment cycles, and search periods speeded up, even appearing to be instantaneous. It is para-doxically sad that with all this time saving going on, we have even less time on our hands. American parents are spending 10 hours less time per week with their children now than they did in the 1960s.[33]

Dimensions are compressed by technology as processors become smaller and faster. The obvious example is computers. My first computer-related job was as Facilities Manager in an installation whose computer was the size of a truck, cost a fortune and was 600 times less powerful than my current laptop that fits comfortably in my briefcase. Of course both machines were designed for different things, so I am comparing apples with pears to some extent. More evidence of miniaturisation is the mobile phone phenomenon, which allows you to surf the Internet on an instrument smaller than your hand.

Geographical distance is compressed by computer networks and increasing bandwidth. India now enjoys the fastest grow-ing software development industry in the world, even though it is distant from most of its clients. Round-the-clock software development is possible by companies with offices in Europe, Asia or Australia, and the USA. Video-conferencing allows face to face meetings across oceans. (If only the earth were flat we wouldn't have the time zone problem.) Indubitably the most profound technology enabling the compression of distance is the Internet which has allowed companies to reach the world as a direct market. Jane Citizen can set up a web-site in Alaska or on Mauritius and be advertising to, and interacting with, customers anywhere in the world in hours. (Except apparently Mongolia which I read had only one PC in 1998.) However, the one thing that technology has not yet managed to compress is the physical movement of goods. This logistics area remains the Achilles Heel of the Internet, and opportunities for effective and efficient logistics operations are manifest.

Costs are also compressed by technology. Moore's law predicts a halving of the cost of processing while doubling the power every 18 months until the year 2020. This cost compression significantly lowers the barriers to entry to most industries. Steel, the 'sine qua non' of large industry takes four man hours to produce one ton, in the largest steel refinery in the USA. Nucor Steel revolutionised steel production with its highly computerised mini-mills, and they produce one ton with 45 minutes of labour[34]. Small 'inexpensive' boutique manufacturers are changing the face of industry.

Data is being compressed into information and knowledge. Not very well in many of the organisations I have worked with, but that's more a function of people's inability to think differently than any fault of the technology. With the combination of mobility and networking, the corporate memory is now available to everyone in the organisation whether they be at a customer site or in some remote geography. The ability to filter through the mass of data and focus on trends allows a new level of modelling and 'what-if' exercises.

Technology allows displacement of costs and activities, as we are able to shift the burden of work onto suppliers and outsourcing companies without compromising our own operations. So the assets we are forced to use to run our businesses are directly linked to the core business. All the rest can move off the balance sheet onto the profit and loss statement as expenses. Displacement of activities away from the core business is creating new forms of companies, which combine disparate organisations, each focusing on what they do best, to produce an apparently complete service to customers. This new arrangement of endeavour has bred entrepreneurs who act more as composers and conductors than as musicians – they capture an idea, and assemble all the parts necessary to make the idea work, and orchestrate the activities of the parts. Although they work like demons, they don't actually do any of the direct work.

Further displacement occurs when technology allows us to cut out steps and middlemen in the production or sales process. This process of 'disintermediation' has connected suppliers directly with customers, removing agents and handlers from the process. But it has given rise to a new form of middleman – the 'infomediaries'. People or organisations who set up portals and hubs to allow more suppliers to reach more customers directly.

It is clear that people will continue to find more and varied mechanisms for using technology to make life faster. When all's said and done I am not sure whether life is any easier though. Perhaps I am a closet anti-technologist. I certainly know that technology is responsible for many hidden ills, shortcomings and devastations in the world. I have already cited the fact that a battery takes 50 times more energy to produce than it delivers. Computers generate toxic waste. Silicon Valley has become one of the most polluted areas of the USA[35]. Chip manufacture requires the extensive use of ozone-depleting gases. And this ignores the increasing social ills like increased surveillance, decreased privacy, hacking, freely available pornography and the list goes on. We have yet to met the consequences of the current wave of technological advance, whether good or bad.

2.4.2 The law of unintended consequences

When Johann Gutenberg produced the first printed Bible in 1456, he believed that the ready availability of the sacred book would strengthen the position of religion in society. In fact, an unintended consequence of Gutenberg's printing press was the spread of all knowledge, religious or otherwise. Knowledge was no longer bound by location, locked up in rare books or in people's heads. It was from this point on, that an exponential proliferation of knowledge ushered in the scientific revolution, which ultimately led to the erosion of religious dogma and the subsequent weakening of the church.

There are significant unintended consequences to be found in the technological innovations manifesting themselves in the world today. For example, in the same way that the printing press led to the scientific revolution in the fifteenth century by enabling knowledge to be independent of geography, what revolution is being launched right now by the Internet, which to a large extent, allows people to operate independent of geography? In 'The Sovereign Individual'[36] Davidson and Rees-Mogg predict the end of governments as we know them, and the rise of the 'city-state', as a direct result of the Internet. Having read the book, I can't say I disagree with them – but I get ahead of myself.

I am not a futurologist or a soothsayer, but I would like to look, in a deferential way, at some specific technologies, considering the intended and unintended consequences, and offering some thoughts on where technology is taking us.

- I'll look at the trend of technology in becoming both cheaper, smaller and more connected. I'll particularly examine 'personal' technology.

- Another linked technology lies in the growth of the Internet, and in not just the access to information, but the ability to conduct transactions outside the established structures. The Internet will affect the way the world works and governs itself.

- Finally, an important 'technology' for companies lies in their ability to assimilate, organise and use information.

2.4.3 Everyone has one – smaller, faster, cheaper: personal computing – personal empowerment

A personal computer, in all its forms, is more than a tool. It frees up time so people can do other things, it gives access to information so people can decide for themselves, it increases the scope of influence so people can work in more areas, it is location-independent so people can work wherever they are. The list goes on. PCs will change how work is allocated, the way work happens, where it happens, and how it is measured and rewarded. It will therefore change how we plan, lead, organise and control people. Personal computing will aid and abet to a revolution in management and empowerment. I'll look at a few aspects of personal computing as they affect the way work is done in organisations.

There is no entrance fee – access to computing is nearly limitless

Individuals are being empowered by technology. More computing is available to more people. This means that computer literacy rates are increasing, but particularly among the young. As the saying goes: 'it's difficult bringing up a 12 year-old kid, but someone has to understand the technology.' These youngsters learn to program almost as a second language, with none of the angst or formality that I remember from when I learned. Computing is less of a learned skill, and more of an acquired competence.

I sometimes lose sight of the fact that personal computers have only been around for 20-odd years. I remember when I was a geologist, and I motivated for the purchase of our company's first PC: the Managing Director, Financial Director and myself went off to the supplier to examine the options and buy the machine. And the sales assistant asked us if we wanted 10 megabytes of disk drive, or 20? We opted for 10, because we couldn't foresee the situation in which a 20 megabytes of storage would be necessary. I'm dating myself here, but the point is that now a PC is largely viewed as an essential piece of office or home equipment, the bigger the better. The problem is that many 'captains of industry' remain PC illiterate.

I see a number of consequences here: I view with some eagerness the first ground-breaking programming from youths for whom computing is an acquired (rather than learned) skill. Such people won't be constrained by what we oldies regard as 'rules' of software. For example, spreadsheets, reporting, word processing and graphics are all fairly neatly compartmentalised in my mind. And it seems, in the 'mind' of the software I use. I can foresee 'learning software' which looks at the way I work and constructs a package that fits my work patterns, from input handling objects. For instance, in my writing, I use a thesaurus more than most, and my word-processors' thesaurus is fairly basic. I would really like my software to wake up, smell the coffee, and give me a good thesaurus.

Wherever you go, there you are – portable computing

Personal computing is becoming more portable. My wife, who is not computer literate, took one look at my new laptop and said: 'now that's a computer I can use. It's more human and friendly than the great big box you have on your desk.' Laptops are getting smaller, and more manageable. But not only more manageable, computing is now getting closer to where the work happens. On site, at the customer's premises, and at home.

What happens when you can work from home, or from your client's premises, or from your hotel room or the airport? Well the intended consequence is that more work should be done. The unintended consequence is the loss of 'humanity' and contact. Humans are social beings. We like people.

I was involved with a forward-thinking supplier of software who asked the question: 'if successful employees spend most of their time on the client's premises, why do we need offices?'

Interestingly, we explored the idea and found that most people in this situation would use the office not as a place of work, but rather as a place to socialise, test ideas, relax away from the 'frontline', and to brag or commiserate as the need arose. Consequently, this software supplier's head office had casual sitting rooms rather than offices, a good library, an Internet Café rather than a canteen, and a pub in which the only rule was: 'don't run out of my brand of beer!' A few years later I checked with them and was pleased to find that rather than take clients out for a drink, they much preferred bringing clients 'back to their place' because there were always like-minded souls inhabiting the pub. They naturally made more sales. Portable computing allowed them to examine the basic assumptions about work and the work place, and they changed, radically. I salute them.

Assessing the value of contribution – measuring work

Portable computing will change how we measure work. Rather than being a place to which you go, work will be a thing that you do. This in turn will unequivocally change the way we measure people's performance. At the moment, most people are paid 'attendance fees': paid for the time they are present at the workplace. If you want to test this, just suggest to your boss that you will only be working five hours a day from now on, but not to worry, your outputs will go up. The standard answer will undoubtedly be: 'you're paid for eight hour's work and that's what you're going to do!' But if people work from home, or from the road, or their client's premises, then how do we measure their performance? By their outputs, of course. This in turn has a major impact on measurement and payment systems. Also, you can no longer practice 'line-of-sight' management. 'Line-of-sight' management requires you to 'manage by walking about', to 'catch someone doing something right' and all the other progressive management techniques that we have come to know. We will now have to develop 'out-of-sight' management techniques. I would like to suggest that management techniques will have to become more like 'self-management' techniques, and that central management will concern itself with *what* is done, rather than *how* it is done.

Management of distributed workers will also become an issue of balancing the attractive forces (those that draw employees towards your culture, vision and values), and displacement forces (those which pull people away from the way your organisation works).

Computers get cheaper, people get more expensive – a system under strain

If computing is becoming cheaper, and people are becoming more expensive, what consequences can we expect? You don't have to be a mastermind to work out that computing will replace people. And then what?

> Taken to extremes, the perfectly efficient corporation would entail computers and machines making things. People would be unnecessary. We are acting as if this is the world we wish to create[39].
>
> (Korten, 1995)

The good news is that computers can't feel, empathise, or 'be there' for people. This balances nicely with the move towards differentiating on customer service. We still need people to be nice to people. Our jobs will become more people-centred and more service-orientated, but at the same time we will have to be masters of the technology which does all the mundane non-people oriented work.

The unintended consequence of customer-centred service is likely to be a rise in customer power, and we may be faced with customers who abuse this power with a possible corruption of customer service principles, which may force organisations towards shady dealings in the interests of making the sale.

Personal computing – all change

I have touched on a few trends in personal computing, and extrapolated a few consequences, but it becomes obvious that the personal computer represents a significant factor in how our companies will be operating in the near future.

One of my favourite quotes as I sit at my laptop, either at home or on an aeroplane or in a hotel room, comes from Ken Olson, President, Chairman and Founder of Digital Equipment Corporation (DEC). In 1977 he said:

> There is no reason anyone would want a computer in their home.

How we marvel at the near-sightedness of it all. But of course we would probably nod in agreement if someone said, 'every company needs offices'. Or do they?

2.4.4 The internet

It is a daunting task writing about the Internet. So let me surrender to a mind much greater than my own – Peter Drucker[38] who says:

> The first lesson of the world economy is that the two most significant phenomena – money flows and information flows – do not fit into any theory or policy we have. They are not even 'transnational'; they are outside altogether, and 'non-national'.
>
> (Drucker, 1999)

In short, Drucker is announcing a new world economy based on the Internet, of which the greater portion is made up of money, information and services, none of which conform to traditional economic principles.

New laws define this new economy. For example there's Moore's Law (processing power will double every 18 months while processing costs halve in the same period) and Gilder's Law (bandwidth will triple every year for 25 years) both of which are linked to Metcalfe's Law (the power of the Internet is equal to the square of its nodes). Taken in parallel with the fact that technology is changing faster than our behaviours are, we're in for a roller-coaster time in the Internet economy.

Access to the world

There are pros and cons in having ready access to information. In organisations, access to information allows you to cut out layers, and to bypass gatekeepers. It is causing a shift in power in organisations away from the power people hold because they have access to certain information towards power that people have because they know more than the others do.

Access to information also affects who can participate and how they can participate in an organisation's affairs. The 'empowerment' movement is less about management giving away power, and more about self-empowerment. I'll give you an example: a friend of mine is an engineer working for a utilities company. He, and two work colleagues believed that their department could provide services to the outside world, and a scan of the Internet supported this belief. They designed a web page offering their services, and then went to the utility's management to discuss their future relationship with the company. Management was aghast. If they didn't like the friends' proposal, they knew they would lose the entire department. So they came to an arrangement in which they would 'pay' market related rates – less a preferred customer discount – and the team would be free to seek work outside. Sound like blackmail? You bet! Who said business was fair? But now, thanks to the Internet, the boot is on the other (worker's) foot.

It's easy to gain access to information. I was talking to an executive on an aeroplane yesterday, and he showed me a project his son was doing. All the diagrams and much of the text came from the Internet. I'm not sure how the teacher marks such projects. In my day I had to go to the library, and search through books until I found the one that served my purpose. I would then check the book out and re-write the text that I believed was pertinent, and I would trace pictures, and re-draw them into my project. I don't mean to sound overly nostalgic, but I do wonder if this ease of access to information makes learning any easier. I think not. I would spend hours on one particular drawing. Now it's a case of 'cut and paste'.

Which brings us to the information overload problem. A local ISP advertises its services with the slogan: 'there's so much good stuff out there'. I always want to shout 'Where?' because every time I get out there I either find a load of nothing, or so much that I can't even begin to assimilate it. Margaret Wheatley[39] suggests that self-organisation will take over when information overload becomes too great. The problem with this idea of self-organisation, which I actually support, is that you need to provide frameworks and methods for people to adopt in order to cope with the information at their disposal. Such a framework would take the form of a vision, your mission, and of course your strategic objectives. There is a need to have a framework which will allow individuals to integrate all the many initiatives that the organisation has undertaken. This is probably one of the most important forms of information management that a company can undertake.

The Internet separates the work from the location in a way that has never happened before. I am writing this book in various locations around the world as my work takes me there, and my publisher, with whom I have frequent discussions, is based in Oxford, England. I've never met many of the people who are involved in the production of this book. Perhaps less trivial is the fact that the Internet compresses distance to zero and shrinks time. This means that an organisation can offer a service to anyone in the world any time of the day. There are practical issues associated with this manner of doing business of course but as a good (and very successful) friend of mine says, 'that's just logistics, man.' It is a little more than 'just logistics' but I take his point. Once you have the enabler in place, the rest is just a case of making it happen. And the Internet allows organisations to think 'global and immediate' and that's the breakthrough thought for the Internet revolution.

Associated with the separation of work from location is the mobility that the Internet provides.

Business boundaries

The Internet changes business boundaries, and this will change the way businesses see themselves and the work they do. Changes in boundaries involve the geographical boundaries, the physical boundaries, and most importantly, the mental boundaries. Geographical location is less of an issue with the Internet, especially if you are a provider of services. But the physical boundary changes are profound. Many companies are doing business with their competitors in order to supply a seamless solution to their customers. The Internet is not solely responsible for this of course, but again it is an enabler. Some exciting breakthroughs are being made with companies that are extending their boundaries up and down the supply chain. The Internet gives you access to your customers and to their customers as well. I was recently involved in assessing the purchase of a medical health insurance company by an IT company. It made sense: combine the medical knowledge and product suite of the health insurer with the one thing that troubles most such companies – processing capacity. That's where the IT company came in. But we saw a hidden opportunity. This health insurer had some 500,000 clients. 'What if,' the IT company reasoned, 'we could use this channel of medical insurance to offer 500,000 known clients other services, such as banking, buying, and financial services?' And they went ahead and put in an offer to purchase the medical insurer as much for its ongoing business as for access to its customers. Now this doesn't have to be an acquisition scenario, it could also be a joint venture or a contracted agreement.

In the same way it is possible to do business with your suppliers' suppliers. This doesn't mean bypassing your suppliers (although that is an entirely valid scenario), but usually companies will work with their suppliers to ensure that their supply chain is stable and of the correct quality.

Another boundary issue raised by Davidson and Rees-Mogg in *The Sovereign Individual*[40] is the erosion of national boundaries. This has implications. Individuals will become more powerful than organisations, and movement of these individuals will flow to locations guaranteeing the best quality of life. Thus boundaries may shift inwards, as smaller city-sized units make these guarantees, and attract the right people to their location. Once you have the people, they generate income, and you can improve the quality of life further. The rich will get richer and the poor will get poorer. The Internet will speed this process up.

Encryption

The Internet worries authorities. Already trade is occurring in great volumes across borders, and only when it involves a physical good, can governmental authorities detect it. Anything that can be digitised can pass through the Internet without governmental and tax agencies being able to assess its value or indeed its content. Cash can be digitised, as can financial and retailing services, higher education, tourism, books, videos, technology and professional services. How will authorities tax this, or even know it is happening? Tax authorities in Australia became concerned when their tax revenues from a number of isolated towns dropped to about half of the previous levels. When they investigated they found that these towns had reverted to LAN-based barter. If you were a dentist, work you did for the plumber would be paid back by the plumber at some later date. This very soon evolved into a crude form of e-cash, where one hour of a dentist's work generated x units and an hour of a plumber's work generated 2x units. (No disrespect to dentists, but have you seen your plumber's bills lately.) If this was all a local system, then real money would begin to disappear (or more precisely not appear), from the system. Cash would only be used for goods which were unavailable in the town, and earnings would only be generated for work done outside the town. And so what was there to tax? Only boundary goods – those that came from outside the town, and boundary earnings – those that were earned outside the town. And if you encrypted the 'in town' e-cash, how would the authorities have any way of knowing what went on, much less tax it. And the same is happening across boundaries with the assistance of encryption.

2.4.5 Organising information

I have discussed the information overload brought about by the Internet. But what about the opportunities brought about by information overload. The largest selling magazine in the USA is purely an information overload organiser. It is called the TV Guide[41] and its sole purpose is to organise the TV schedules from the various broadcasters into a digestible form for TV viewers. The information is available already – each station puts out their schedules free to the public – but people are prepared to pay for it to be organised for them. Bill Davidson and Stan Davis[42] call this 'Information Exhaust' and point out that in 1987 Rupert Murdoch bought TV Guide for $2 billion, which was more than any market valuation of any of the major American TV networks, CBS, ABC, or NBC at the time. In other words, organised information about TV was worth more than any individual TV broadcaster.

If organised information is saleable, then database design and data warehousing will be equally saleable. As will knowledge, and the management of knowledge. And the exciting part of this is that it can all be done over the Internet. I have a friend who met someone who had just been fired from a software company for being too radical, and between them they developed the tightest data compression tools available. They combined this with world-class encryption and are able to offer an Internet-based backup facility to medium-sized organisations anywhere in the world. So alluring was the idea that they have been made offers for their company even before it opened its doors for business (funnily enough by the company that fired the developer a year or so before). They are prudently taking their idea to market and running the operation before they are even prepared to consider selling.

Another form of organisation of information is the education industry that seems to be migrating wholesale onto the Internet. Here educators can offer their services anywhere in the world. Their academics organise they latest ideas and research and the body of knowledge into courses and offer these courses and associated mentoring and guidance to anyone with a connection to the Internet. Education is an ideal candidate for the Internet, although the face-to-face interactions between teacher and student and between students themselves are found wanting. Nevertheless education is no longer the preserve and limitation of a national body. This will have profound effects in the near future, as people in educationally backward countries gain their world-class degrees and either emigrate to more welcoming economies or stay and challenge the status quo. And there's nothing the home nation can do about the ongoing education of their people.

2.5 People

Do you ever hear something that just rings so true, so substantial that it changes your whole perspective from that moment on? Such a moment happened to me in 1993 when I read the foreword to Peter Block's book: *Stewardship*[43]. The foreword was written by Joel Henning, and I'll paraphrase it as follows: we in the Western World have proclaimed victory with the demise of the totalitarian regime east of the Iron Curtain. Anyone could see that these 'drab grey societies' exchanged their freedom in return for central control and supposed security for their citizens. Whatever their intentions, these 'drab grey societies' strangled the human spirit, enfeebled hope, and created dependency in the general population. But in our smugness, we fail to see that this is precisely how we run our companies, our schools, and our public institutions: we run our organisations through central control, central planning and the offer of supposed security for our employees.

That struck a chord. It's almost as if most of our companies have an invisible sign nailed above their entrance saying: 'abandon democracy, all ye who enter here!' Now I'm not sure that democracy is an appropriate form of corporate governance: democracy is slow, wasteful, redundant, expensive, and inefficient. The antithesis of everything that good management stands for. And, as a friend of mine says: 'if you're in the middle of the road with a 16-wheeler bearing down on you, you don't form a committee'. So there is a place for democracy, and that's in government. It must be said however, that there is room for more participation in the workplace. The forces driving organisations towards participation[44] include:

- people have direct access to information and don't need layers of 'information processing' management between them and the organisation's decisions;

- boundaries between organisations and countries are being rendered irrelevant, and artificial hierarchies and structures get in the way of interactions across borders;

- technology has transformed labour, freeing people up to do more, act across a wider front, make more decisions, and work from wherever they find themselves;

- access to better information allows competent individuals to choose their employers in a way not possible a few years ago. People choose organisations which allow them to have a say in their work, exercise autonomy themselves, and share in the successes of the enterprise[45]. This is not the traditional 'they will do anything for money' perspective;

- the rise of customer power requires employees to respond to customer expectations in an innovative and often counter-policy kind of way. Companies which do not encourage their staff to bring their brains as well as their bodies to the workplace will soon be in difficulty.

2.5.1 Changing people environment

There are numerous changes in the way people work. I present those I believe to be the most important as follows:

From standardised mass production to specialised knowledge work

It is fairly simple really, customers now have the power, suppliers must compete among themselves for customer attention (and dollars), or go under.

A brief history lesson in the growth of customer power is provided by Nicholas Imparato and Oren Harari in their book *Jumping the Curve*[46]. At the depth of the depression in 1933, one third of the labour force was unemployed. They had no money to buy things. Recovery only came in 1940 with heavy military spending. Then there was money, but no goods. After the war, the vast war engine converted to peacetime products and supply rose to meet world demand. There was a proliferation of global competitors, which caused the world supply of goods to exceed the demand for them. Because of this, during the late 1970s the customer gained power over the supplier. Customers could now afford to reject poor quality and lousy service. And it is no accident that most customer-centred business initiatives take root in the 1980s. It is also not totally unpredictable that more and more staff are being allocated to finding out what the customer wants, and getting it for them.

Organisations are depending on their staff to think about how best to serve customer needs. Combine this with almost totally free access to information, and *voila* you have a knowledge worker.

From paternalistic management to peer deference

Paternalistic management sounds quite noble, and very often is noble, sympathetic and well-meaning. However, it also suggests an authoritarian approach, which if not guided by the greatest philanthropy, can become distorted into a dictatorial, autocratic and unyielding relationship. More organisations are recognising that peer-to-peer relationships work better in the information economy. Deference is important, and everyone has a role and is expected to perform that role, in a collegiate environment. Collegiate conditions do not imply some form of academic institution, rather they suggest that colleagues work together towards a well structured goal, on an equal footing. This sounds a bit too utopian, and it is. Working together as colleagues and peers is difficult and fraught with setbacks, but the rewards are clear: if everyone has their work based on their expertise, and employs their brainpower and their energy to work towards a common objective, then the effort required keeping everyone in line and working is significantly reduced. Each person can concentrate on his or her task without more than peer group involvement. I will deal with this collegiate environment in more detail in Chapter 13 where the focus is on organising IT.

Another downside of paternalistic management is that the decision-cycle is stifled by bottlenecks as problems flow up the organisation waiting for a decision to be taken at the right level. (Often the right level is on leave, or away on business at the time.) How much faster if a colleague takes a decision using good judgement based on the organisation's vision and values? Good judgement is the issue here. And you create good judgement by openness and trust, not by absolute control.

In a study by Management Centre Europe, less than half of the managers polled believed that their CEO was up to the challenges facing their company. And 98% believed their CEO to be motivated by money, power and ambition – and a long way from the new roles proposed by the new thinkers.

Probably another significant negative factor in paternalistic organisations is what I call the 'bull of the herd' mentality. Here I draw the analogy between a wild bull fighting to maintain his right to lead the herd. He must be stronger, know more and be craftier than any possible challengers. This sounds dramatic, but I have seen substantial effort in organisations going into either defending territory or assaulting other territory – all within the company. This has nothing to do with making sales, and everything to do with climbing the ladder to where paternalistic power can be wielded. Collegiate organisations will expend less energy on such power struggles, although it depends on having an inspiring and motivating vision and mission.

There are numerous analyses of the types of power that people use in an organisation. I have isolated a set of seven power types that I see in operation. Understanding people-power gives you an effective tool for managing people and relationships. I go into the types of power in some detail in a later chapter which deals with relationships.

The main driver behind the shift from paternalistic management style is the shift from organisational power to expert power. Organisational power draws its authority from the company position that they hold – 'I am the CEO, or Head of Marketing or Head of IT, so people must listen to me'. Expert power is based on what people know and are able to apply in the furtherance of company goals – even the CEO and Head of Marketing and Head of IT can be rendered powerless by a failed system, until the experts get involved. This shift in power is profound. More and more organisations depend on experts who have the knowledge and can apply it to their circumstances. And the nature of knowledge has been set free by technology. The Internet is the obvious feature of the freeing up of knowledge in the world, but it does more than make knowledge available to everyone. It frees up people from being bound by a location or time in their creation and application of useful knowledge. (As I write this paragraph, I am sitting in a holiday cottage, with the wind blowing across the mountains in the distance, and wild birds visiting the shrubs outside. Hmm, I think I'll go down to the beach.) . . . I'm back. It is an hour later, and unless I had pointed this out to you, you would not know that I had been away (there's some beach sand on the keyboard, but I hope you can't see that!). Knowledge knows no boundaries, or time or place. How then will authoritarian managers control it, and with it the development of experts right under their noses? Because those experts are gaining the power not only within the organisation but also throughout the world.

> Leadership systems currently in use are designed to control relatively uneducated, mostly untrustworthy people in an environment of very slow change[47].
>
> (Belasco and Steyer, 1993)

I'll leave this section with these questions: What if farmer Brown's cows were free to go where they would best be looked after? If there were no fences? If the cows had access to information about where the pastures were greenest, the grass sweetest, and the milking gentlest? And what if farmer Brown's cows were regularly and actively being solicited to go across to other farms? What indeed, if there were a whole industry set up to ease the movement of cows between farms? Would farmer Brown have to change his thinking? Clean up his act? Do more to attract and keep cows? You bet.

Would farmer Brown survive long if he tried to control his cows, fence them in and tell them what they could or couldn't do? You decide.

Layered decisions so everyone decides

Bureaucratic companies are often remarkably unable to sense what is going on around them: front line employees are focused on the rules and chain of command, with the customers being a distant inconvenience. Management are focused on reports, meetings and politics. These are the observations of Gifford and Elizabeth Pinchot in their book *The End of Bureaucracy and the Rise of the Intelligent Organization*[48]. They point out that when information does flow in such organisations the process is more akin to a confectionery than a company, as each successive level adds more sugar-coating to unpalatable information.

In a bureaucratic company information is power, and this power has corrupted any chance of the organisation being responsive or even sensitive to their customers or to their environment. Because, in spite of rigid procedures, job descriptions, and bureaucratic guidelines, employees have vast freedom in one area: how much information do they pass on, and in what form should it be presented?

By having a net upward flow of information, companies effectively separate the thinking from the doing. In the old command and control organisations this impediment may have been excusable, but these days customers are also demanding to be left in the hands of staff who do not have permission to think.

The pace of business change is so great, and customer demands are so diverse, that organisations have to allow their staff to take decisions on their behalf, or they will stagnate and wither.

From command and control to results controlled rewards

There is a move from line-of-sight to out-of-sight management. And it is a difficult one to make. Our entire organisational and management process has been structured around people working in close proximity to their supervisors and to each other. We have come to accept that this is the natural order of things. But managers are actually a recent phenomenon, dating from the late nineteenth century. Before that, you might have found masters and gang bosses, owners and overseers, but no job existed which could be described as getting work done through others. But from the industrial revolution onwards, people have gathered near the means of production to get their work done. Now the advent of the information revolution and the migration of people away from industrial work towards service work allows for people to work from various locations not connected with the physical address of the organisation. For example, a British airline has a significant portion of its reservations staff located in the Bahamas. Also, financially astute people are very expensive to employ in New York, but in Ireland, their quality of life and their rates are much more acceptable. Which is why a number of New York-based insurance companies have their claims processed in Ireland. A Slide-Presentation preparation company located in Reading in the UK has its work done in the USA. That way they can make use of the turning of the earth to offer an overnight service, which of course isn't really overnight because the people working Stateside are doing so during their day and England's night.

Managing people at a distance is difficult and has resulted in a shift from monitoring activity towards paying more attention to deliverables. This means that managers become less concerned with the way things are done. For example there is less monitoring of the time, the place, and to some extent the method, (or even monitoring how people are dressed when they work). More attention is being placed on defining the deliverable unambiguously and clearly, and then assessing whether the deliverable meets the agreed criteria.

From POEM to AMTS

I can't claim ownership of these acronyms. I don't know where 'POEM' comes from, but AMTS is my acronym for a suggestion by leadership guru Warren Bennis[49] as to the future work of leaders. I do know that when I read the paper by Bennis, his thinking made such sense to me that I have added to his principles over the years.

POEM used to be the work of managers. It means Plan, Organise, Execute, Monitor/Measure, and covers the ground pretty neatly. But to my mind it is an outdated model of management. Managers today must manage other domains.

The new role of management is AMTS or the management of attention, meaning trust and self.

Managers need to manage the attention of staff. This means the vision, values and principles that guide the organisation. They should also map out the direction in which the organisation needs to be going, and should pay particular attention to what the destination will look like. Particularly what behaviours are appropriate if that destination is to be reached. Finally and to my mind most importantly, the new manager has a job guiding staff to pay attention to the right things, and to stop paying attention to the wrong (but often comfortable) things. The management of attention involves being up the tree, and seeing the forest for the trees.

Managing meaning involves initiating and sustaining the dialogue around the company vision. For example: 'what does "Customer Focus" mean? How will our behaviours change? What will we look like?' Management of meaning has a wider purpose – the new manager provides meaning to work. For truly effective staff, their work means much more than a pay-cheque. Managing meaning involves fostering dialogue, and reinforcing positive messages.

The management of trust and self are closely allied. The primary cause of cynicism in the workplace is the difference between the espoused vision and the behaviours of the executives of that company. New managers understand that their personal vision must be closely aligned to the corporate vision, so that they can live the vision. People are not stupid; they hear what is said, and they see what is done. If there is a gap, then you can forget about being world-class. Management of trust also involves ensuring that rewards are appropriate to behaviours. Often companies declare a new vision, define the new behaviours, and then continue rewarding the old behaviours. Imparato and Harari[50] say this of rewarding staff:

> The new manager has to actively discriminate according to different staff responses.
>
> (Imparato and Harari, 1994)

Staff who agree with the new world-class vision and show commitment and results must be satisfied and rewarded, and must be seen to be so. Staff who stick with the old, must be dissatisfied and must not be rewarded. This requires courage on the part of the manager.

From shareholder value to values

There is recognition that there are multiple stakeholders in the enterprise, bound by a set of values or principles. The shareholders are not the only stakeholders. Both Handy and Reich agree that the prime stakeholders in a business are the employees, because the prosperity of the business depends on more than employee actions, but also because knowledge-workers are more likely to have an ownership stake in the business[51]. And businesses are starting to realise that they need more than ever for their staff to bring new ideas and innovations to the table. They need their staff to meet customer requirements in new and imaginative ways. This makes most employees into knowledge-workers. More and more companies realise that they need to look after their staff, treating them less as expensive production units and more like people. People need reasons to do things. They need to align their vision with that of their employer because if they are to innovate and delight, then employees need to feel an affinity to their company, to feel that they are all working towards a common goal. If companies require their people to think they need to give them a framework in which to do so. More importantly, if employees are expected to use their judgement in serving customers or in their daily work, then that judgement needs to fit into a context. Vision, mission and values provide that context, whereas in the past, rules, procedures and job descriptions were sufficient.

Values also link suppliers and organisations. Many companies are starting to find that entering into longer-term partnerships is a more robust way of dealing with suppliers. In the short run, entering into a 'partnership' reduces costs for the customer, as they tend to hand off cost elements to their suppliers. Suppliers tend to accept this cost because they want to keep the business, and because the partnership brings consistency to the relationship. I know of one particular supplier who cut their tariff by 1% merely because their customer was willing to dispense with a clause in the contract that allowed the customer to cancel on one month's notice. And this was an 80-million dollar contract, so 1% was a significant amount. Removal of that clause brought some faith and stability to the relationship. After a while the partnership reaches a stage at which the supplier can no longer absorb the costs of the relationship. If the parties get through the next turbulent negotiation, the partnership moves on to a point in which values start to play a role – what's important to us is important to our suppliers and vice versa.

Businesses are also finding that their values are important to their customers. Many German companies will not do business with potential suppliers until they have examined their position on the environment or diversity management, or other values close to themselves. Certainly I don't buy from a number of companies because I don't like their approach to the environment (or lack of approach).

From tangible production to intangible outcomes

Many company objectives include not only serving and retaining their customers, but also focusing on the intangible elements of their customer relationship. Sveiby[52] puts the case that customers provide valuable references and if companies use this feature of their relationships properly, they can greatly strengthen their sales effectiveness. Blue chip customers also enhance a company's image that not only improves their market position, it also assists them in staff recruitment. But customers also provide two largely overlooked benefits to companies: firstly they act as a measure of the company's products and services and their feedback should form an integral part of a company's relationship with their customers. Secondly customers provide an important training ground for employees. Customers are 'external assets' and as such are often not included in benefit calculations. There is a move away from a need to see tangible production and short-term objectives being met, with the understanding that if you look after the intangible things – referrals, prestige, R&D leverage, learning, and ideas – then the tangible things will follow. Don't take this too literally, you still need bread on the table, and a cash-flow to sustain you, but rather see this as a shift in emphasis.

From economies of scale to economy of scope of network

Research in the European Union showed that while economies of scale hold true for capital intensive industries like mining and manufacturing, in the service sector, efficiency seems to decrease with unit size. Sveiby again explains that the provision of services requires creative and knowledgeable employees who dislike routine and structure and prefer to operate in a close-knit group where everyone knows what's going on. Their network defines how effectively they can perform their tasks. These networks are largely informal and require little maintenance from the organisation. What is required from the organisation is the infrastructure and facilities to allow staff to set up these networks. What is also required is an attitude from the company that promotes and supports such networking activities.

On a corporate level the scope of their network, the access they have to suppliers and that customers have to them, defines their success.

2.5.2 The changing relationship between employers and employees

We've no use for intellectuals in this outfit. What we need are chimpanzees. Let me give you a word of advice: never say a word to us about being intelligent. We will think for you, my friend. Don't forget it[53].

(Louis-Ferdinand, 1932)

These are reportedly actual words said by a supervisor to a worker in the Ford factory in Detroit during the 1920s. Of course methods have changed, and Ford have certainly evolved way beyond such unenlightened practices, but sometimes I get the feeling that this may still be the sub-text going on in some managers' heads, while they're exhibiting caring and concerned management behaviours.

There are many drivers in business, society, technology, and government which are forcing a substantial change in the way employers select, employ, manage and reward people, and similarly in the way employees choose their employer, work, and in what treatment they will accept from their employees.

Employers are being driven by an increasing need to cut costs, improve customer service and quality, speed up their reaction time and ability to change, and transform their capacity to respond to chaotic market conditions.

Employees on the other hand are being freed up by technology.

However, there are some issues between people and the organisations for which they work, that are going to change fundamentally in the next few years. The drivers of this change come from both employers and employees, and I'll deal with these drivers in a moment. But back to democracy in business.

> Power tends to corrupt, and absolute power corrupts absolutely. Great men are almost always bad men[54].
>
> (Acton, 1887)

And it is a question of power that forces us to look at how companies and management in organisations transact their business. Earlier I discussed how shareholders no longer behave like owners and I commented on the fact that 'short-termism' and the profit-at-all-costs motive represent a major threat to the sustainability of current business practices. Heavy stuff really. What has become obvious to me and other authors[2,6,9] is that the business/employee relationship is undergoing radical change. ('Radical' has its origins in the Latin word 'radix' root – and it is the root of why people are employed.)

But Charles Reich[55] a Professor at Yale University Law School, worries that the power of business over individuals is way out of hand. Can you imagine, says Reich, if a country was to behave like a company? Its constitution could read:

> Policies or choices made by voters shall be subject to review by a Board of Managers. The Board may, at its absolute discretion, confirm or reverse decisions made by the electorate.
>
> (Reich, 1995)

As for efficiency, says Reich:

> Rights are inefficient. Fair procedures are inefficient. Limitations are inefficient. Democratic dialogue is inefficient. Self-government is inefficient. Non-conformity is inefficient. Dignity is inefficient.
>
> (Reich, 1995)

Implementation ideas

The implementation thinking for this chapter follows the path of thinking about the environment in which your IT function operates. I deliberately stay away from technology-specific suggestions because CIOs think too much about technology. Think about your business and the economy.

1 Where are the frogs and sails on the horizon for your company? Frogs represent incremental change that has been happening for some time and sails on the horizon represent something which is in plain sight but that you can't see. Sails are difficult to identify because you can see them but are choosing not to do so.

2 Do some research on chaos theory. It will form the basis of your understanding of world economic trends. In Chapter 3 I deal with complex adaptive systems, but this represents a small part of the chaos body of knowledge. Buy an 'infotainment' book on chaos – one written for the lay person.

3 Examine your organisation looking for 'information exhaust.' Information that is currently being ignored but with some organisation can add significant value to the company. An example is a motor vehicle finance company that I worked with. About 30% of people taking financing plans from them defaulted at some stage. *All* their effort went into managing these defaulters. Which left 70% of good, non-defaulting customers out in the cold. They did *nothing* for these people. Information about when contracts are coming to an end now allows this company to thank their customers for their loyalty and faultless record, and to offer a discount on their next finance transaction.

4 Perform a stakeholder analysis. Firstly for your organisation's stakeholders, and secondly for the IT function. This will help you in both relationship management and in strategy development, both of which I deal with in later chapters, and both of which will use stakeholder analyses as their base from which to work. Identify stakeholders, describe them, find out what drives them, and find out what their expectations are of you and of your organisation.

References

1. Handy, C. (1989) *The Age of Unreason*. Arrow Business Books, London
2. Davidson, J.D. and Rees-Mogg, W. (1999) *The Sovereign Individual*. Touchstone Books
3. Smith, A. (1993) The Wealth of Nations, Vol. 1, Bk. 1, Ch. 2 (1776). In: *The Columbia Dictionary of Quotations*. Columbia University Press
4. Keynes, J.M. (1936) *The General Theory of Employment, Interest and Money*, Ch. 24, 'Concluding Notes'
5. Drucker, P.F. (1995) *Managing in a time of great change*. Butterworth-Heinemann Ltd, Oxford

6. Korten, D.C. (1995) *When Corporations rule the world*. Kumarian Press & Berrett-Koehler

7. Drucker, P.F. (1995) *Managing in a Time of Great Change*. Butterworth-Heinemann, Oxford

8. Davidson, J.D. and Rees-Mogg, W. (1999) *The Sovereign Individual*. Touchstone Books

9. Cannon, T. (1997) *Welcome to the revolution*. Pitman Publishing

10. Drucker, P.F. (1995) *Managing in a Time of Great Change*. Butterworth-Heinemann, Oxford

11. Firmage, J. (1999) In: *Brave New World – an interview with Joe Firmage*. Intelligence Magazine, Volume 5, No 9, Imagine Media, CA

12. Mathews, D.H. *et al.* (1972) *The Limits to Growth*. New York Universe Books NY

13. Meadows, D.H., Meadows, D.L., Randers, J. and Tinbergen, J. (1992) *Beyond the Limits*. Earthscan Publishers

14. Reich, C.A. (1995) *Opposing the System*. Little, Brown, London

15. Sveiby, K.E. (1997) *The New Organizational Wealth*. Berrett-Koehler, CA

16. Stewart, T. (1998) *Intellectual Capital*. Nicholas Brealey Publishing

17. Firmage, J. (1999) Brave New World – an interview with Joe Firmage. *Intelligence Magazine*, Vol. 5, No. 9

18. Reader's Digest (1990) *How is it done?* Reader's Digest Association Limited, London

19. Elgin, D. (1993) *Voluntary Simplicity*. William Morrow and Company, New York

20. Bierce, A. (1906) *The Devil's Dictionary*

21. Handy C. (1994) *The Empty Raincoat*, Arrow Business Books. London

22. Reich, C.A. *Opposing the System*. Little, Brown, London

23. Handy, C. (1994) *The Empty Raincoat*. Arrow Business Books, London

24. Reich, C.A. *Opposing the System*. Little, Brown, London

25. Firmage, J. (1999) Brave New World – an interview with Joe Firmage. *Intelligence Magazine*, Vol. 5, No. 9

26. Albrecht, K. (1994) *The Northbound Train*. Amacom, NY

27. Mintzberg, H. (1987) Crafting Strategy. *Harvard Business Review*, July-Aug

28. Remenyi, D.S.J., Sherwood-Smith, M. and White, T. (1997) *Maximising IT Benefits: A Process Approach*. Wiley

29. Schwartz, P. (1991) *The art of the long view: planning for the future in an uncertain world*. Currency & Doubleday, NY

30. Kaplan, R.S. and Norton, D.P. (1996) *The Balanced Scorecard*: *Translating Strategy into Action*

31. Handy, C. (1995) *Beyond Certainty*. Hutchinson

32. Schwartz, P. (1961) *The Art of the Long View: Planning for the Future in an Uncertain World*. Currency and Doubleday, New York

33. Bryson, B. (1994) *Made in America*. Martin, Secker & Warburgh

34. Stewart, T. (1998) *Intellectual Capital*. Nicholas Brealey Publishing

35. Mander, J. (1997) The Electronic Revolution: Virtual Empowerment. In: *Turning Away from Technology*. Mills, S. (ed.) Sierra Club Books

36. Davidson, J.D. and Rees-Mogg, W. (1999) *The Sovereign Individual*. Touchstone Books

37. Korten, D.C. (1995) *When Corporations Rule the World*. Kumarian Press and Berrett-Koehler

38. Drucker, P.F. (1999) *Management Challenges for the 21st Century*. Butterworth-Heinemann, Oxford

39. Wheatley, M. (1993) *Leadership and The New Science*. Berrett-Koehler, San Francisco, CA

40. Davidson, J.D. and Rees-Mogg, W. (1999) *The Sovereign Individual*. Touchstone Books

41. Davidson, W.H. and Davis, S.M. (1991) *2020 Vision – Transform your business to succeed in tomorrow's economy*. Simon & Schuster, NY

42. Davidson, W.H. and Davis, S.M. (1991) 2020 *Vision – Transform Your Business to Succeed in Tomorrow's Economy.* Simon and Schuster, New York

43. Block, P. (1993) *Stewardship.* Berrett-Koehler, CA

44. McLagan, P. and Nel, C. (1995) *The Age of Participation.* Berrett-Koehler, San Francisco, CA

45. Tampoe, M. (1993) Motivating knowledge workers – The challenge for the 1990's. *Long Range Planning*; Vol. 26, No 3

46. Imparato, N. and Harari, O. (1994) *Jumping the Curve.* Jossey-Bass

47. Belasco, J.A. and Steyer, R.C. (1993) *Flight of the buffalo.* Warner Books, NY

48. Pinchot, G. and Pinchot, E. (1993) *The End of Bureaucracy and the Rise of the Intelligent Organization.* Berret-Koehler

49. Bennis, W. (1993) Learning some basic truisms about leadership. In: *The New Business Paradigm*, G.P. Putnam & Sons, NY

50. Imparato, N. and Harari, O. (1994) *Jumping the Curve.* Jossey-Bass

51. Brynjolfsson, E. (1994) *Incomplete Contracts Theory of Information, Technology and Organization.* Center for Coordination Science, MIT

52. Sveiby, K.E. (1997) *The New Organisational Wealth.* Berrett-Koehler, CA

53. Louis-Ferdinand, C. (1894–1961), French author. Examining doctor at Ford auto factory in Detroit, where the narrator Ferdinand Bardamu (and Céline) worked, in *Journey to the End of the Night* (1932; tr. 1934; 1966 repre., p. 196).

54. Lord Acton (1993) Letter, 3 April 1887, to Bishop Mandell Creighton (published in *The Life and Letters of Mandell Creighton*, 1904). In: *The Columbia Dictionary of Quotations*, Columbia University

55. Reich, C.A. *Opposing the System.* Little, Brown, London

3 | Radicals and revolutions – anarchists in our midst

3.1 The revolution within a revolution

This is the information revolution. Or so we've been told by those who profess to know. Interestingly we haven't yet settled on a name for what's happening: some call it the information revolution, others call it the service revolution and still more call it the age of the customer. Hindsight will probably allow us to identify another world-changing trend that truly identifies what's happening now. Time will tell.

Let me briefly trace the 'revolutionary' path of man and business, before I deal with what I believe the breakthrough idea of this current revolution thinking will be.

3.1.1 A brief history of men's revolutions

At the height of the agricultural development of the American landscape, some 70% of Americans worked on the land. In 1930 the figure had dropped to 15%, and in the year 2000, fewer than 5% of American workers were involved in agriculture.

The agricultural revolution was about taming nature – the domestication of animals and crops. The industrial revolution was about the taming of energy – replacing muscle with machines. But in spite of these new machines, you still needed people to provide the brain, eyes and ears. Machines in the industrial revolution were large, cumbersome, and in general fixed in one place, so people were required to move off the land and out of their villages to where the machines were located. And the person who owned the machines, who provided the capital, was the lord of all he surveyed. He was the capitalist.

Most commentators agree that the agricultural age, which lasted 10,000 years, was supplanted by the industrial age in about 1750. Now the industrial era is also regarded as past, as suggested by the following statistics: at the height of the industrial age, some 50% of American workers were engaged in manufacturing activity. Now only about 20% remain. These statistics do not consider the number of industrial and manufacturing jobs that have been exported to the 'Eastern Tigers' and other emerging economies. (Slavery is alive and well, but luckily for the West they have exported it to developing nations. Consider that a cotton labourer in Central Africa only earns enough in one year to buy one of the cotton shirts sold in Western boutiques. But this book is not about the increasing gap between the rich and poor and the revolution that will occur because of the instability of this system.) Be that as it may, it can be said that the number of manufacturing and industrial workers in the Western World is decreasing.

There is of course now a second industrial revolution accompanying the information revolution in which machines are becoming smaller and more portable and are starting to see and hear and act without the need for human intervention. Where then are people to be employed? In the service industry – machines haven't yet mastered empathy and caring.

William Halal[1], author of *The New Management*, from which book the above statistics are taken, suggests that between the Industrial Age and the Information Age which is debatably upon us, there lies what he calls the 'Service Economy.' His statistics show that in the 1950s the number of white collar workers exceeded the number of blue-collar workers, and this number continued to grow into the 1980s. But the Service Economy has deeper roots than a simplistic count of American workers would suggest. It grows from the ascendancy of customer power.

I have covered the rise of customer power and that this 'customer' revolution has not run its course. Because employees will become customers of organisations as they shop around for the best employer who will value and pay for their intellect and services. That revolution is just taking off.

3.1.2 The 'information' information revolution

What can we learn about information technology through the study of economic revolutions? As you know, there have been some hilarious gaffes made by so-called experts in information technology, probably the most famous coming from Thomas Watson of IBM in 1943 when he said:

I think there is a world market for maybe five computers.

(Watson, 1943)

It would be a pity if we were to make a similar blunder in our thinking about IT. And thinking about revolutions, I wonder if the average IT function has moved out of the factory mode of operation into the service organisation mode yet?

It bothers me when I see 'factories' of IT support and development staff, all located in one place. There are reasons for a centrally located office, but I am sure that IT could be at the forefront of networked and virtual organisational developments if it was so minded. I will go into IT organisation and location in a later chapter, but for now it might be worth thinking about how the world information revolution seems to be bypassing many in-house IT functions. This will be a task under 'implementation ideas' at the end of this chapter.

3.2 Complex adaptive systems

Since the early 1990s an approach to thinking about complex systems has been finding its way into the workplace[2,3,4]. It is a topic that spans all areas of business, if you choose to see it that way.

3.2.1 Linear systems and complex systems

When I was at school, physics problems represented something of a challenge: 'a body with density "x" falls distance "y" through a medium with "z" density. How long would it take the body to fall distance "a" if the density of the medium was "b"?' I never knew where to start. All this talk of bodies sounded faintly macabre. But what I didn't realise was that in spite of my difficulty with it, this was actually a simple linear problem. Things could get much more complex. What scientists have been pondering for some time is the question of how really complex systems operate. The physics problem I described is relatively simple and linear – its solution is fairly easy to derive. Scientists have come to realise that linear thinking only explains a very small part of the world. It cannot answer questions on how ant colonies behave, or how ecosystems operate, or how weather patterns form, or how people interact. They have recognised that there is a difference between complicated and complex. Complicated systems have many parts, but each system works exactly the same way over time. Your watch is complicated, as is your motor-car, as is the space shuttle, and indeed your laptop computer (although sometimes I wonder). But they operate exactly the same way every time you use them. Complex systems on the other hand react differently all the time. They appear to generate more than the sum of their parts, and when viewed at a large scale they appear to be intelligent, learning systems that constantly change to meet new circumstances. Which of course interests business men and women. They have looked at complexity science and seen in it, a way to organise and to nurture their organisations.

Complex systems have a large number of components which interact with each other and their environment. The sum of these interactions creates a pattern or form which constantly adapts to conditions in which the system operates. That's why they are called 'complex,' because they exhibit many independent interactions, 'adaptive' because they respond to their environment, 'systems' as they are linked in some way. Imagine if you could create an organisation that constantly adapted to the environment (customers specifically) in a coherent yet independent way?

Business is a complex adaptive system, not a linear complicated one. Employees interact with each other and the environment, and adapt to changing conditions. Outside of this, the economy is also a complex adaptive system, as is society. In order to find some way through this maze of complexity and chaos, forward thinking business people are applying complexity science rules to their businesses with gratifying results. It's hard work, much harder than the old command-and-control management model, but the rewards are surprising. The emphasis is on the word 'surprising.' It would be good to say that the surprises are always agreeable, but in some cases they are not. However all business people who have embarked on this route agree that the rewards are ultimately worth it.

3.2.2 Driving complex adaptive systems

At first sight, it would seem that you need complex processes to produce complex adaptive systems. On the contrary, scientists have found that a few simple rules which govern the behaviour of individual components of the system tend to generate complex systems.

There are some features of complex adaptive systems which are applicable to business environments, but be warned, complex systems cannot be managed in the old way. Rather, people are finding that their management role changes to one in which they set the direction, specify the few rules required to operate in the system and then get out of the way. This doesn't mean they disappear from the scene, rather that they guide, support and nurture the environment, and that they resist the temptation to interfere with people trying to get their jobs done in their own way. Much like a farmer prepares the field, plants the seeds then lets the crop grow.

Complex adaptive systems have components or agents which interact with each other and their environment according to a few simple rules. Let's break this down a little further:

Roger Lewin and Birute Regine[5], describe an experiment by a complexity scientist Craig Reynolds, who modelled the behaviour of a flock of birds, wheeling, diving and swooping in unison. Reynolds developed a computer simulation which replicated the action of the flock by giving each 'bird' three rules to obey: (1) fly in the direction of other birds; (2) try to match the velocity of neighbouring birds; and (3) avoid bumping into things. After a short while, the 'birds' having been randomly placed in space, had 'formed' themselves into a 'flock' that behaved in a very similar way to real flocks of birds.

A lesson for business is that, if people have a few simple rules and guidance, they will tend to organise themselves to get the job done. The first prerequisites for complex adaptive business systems is to recognise that business is just such a system. This is not trivial, because just as Reynolds specified the few rules, then got out of the way, so must business leaders. Complex systems are managed by 'distributed control' rather than 'central control'. This spells the end of 'command-and-control' and insists on more human, personal relationships. Some managers won't be able to handle this personal management style.

To create and manage a complex adaptive system is difficult and takes time. The essential elements of such systems are:

- a driving sense of purpose that binds all system components;

- a few rules (only three or four);

- trust that solutions will emerge from the process. Complex science calls this 'emergent behaviour.' It can't be fully predicted, and it adapts to its environment constantly;

- constant attention to relationships and the environment in which the system operates.

The new role of leaders in complex systems is to see the world. This doesn't mean that you get to go on a world cruise, rather it means that a leader is expected to see through all the complexity and chaos both inside and outside the organisation and translate what they see into a compelling business direction. Then they draw the attention of employees to what they see. The purpose needs crafting – simply saying something like 'make profit', or 'serve customers' is facile and pointless. The aim of the common purpose is to allow individuals to align their own sense of purpose behind a driving organisational purpose. This alignment of purpose occurs all the time – clubs, societies and special interest groups form and regularly attract people with the same interests and values. And it is instructive to see just how much time and energy people put into their non-work activities (often at the expense of the activities for which they are being paid). The burden is on the leaders of organisations to draw the same sense of excitement and dedication from their employees by crafting a compelling sense of purpose. I'm not suggesting you necessarily form a club here, but allow the club and society purpose to inform you. What interests people? Can they bring that same individual's interests to work? Finally pay attention to the alignment of visions, the organisation's and the individual's.

The job of leaders is to create the driving sense of purpose in the organisation, to monitor that purpose and help the organisation to adjust when the purpose needs adjustment. But they need to let everybody follow that direction on their own.

This is not abdication of their responsibility, neither is it abandoning their 'hand on the tiller'. But the new tiller is not the old POEM of the past. 'POEM' is the old 'plan, organise, execute, monitor,' domain in which command-and-control managers operate. How can you plan, if you let the organisation respond in a complex and adaptive way? How can you organise when staff are expected to respond to stimuli that you can't even see right now? And the principles embodied in complexity science suggest that if the conditions are right, then rich and focused solutions to customer and business conditions and events will emerge. So the 'execute' in POEM is replaced by emerge, or self-organise. Finally the 'monitor' focus shifts, provided you have effectively defined the purpose. The manager now monitors the environment, while the self-organised teams monitor their own progress and results.

You are moving from management in the system to leadership of the system and they are different activities. Barry Oshry[6] writes this about system leadership and management:

> Management has to do with working within the accepted mission, structure and direction of the system – smoothing things out, marshalling resources, removing roadblocks, motivating the members, streamlining processes, increasing efficiency, and so forth. By contrast, system leadership has to do with breaking the system out of its

current patterns, radically transforming the systems mission, direction, traditions and culture, elevating the system to previously unattained levels of performance.

(Oshry, 1999)

However, the second condition for complex adaptive systems still needs to be met. A few 'rules' need to be defined. Here leadership is important. In complexity science there is a concept of fractals. A fractal is the smallest part of a system, which when multiplied by itself develops into complex systems. Or looked at another way, fractals are components of the whole system which look the same as the whole system. For example, the human circulatory system is a fractal. If you look at the blood vessels in your hand, they resemble the overall shape that the complete system takes on. A tree has a fractal nature, because each branching twig is seen on different scales throughout the tree.

The management fractal question is this: what rule or rules, if multiplied throughout the organisation will result in complex adaptive behaviour that serves the purpose of the organisation? An example that comes to mind is one that a friend of mine implemented in his company: 'absolute honesty at all levels.' This meant between management and staff, between people, with customers, and honesty with performance, company and performance. The results were traumatic and fiery in the beginning, but created an enormous sense of trust and openness over time. Another fractal element of a business comes from a consultancy I once did some work for. The rule was that everyone had a profit and loss statement. This was discussed at a meeting every month. That doesn't sound too radical, but when combined with their two other fractal rules of learning and sharing, some very powerful teamwork emerged. Because one consultant knew he was no good at sales, he would enlist the support of the others to set up work for him. He would of course 'pay' them for their leads.

By the same token, consultants would often sell work that they could not do, or would need a team to do, and they would have to set up and 'pay' a project team. Finally, (although this didn't actually happen), if a consultant decided that he hated consulting, he could 'sell' research services to the others if he so chose. And yet all these consultants earned base salaries, and their bonus was calculated on the firm's success. This is of course not an ideal environment for every consultancy, but for this medium-sized firm it worked well.

So the art of leadership is to choose the fractal rules that will create new and adaptive behaviour in the organisations, apply these few rules rigidly, and let behaviours emerge.

Trusting in emergence from setting a strong shared purpose and setting fractal rules is an enormous leap of faith that many struggle with. Those that have tried and endured with it have reaped benefits that they never foresaw.

Finally the role of the leader in complex adaptive systems is to facilitate and expedite appropriate emergent behaviour. This is close to the old 'management by walking about' or MBWA concept, but it has subtle differences. Firstly the purpose of MBWA differs. It is not to monitor performance, rather it is to monitor the environment in which people operate. It is not to direct people, rather it is to provide constant purpose and guidance. It is not to check up on (or in more draconian management styles, to catch them doing something wrong), rather it is to provide safety – to know that it's all right to experiment, to translate 'mistakes' into learning experiences, to be there.

If this style of management sounds wishy-washy, it is not. It is the hardest thing to do, because it demands constant attention and energy, it demands self-examination and control, and it demands complete openness. Probably the most difficult element is that it demands humanity from leaders.

Implementation ideas

1 Has your IT function come out of the industrial revolution into the service revolution. 'Industrial' IT functions will locate people at a central point. They command by 'line-of-sight' and not by outputs. They manage people rather than lead them. They regard the hard workers as those who visibly dedicate time and overtime to the enterprise, rather than adjudge hard work by its effectiveness, irrespective of the time spent.

2 Fill in the following table. There is one completed in the final chapter, but try it for yourself first. Identify an area in IT or in your business. Think about what drives the purpose. (Not what the actual purpose is, but what drives that purpose. Here the implementation idea in Chapter 2 of performing a stakeholder analysis will prove useful.) Think about the 'fractal rules' which will govern the area or function. Finally think about what the environment must look like if these rules are to serve the driving purpose. The goal is the emergent behaviour in the final column.

IT Domain	Informer of Purpose (Build it)	Fractal Rules (Live & Die by it)	Environmental Actions (Nurture it)	Emergent Behaviour (Trust it)

References

1. Halal, W.E. (1996) *The New Management*. Berrett-Koehler, San Francisco, CA

2. Wheatley, M. (1993) *Leadership and The New Science*. Berrett-Koehler, San Francisco, CA
3. Sanders, T.I. (1998) *Strategic Thinking and the New Science*. Simon & Schuster, NY
4. Zohar, D. (1997) *Re-Wiring the Corporate Brain*. Berrett-Koehler, San Francisco, CA
5. Lewin, R., and Regine, B. (1999) *The Soul at Work – Unleashing the power of complexity science for business success*. Orion Business Publishers
6. Oshry, B. (1999) *Leading Systems*: Lessons from the Power Lab, Berrett-Koehler, San Francisco, CA

4 | Stop the revolution – IT wants to get on board

4.1 Do we even understand the information revolution?

> A new Information Revolution is well under way . . . It will radically change the *meaning* of information for both enterprises and individuals. It is not a revolution in technology, machinery, techniques, software or speed. It is a revolution in *concepts*. It is not happening in Information Technology (IT), or in Management Information Systems (MIS), and it is not being led by Chief Information Officers (CIOs). . . . And what triggered this revolution and is driving it is the failure of the 'Information Industry' – the IT people, the MIS people, the CIOs – to provide INFORMATION[1].
>
> (Drucker, 1999)

It seems that one of the greatest commentators on business this century believes IT people share their future with the dodo. This is not old criticism, Peter Drucker writes this opinion of IT and its people in 1999, so perhaps we had better take notice. Interestingly he is not really critical, rather he's dismissive:

> They will not disappear. But they may be about to become 'Supporting Cast' rather than the 'Superstars' they have been over the last forty years.
>
> (Drucker, 1999)

Drucker's reasoning comes from a perspective I hadn't considered in any depth, and it certainly changes my view on the 'Information Revolution.' For Drucker explains that the current information revolution is in fact the fourth information revolution in human history. The first was the invention of writing between 5000 and 6000 years ago, the second was the invention of the written book in China some 3000 years ago, and the third was the invention of mass printing by Gutenberg in 1450 to 1455. As Drucker explains, there is no written record of the first two revolutions and their respective impacts on society, but the third is well documented. And this gives us some food for thought.

Drucker points out that there was a large information industry in Europe before the printing press. It consisted of hundreds of monasteries housing highly skilled monks, probably more than 10,000 of them. There they toiled at copying books by hand. Their output was about 1250 pages per monk per annum. After the invention and bedding-in of the printing press, and the learning curve of the new breed of craftsmen called 'printers,' annual productivity was about 250,000 pages per craftsman. This is a 200-fold productivity increase, truly worthy of the appellation of 'revolution.'

But of course the real information revolution, the one being predicted by Drucker, had its historic equivalent not in the invention of the printing press, the technology, nor in the gigantic leap in productivity, but in what was being printed, and who had control over it. Hitherto, all printing had been religious in nature, and in Latin. Within a few decades of the invention of the printing press there were books on verse, prose, law, mathematics, philosophy and science. Knowledge was being freely passed for the first time in human history. The printing press ushered in the Protestant Revolution, and the Scientific Revolution. Gutenberg's aim was to strengthen the position of the church through the mass availability of Bibles, but he actually hastened the weakening of the church. Society, education, science and religion were all radically affected. Easily as great a revolution as the one we are going through now.

And where do IT people stand in all this? Are we the monks? Or the Gutenbergs? Or are we the people who see the potential in the technology and who use it to change the way the world works? Drucker thinks we are the technicians who will pave the way for the truly visionary thinkers in this revolution. And technicians we will remain.

I suppose it really is the old FIFO principle: Fit In or Find yourself Outsourced, or something like that. But the problem for IT people is that to fit in to business-thinking and speed of change, they need to do most things differently. Drucker would have us believe that it's simple. IT must put the 'I' into the 'IT', or must start to provide meaningful information to management:

> The people in MIS and in IT tend to blame this failure on what they call the 'reactionary' executives of the 'old school.' It is the wrong explanation. Top executives have not used the new technology because it has not provided the information they need for *their own tasks*.

Drucker explains that IT people are far too focused on cost data and internal data. A simple ROI (return on investment) equation – net income divided by net assets – has led us astray[2]. Because it is always easier to measure and manage the denominator (assets, capital employed, costs, headcount, etc.) than to take a position on the numerator (income, new business, etc.). Because nearly everything in the denominator is internal to the organisation – and in general in the past – while the numerator deals with the creation of value, of risk-taking, of abandoning the old and taking on the new. Ask any executive where his or her information needs really lie. It is in the numerator, in the external, in the future. Then ask the average IT person where they spend their efforts.

4.2 The business 'Bill of IT Rights'

Drucker's appeal for IT people to have an honest marriage between the 'I' and the 'T' is, from the perspective of IT people, somewhat simplistic, even though its validity cannot be doubted. So let's unpack this requirement a little. IT needs to do the following things if it is to match business needs, and if it is to cease its production of misbegotten solutions and avoid its relegation to 'supporting cast'. Look upon this as a business 'Bill of Rights' or prerogative.

4.2.1 Stable platform

Give the business a stable platform from which to run their computing applications. Business people have a right to expect stability from their existing systems. This has major implications on change control and the allowing of customisation and non-essential changes to standard applications. Especially in the light of the next business 'right.'

4.2.2 Flexible future

This same stable platform should be flexible enough to accommodate as yet unforeseen systems. Not only should IT people provide the environment into which new technologies and business solutions can be easily injected, but they should welcome such initiatives by the business.

4.2.3 The same time-frame

Provide IT solutions to business problems or opportunities in the same business time-frame. The days of business wanting a solution in 6 months, and IT providing it in 18 months are over.

4.2.4 Technological leadership

Identify technologies which provide business opportunities, and lead the business in exploiting these technologies.

4.2.5 IT education

Improve general IT competence and understanding at all levels in the organisation. This business competence in IT will dictate the successful usage of IT in the organisations, but will also be necessary if IT is to make a success of most of the other points in this list, particularly the necessary application of standards, and the solving of business problems in business time cycles.

4.2.6 Strategic IT leadership

Provide guidance and leadership to business within the strategic intent of the organisation. Traditional views of IT strategy development require the IT strategists to take the company strategy and provide IT solutions around it. This will have to change to a co-creation of strategy, and a strategic positioning of all IT efforts within the strategic domain of the organisation as a whole. Furthermore, now more than any other time, technologies have the ability to change what Peter Drucker[3] calls every organisation's 'Theory of Business'. These are the assumptions, objectives, customers, value proposition (or why people buy stuff from us), and definition of success. Technology can redefine all this within a business, and the technologists should have both the ability to identify opportunities and to sell these opportunities to the business. Unfortunately this latter capability is often lacking in many technical people.

4.2.7 Alignment

Align system processes with the organisation's vision, mission, strategic intent, values and culture. Thus an organisation which chooses operational excellence and lowest cost production as its strategic platform will have a significantly different computer architecture than one in which customer intimacy and service beyond expectations predominates[4].

4.2.8 Relationship

Manage the relationships. This is probably one of the more challenging requirements of the in-house IT department. There are numerous stakeholders in the successful operation of an IT environment. It is the belief of most CEOs that their CIOs tend to concentrate more on the technology and less on the understanding and support of the various stakeholders in IT[5]. The management of relationships provides the key to unlocking IT's position in the organisation.

4.2.9 Changing requirements

Allow business to change their minds after they have specified a system. This requires a significant mind-set change in how we specify, build and implement systems. In Chapter 11 on providing solutions, I detail a way of managing solutions provision with constantly changing requirements.

4.2.10 Meet the need

Above all give business people what they need; both information and functionality. And to do that, your first step must be to ask them. By the way, when was your last needs survey? (I certainly remember being a trifle intimidated by any business needs surveys I did. Their demands were always so outside the realm of what I could provide.) But in this age it is generally agreed that customer requirements shape the product. In Chapter 7 on relationships I'll expand on my thinking about internal customers, but for now, let's accept that the people who pay for the services we provide have the right to expect us to meet their needs.

I have not listed these 'Business Rights' in any specific order, because their priority will change over time, as business needs change. Neither are exhaustive, rather that they should be looked on as a list which includes both strategic, operational and 'hygiene' factors.

4.3 Bill of Responsibilities

A 'Bill of Rights' is a dangerous thing without a corresponding 'Bill of Responsibilities.' However, I am reluctant to give a list of responsibilities here. Because in my experience, the majority of IT people I have spoken to, tend to get the wrong picture here. They want to use these 'responsibilities' as a sort of 'big stick' in the vein of: 'if *they* meet their responsibilities, *then* we'll provide them with the services they need.'

The reframe of the responsibilities issue is rather to collect the business needs first. Manage expectations while you're doing this! Then collate these needs, prioritise them and develop them into an IT strategy. Add your own IT leadership wisdom. Develop time-frames and resource requirements. *Then* look at business responsibilities, which will be needed if the IT strategy is to be carried out. Now you can take an instrument to business decision-makers which empowers both parties to see the trade-offs required. Be prepared to negotiate and compromise.

4.4 Ask the winners – successful new approaches to business

All truth passes through three stages:

First, it is ridiculed;

Second, it is violently opposed;

Third, it is accepted as being self-evident.

(Arthur Schopenhauer 1830)

In general there are a number of 'truths' of modern business success, which, while easily espoused by consultants and authors, are incredibly difficult to implement. Nevertheless, I can't resist the temptation of listing my particular truths of business success. It doesn't really matter whose truths you use, provided they are based in sound reasoning in the present and future context. The point of this exercise is rather to take a set of truths, themes, ideas, or success strategies as they apply to business, and apply them to Information Technology. I certainly do not intend to cover business truths in any detail, that's the subject of many other books. Rather I would like to look at four ideas, and then extrapolate them into IT.

4.4.1 Some truths of business success

There are at least four things you have to get right if you want to be successful in business. Only four truths or principles sounds so simplistic as to be frivolous or shallow, and near useless, but bear with me.

Successful businesses know why they succeed

When you look into this, you come up against a deep-thinking requirement:

- why do (or should) customers buy from us? (And not from our competition?)

- how do we provide what customers need?

- how well do we meet customer expectations?

- what will customers want tomorrow?

- how will we have to be different from where we are now?

This is the rationale of your organisation. Where you ask and answer the deep questions; and you continue asking these questions. (Sadly, in my experience many of the more mature organisations have stopped asking these questions, or more worryingly, don't allow the questions to be asked.) It's really weird, but the more successful organisations become, the less they allow deep questions.

Successful businesses create their own future . . . now

In the past the common saying was: 'I'll believe it when I see it.' These days, more and more personal motivation gurus are promising that you can 'see it when you believe it.' They assure people that they alone can manifest their desires by thinking hard enough about them in a structured way. They believe that a certain mode of thinking attracts prosperity. I am not suggesting that businesses follow these methods, but I am suggesting that businesses are responsible for making their future prosperity. This sounds rather mundane and self evident, but do this little analysis:

Of all the initiatives currently underway in your organisation which are directed at improving the current operation (upgrades etc.)? Which are aimed at implementing some new way of carrying out current operations (e.g., automating some process)? Which are focused on introducing some new process or activity that has not been tried in the organisation yet (e.g., e-business)? And which projects are entirely speculative – where someone is testing some idea that may or may not produce a totally new breakthrough for the organisation (e.g., a new product or service)?

Figure 4.1 presents these categories in graphical form.

The categories on the right are the important ones in this case, because they involve creating a future that is different from the present.

I have done exactly this exercise in a few organisations. Normally the first hurdle is to find all the 'projects' which are

New way of doing current processes (automation)	Exploratory activity that could change the playing field
Operational improvements (upgrades)	New activity for organisation exploiting existing technology

Future / Present (vertical axis) — Operational / Strategic (horizontal axis)

Figure 4.1 Analysis template for activity focus

underway. People hide their favourite projects for fear of having them cut. (Interesting that, makes you wonder if everyone works for the same organisation.) I usually define a 'project' as something that takes more than three months to complete and has a definite goal, but the time period differs with the organisation. Having found all the projects – (my experience has shown me that the hidden projects will only appear once their sponsor sees value in the exercise you are doing) – the next wrangle will be about what fits where. I once had a financial director tell me that his General Ledger was not only strategic, but was also one of the core processes of the business. It took a lot of discussion for him to allow it to be relegated to 'operational' and 'support.' I'm not saying some ledgers aren't strategic, I just haven't found one yet.

Now the fun work should start – the interpretation of all the project activities to see what the 'stance' of the organisation is. I have seldom found an organisation that is devoting sufficient time to its future.

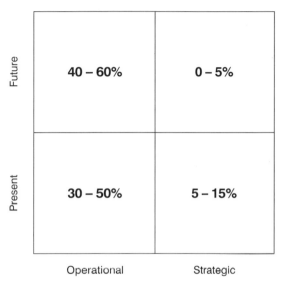

Figure 4.2 Activity focus of organisations

My experience of this exercise can be mapped as in Figure 4.2.

I must stress that this is not academically researched and proven – I have merely taken my findings from a number of these exercises and plotted them. The sample size is not sufficient to claim these statistics as 'proven.'

However, Figure 4.2 does give us cause for discussion. Firstly, who says that everything an organisation does should be strategic? I would argue however that many people mistake 'future operational' work for being strategic. And also, very few organisations allow their people to play with ideas. The 'future strategic' activities have by their nature risk attached. They may or may not produce value. And most organisations hate that kind of uncertainty. They fall into what I call the ROI trap – the Return on Investment trap. If the return on some project cannot be 'proven' then the project never takes off. This is a trap, because most significant breakthroughs are brought about by people playing in this area. I use the term 'playing' deliberately. It appears that very few organisations are willing to pay for play. This is the mindset shift that creates the future. (Sadly many people who do come up with a breakthrough idea leave their organisation because it is unable to cope with such thinking.)

Hamel and Prahalad in *Competing for the Future*[6] ask similar questions. They ask what percentage of your time is spent looking at internal versus external issues. The next question asks what percentage of time spent looking externally is future-looking. And finally they ask how much of your external and future thinking you share and discuss with colleagues. They say:

> In our experience, about 40% of senior executive time is spent looking outward, and of this time, about 30% is spent peering three, four, five, or more years into the future. And of the time spent looking forward, no more than 20% is spent attempting to build a collective view of the future (the other 80% is spent looking at the future of the manager's particular business).
>
> (Hamel and Prahalad, 1994)

Multiply this lot out and you find that 2.4% of senior management time is devoted to building a corporate perspective of the future.

So if you want to create your future today, allow people to play in the future strategic field. There is no other way.

Successful businesses believe that people are important

Most textbooks and articles on business will tell you that people are important, but let's look at it in some detail. Firstly the range of 'people' regarded by successful businesses include all stakeholders: employees, customers, suppliers, investors and

	Multi-stakeholder culture	Narrow-focus culture
Share price appreciation	901%	74%
Revenue growth	682%	166%
Job growth	282%	16%
Net income growth	756%	1%

Figure 4.3 Multi-stakeholder survey

the community. And many are extending their importance classification to environmentalists and by extension to the environment. In a survey of 172 companies in 19 industries over 11 years, Kotter and Heskett[7] reported as shown in Figure 4.3.

Stakeholders are important. People are important. To avoid confusion, important means 'having high rank or status, or great authority' as well as 'of great effect or consequence; momentous' according to the Concise Oxford Dictionary. Really successful companies that regard people as being important believe they have a high status and have great authority in their operations. And they regard inputs from these stakeholders as being of great consequence – they act on input. Sadly I have seen a number of executives receive the results of a survey, either of their customers or of their staff, only to reject the findings (which at least is an honest reaction), or more insincerely, they accept the findings and then do nothing. Successful companies believe that they are in a real partnership with their stakeholders.

Successful businesses look after the nuts and bolts

I have ceased to be surprised that when I propose various innovations, executives buttonhole me with rejoinders such as, 'yes but if we do that, we'll lose control, or our sales will suffer, or our costs will sky-rocket.' It's a little disappointing that these business leaders are unable to concentrate on more than one idea at a time. Nobody said that you have to stop doing the earlier things that made you successful. Flourishing companies understand that you still need to keep some degrees of control, or that you need to look after the hygiene factors. What they also understand is that you should stop doing those things that have ceased contributing to growth, and that you should leave room for some chaos and novelty. If you try to control everything, you will bind the organisation so tightly that growth is not possible.

Some companies that I deal with have mastered 'above and below the line' thinking. They understand that there is a cost in terms of resources, time and cost in keeping the momentum of existing operations going. But they also understand that they need to spend time and money 'above the momentum line' in order to grow and change their business activities to meet new challenges. Finally the really forward thinkers believe that they should devote some resources and time to being 'off the line' completely, dreaming, and playing with new ideas.

More nuts and bolts thinking from growing companies is a belief that they need to have the platform from which their people can help them grow. It is quite worrying to see companies with great plans for the future, but no plans at all to put in the infrastructure that will enable that future. Or they cut corners on infrastructure. Hands-up those who have just read this and thought, 'yes but if we do that our costs will sky-rocket'? Again I come back to the need for common sense. Watch the costs, but don't strangle yourself with over-control.

I've never seen a company with happy customers and unhappy employees. It just doesn't work that way. So prospering companies look after the hygiene factors – the 'tea and toilet' issues. But they do it without fuss and fanfare. I suppose if I wanted to make a law of business it would be that more time in meetings is spent on tea, toilet and parking issues than on future thinking.

4.4.2 Reframing – for IT

The challenge is now to reframe these four ideas for an IT environment. Ideally you should do this before you read this section, or better still, do the exercise with your colleagues. However, I have put together some questions to get you going. The four successful business ideas are:

- successful businesses know why they succeed;

- successful businesses create their own future, . . . now;

- successful businesses believe that people are important;

- successful businesses look after the nuts and bolts.

So the question categories for IT should be:

- why do we succeed, and how can we know this?

- how can we create our own future, . . . now?

- how can we make people important?

- how will we look after the nuts and bolts?

Why do we succeed, and how can we know this?

Here are a few questions and thoughts on each category.

Why do (or should) the business use our services? (And not services from our competition?) If your answer is, 'because they have to', then you're in trouble already. What services do you provide? And what services should you provide? Go beyond the ordinary, obvious services here. Also remember that real businesses don't just set themselves up to provide a product or service and then wait for the customers to beat a path to their door. They advertise; they survey their customers; they promote themselves and so should IT.

How do we provide what the business needs? This question runs to platforms and capacity. It considers internal IT processes. It means asking users what they want.

How well do we meet user expectations? Ask them. That's all. But don't then reject or ignore the results.

What will users want tomorrow? This is the slightly difficult one. There are three tactics available to you here – firstly put in place an architecture that is flexible enough, secondly guide (indoctrinate?) them into wanting what you can accommodate, and finally ask them what they want. This means educating your key users about the architecture so that they don't fall quite so easily into 'magazine management' habits. (In Chapter 1 I talked of 'magazine management' which involves executives walking up to your desk, magazine in hand, pointing at a 'gee-whiz' article and saying: 'I want that'.) I'm not suggesting that you should remove all magazines from circulation just in case a user should get ideas into their heads. In fact the more the merrier, but you can modify their perceptions of what is and isn't viable in your company. When you ask your users what they want in the future, do it in context of the corporate strategy, or else you might spend a lot of time dissuading users from wanting outlandish IT. I once had to show a user of mine how brain implants and head-up-displays were not in the IT arena at the moment. (To be honest, this was a brainstorming session in which anything goes, but he did want to take the idea forward once we started sorting them.)

How will we have to be different from where we are now? In order to meet the challenges of the organisation's strategic future, you are going to have to start doing something now, even if it is only thinking about the future scenario.

How can we create our own future . . . now?

Take the time to assess all the IT projects that are on the table at the moment. Insert them into the framework I describe above, and think. How many breakthrough projects do we in IT have? How many projects do we have that support IT's strategy? An example of a breakthrough project is when a good number of years ago, I asked three of my staff to test object-oriented development for our mainstream corporate environment. I had read a lot (magazine management in practice) and I wanted to know if the journalist's and vendor's claims were valid – because if they were, then we could possibly cut development time in half or better. I gave these three people six months to investigate the technology, and if it looked good to find an IT-friendly user and build a system for him or her. Alas they never went beyond stage one, and were back within two months, showing that the vendors could not get their development systems to operate in a corporate environment – there was still too much string and chewing gum holding things together. No matter, we had tried a breakthrough idea for IT. Of interest is that we carried out the analysis of current projects for the entire company at the same time, and found that the only 'breakthrough' project that the company had was this 'object-orientation' project. I would hardly call it a corporate breakthrough project, but it was the only one we had, so we put it in there.

After doing this exercise for IT, discuss it with the business. The same exercise done in the business tends to lead to more focus and appreciation of the activities that are ongoing in the business.

How can we make people important?

Look at your relationships with the business (your shareholders), your users, suppliers, staff and the community. Ask yourself about the quality of your relationship with them, and how it can be bettered. In Chapter 7 I examine relationships, how to map and track them, and how to improve them.

How will we look after the nuts and bolts?

What are the nuts and bolts in IT? Of course they are the systems and infrastructures upon which the organisation runs its applications. But what nuts and bolts systems do you have that support these infrastructures? I am often surprised to find that an IT department does not measure the performance of its infrastructures. They don't measure and monitor the stability, downtime, MTTR (mean time to repair) and MTTF (mean time to failure). This takes effort and costs money. Many of them have the systems that would do this monitoring, but haven't switched them on. How then can you look after the nuts and bolts if you have no idea how they are performing? I would like to say that it's not difficult to monitor and measure infrastructures, but I would be wrong because to a large degree it is actually very difficult. This is because at infrastructure level, things are no longer seamless. The infrastructure is about creating seamlessness, so measuring across and between infrastructure boundaries and equipment manufacturers is relatively cumbersome and inconvenient. Make the effort. World-class IT functions do.

Implementation ideas

1 Look for the 'Information' that you can put into the 'Technology.' Examine the information that IT currently manipulates. (Never mind that users specified this information. You'll never be seen to be adding value if you merely implement user requirements.) Is the information past or future focused? Is it internally or externally focused? Is it organised and accessible in a people-friendly way? Do you have meta-information (information about information)? Find one or two key executives (remember the stakeholder analysis?) and meet their information needs – honestly and proactively.

2 Test your organisation's business model. These are the assumptions, objectives, customers, value proposition and definition of success. Look for where technology can redefine all this and can add value.

3 Answer the questions asked in the section: 'Reframing – for IT' (Sect. 4.4.2) in this chapter.

4 Investigate your organisation's projects and locate them in the following grid.

Future

New way of doing current process (automation)	Exploratory activity that could change the playing field
Operational improvements (upgrades)	New activity for organisation – exploiting existing technology

Present

The results should give you some idea of where opportunities lie.

References

1. Drucker, P.F. (1999) *Management Challenges for the 21st Century*. Butterworth-Heinemann, Oxford
2. Hamel, G. and Prahalad, C.K. (1994) *Competing for the Future*. Harvard Business School Press

3. Drucker, P.F. (1999) *Management Challenges for the 21st Century*. Butterworth-Heinemann, Oxford

4. Treacy, M. and Wiersema, F. (1996) *The Discipline of Market Leaders*. HarperCollins Publishers, London

5. DeLisi, P. (1998) CEOs look at the IT function. *CIO Magazine*, 29 April

6. Hamel, G. and Prahalad, C.K. (1994) *Competing for the Future*. Harvard Business School Press

7. Kotter, J.P. and Heskett, J.L. (1992) *Corporate Culture and Performance*. Free Press

5 Play up, play up, and play the game

When I was in school I had to memorise a poem by Henry Humbolt about the game of cricket. (Yes people did write poems about the game, probably still do.) The essence of the story involved a tense end-game situation, with time running out, 'ten to make and a match to win,' and the batsman is exhorted to 'play up, play up, and play the game,' to meet the challenge, and take the side to glory. It is now IT's turn to play up and play the game. But it's not the game they are expecting to play or even necessarily want to play.

5.1 Before you play, find out which game you're playing

I have observed many IT re-engineering exercises. They all start to boldly go where no man has gone before (to split an infinitive, mix a metaphor and plagiarise all in one short sentence). Processes are mapped, plans are drawn, functions are centralised or decentralised (whatever they were not before), and yet somehow, not a lot changes. When all is said and done, business people still distrust the IT department, are still dissatisfied with IT service, and still wonder if their investment is worth it. The problem is that IT concentrates on what *has been* rather than *what is now*. While IT has made great strides in communication in recent years, there is still a lot to be said for paying attention. The rules of business have changed, we need to pay attention to these rules.

And perhaps it is time to change the rules of the IT game. No, perhaps it is more appropriate to change the game, the field, and the rules!

In Chapter 4 I looked at what game business wants us to play. I would now like to look at what the playing field looks like.

5.2 What does IT do – really?

When you look at it there are a few things that IT does for the organisation. Firstly, of course, it runs the IT 'factory.' All the applications and the infrastructure, processes and systems to run those applications.

Then IT provides IT solutions to the organisation. It also helps with IT leadership and strategy within the organisation. That, in a nutshell, is it.

Which of course is a vast oversimplification for us IT people. But ask your business partners, they tend to think along these simplistic lines about IT, and why shouldn't they? Test your own notion of what functions another section within your business performs: does the Finance section only keep the company's books; marketing's job is advertising and selling; operations keep the factory running; and Stores? Well who knows what they do, all you know is that nothing's ever there when you need it.

So keep in mind that the average business view of IT is simple, and let's keep it that way. But let's unpack the activities for our own purposes.

I have used the following list of domains to describe the activities of IT departments. There are many models of IT processes available, but I find this the most useful, and least mechanistic model:

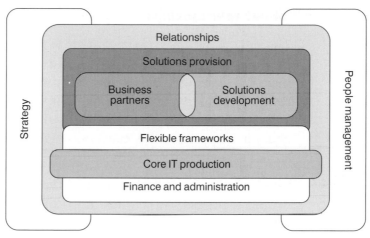

Figure 5.1 Seven IT domains

5.2.1 How to think about the seven domains

These are not processes. I prefer to see these as environments or domains of activity. Why not processes? Because 'processes' have been overdone. Everyone has a view of what a process is, and isn't. Many people have tried process-thinking and many have failed or have been constrained by the limitations of process thinking – with inputs, actions, and outputs, as well as controlling factors and resources applied to the process. Instead, let's think about domains. What happens in the relationship domain? The solutions provision domain? And in the flexible framework domain? These domains require resources, some process thinking, a stakeholder analysis, and a framework in which you can view them. I think in pictures and I would like to believe that picture frameworks will work for business as well. But this depends on business style and needs.

I will go into each domain in following chapters, but here's a summary of my IT domain thinking.

5.2.2 It's all about relationships

The new game of IT management is talking. The success of IT within organisations is largely defined by the relationship that the IT department has with the community within which it resides[1]. The community includes the business, but also includes the employees of the department, the IT community in general, suppliers, the business' customers and finally the society within which the business operates.

Now 'relationships' don't mean all the soft fuzzy stuff that hard business people sometimes find difficulty with. Rather IT relationships can be made hard, measurable things. I will go into this in much more detail, but briefly, relationship management for IT means:

- marketing, with appropriate market penetration and retention plans (even if, no especially if, the marketing plan addresses the business for which the function works). Far too little attention is paid in IT to formal marketing of IT within the business;

- account management: including account structuring and organising, bringing the right people to bear on the right accounts, visit schedules and reporting, etc.;

- measurement: in my experience of IT departments surveying their business opinions of their service, they invariably give themselves a worse score than the business itself. This indicates that IT tends to know where its problem areas lie, and that often organisations have lower expectations of their IT department than the IT department has of itself. Not only is regular survey of the business essential, but independent surveys of IT effectiveness, benchmarking studies and other measurement techniques are essential to maintaining a credible relationship between IT and its business partners. But the feedback loop must be completed. You need to communicate your measurements to the business in a credible way.

- communications: let me tell you a story. For this story we need to be politically sensitive by inventing an occupying and oppressive regime, let's call them the 'Oppressors'. We also need an occupied, generally peace-loving nation which has a small band of troublesome but effective secret band of freedom fighters. Let's call them the 'Liberators'. In a compartment on a train sat an Oppressor soldier, an old Liberator lady, a young and beautiful Liberator lady, and a Liberator freedom-fighter. The train goes through a tunnel. This being an occupied Liberator train, there are of course no lights. In the darkness, there is the sound of a smacking kiss, and then the sound of a resounding slap. When the train emerges from the tunnel, the Oppressor soldier is nursing a black eye. The old lady thinks to herself: 'quite right for that young girl to slap the Oppressor soldier when he tried to kiss her in the dark.' The young girl thinks: 'how strange that the Oppressor soldier tried to kiss the old lady in the dark, and not me.' The Oppressor soldier thinks: 'that freedom-fighter is a lucky chap. He kisses the young girl in the dark, and she punches me!' And the freedom-fighter thinks: 'how lucky I am. I kiss the back of my hand, punch the Oppressor soldier in the eye, and get away with it!'

The story serves to illustrate that you could be doing great and noble things in the dark, but until you shed some light on your activities, everyone is going to have their own interpretation of your actions. And most of these interpretations will be wrong.

So IT, more than any other internal department, needs to have a subtle and effective communications plan.

After all is said and done, relationships go deeper than a surface attempt at internal marketing, account management and communication. The measure of success of your relationships will be the amount of trust that the business puts in you, and their knowledge that you can provide solutions within their desired timeframes. How much time IT people spend in business and customer offices, working with the business to solve business problems, will be a key performance indicator of the success of your relationships.

5.2.3 Providing solutions – in-house or out-house? – there's still work to do – supply/demand

Ultimately the role of IT departments is to provide IT solutions and to operate and support these solutions. Solutions can be interpreted as wide or as narrow as you like. I prefer the wider definition, which involves both proactive and reactive IT initiative. In a wider context, providing solutions would involve setting strategic IT direction in which such solutions can bear fruit.

There are two main activity areas in the solutions provision domain: the first involves the nature of the partnership that you have with your organisation. Jordan Lewis[2] mapped out different types of partnership, referring to organisations and supplier/customer relationships. But there is no reason why we shouldn't extend that thinking to the IT/business relationship.

I will deal with the types of partnership and their development in a later chapter, but one observation of Lewis is worth noting. He says that the development of partnership relationship is exploitational up to a certain point. That's when the supplier of a good or service can't take any more cost into their structure. After this point the supplier either folds, fires the customer or comes to an understanding with their customer. The same holds true of IT as a supplier, although they can't fire their 'customer'. A folded IT function is running on empty. They do what they are told, don't contribute to wider corporate strategy, and keep their heads down at budget time. Often the IT manager has sought pastures greener, and the department is being run by someone who really believes that the role of IT is to keep their heads down, and to scrape by on the dregs. Of course no-one is happy.

The business isn't getting what they believe they need, and the IT function can't get the best people or make an impression on the business.

So the foundation of the IT solutions domain rests on the nature of the partnership between IT and their business companions. I discuss this in Chapter 7 on relationships, but briefly if the relationship is adversarial, or one of customer/supplier then the kind of solutions developed will be different from those developed in a trusting and mutually advantageous relationship. Another aspect of the relationship and solutions development process involves how IT sees the business. Again, if they see the business as unreasonable in their demands or quixotic in their vision, then their solutions development activities will be significantly different from one in which IT sees themselves as enablers of, and participants in, the business vision.

The second part of the solutions-provisions domain involves the mechanics of providing solutions. Rapid application development, object orientation, mainstream coding methodologies, customised enterprise-wide solutions, and any other number of solutions-provision mechanisms are available to suit the situation and relationship. I am not a developer and cannot prescribe any solutions-provision mechanism over another, but I can draw your attention to the need to fit the mechanism to the circumstance. To examine the external factors as well as the internal ones before adopting a method or methods. That seems to me to be the trick to solutions provision, rather than getting into a debate on the merits and demerits of methods.

5.2.4 The difference between creating space and creating a vacuum – providing the framework

It's all very well getting philosophical about wonderful ideas and esoteric models of IT and business. But it doesn't answer real and practical problems. So there is a difference between merely getting people worked up about an idea, and providing, if not the answer, then at least a framework in which they can excel.

What is a framework? Well it's a representation of an artefact, a system or sequence of events. Normally the representation is abstracted into symbols, equations, pictures or sometimes a fabricated likeness (as in a model of a building). Frameworks decipher complex concepts to allow people to make decisions, without the need to delve into the complexities and nuances of the technical environment.

So part of IT's job is to provide frameworks for business. And here we are talking about more than just an architecture, which in my view is the core framework responsibility of IT, but not the only one. There are other frameworks which need to be provided. Ask your business what frameworks they would like to have from IT.

They probably would provide a list as follows:

- frameworks for how to think about IT. How does it fit into business. What about e-business? Are all the magazine articles to be believed? How should we fit all the IT innovations that are thrown at us together? This is more than a high level architecture. It is a layman's guide to IT. It includes something like Anthony's triangle, but also how to think about networks, infrastructure, applications, etc.;

- how to fit business strategy and IT strategy together: many business and IT people are unsure about how business and IT strategies fit together. So offer a framework for both the place that IT strategy plays in business strategic decisions, as well as for the timing of strategic initiatives. Such a framework would include different levels and timings for strategic thinking. It would also try to represent the fit/misfit between business and IT cycles;

- the future framework. This framework would link the company's strategic positioning with an IT positioning. If the organisation is an innovator, then how should it think about IT innovation? If the company sees itself as a fast follower, then how should IT enable fast following, rather than bleeding edge IT solutions. Some organisations are traditional in their approach to business. And a fit between IT and this traditional approach may be appropriate. How will that fit happen? Finally, an organisation may be transforming itself. And how would IT contribute to this transformation? Each of these frameworks has implications. If your organisation is treading the innovation path, it must be prepared to pilot many new ideas. And scrap ideas if they don't work out. If they are traditionalists, they must be prepared to forego innovation in favour of stability. Probably the best reference for this framework would be Geoffrey Moore's: 'crossing the chasm'[3], which deals with how to market and sell technology to customers. It deals with analysing where the customer is in the technology cycle, and offers strategies for selling to the customer based on their strategic positioning;

- architecture: this is the standard view of IT frameworks. But strangely most IT people think this is a deep technological view, not for consumption by mere mortals. Which of course, from an IT viewpoint is true. You need this deep technological thinking. But you also need a translator. To take this technological thinking and offer it to the business in an accessible format;

- applications portfolio: allow your business to see how business environments and processes fit together. Show them how applications often overlap. A number of good report-writing tools come with ERP systems, but somehow we have to repeat functionality. I'm not suggesting that anyone necessarily pulls the wool over anyone's eyes, but money is often spent on applications for want of a better understanding of what current applications can do. Another aspect of the applications framework is also the development process. How is the business to look at development? What types of development apply to which circumstance;

● I've often worked with executives who are not sure what value IT is. How should they compare IT justifications with other business cases? So your average business person needs a framework, or way of looking at IT justifications;

● help the business understand how your IT budget works. I will deal with budget thinking in Section 5.2.8, but the way in which you present your IT budget not only affects your allocation of an often scarce resource, but also affects where you get to apply that budget in the pursuit of IT excellence;

● the organisational framework: show how different IT organisational forms allow different domains and processes to dominate.

All of these frameworks look a little like you have to become a 'University of IT' for your business. It's not that at all. If you and your IT personnel have the kind of relationship with the business that unlocks your success, and you also have to hand these frameworks around which various discussions can take place, you'll find the 'education' of business happens without effort.

5.2.5 The core of IT – factory thinking needed

I use the term 'factory' with deliberation: the industrial revolution started in the eighteenth century in Britain. Similar revolutions followed in other European countries, in the USA, and in Japan during the nineteenth century, while in the twentieth century Eastern Europe, China, India, and Southeast Asia have undergone a similar industrialisation process. But to me it doesn't seem to have reached the IT machine room. We don't run our IT factories like factories. We invent our own IT operations methods and measures, when for 200 years a wealth of knowledge and experience has been available for us to use and adapt.

In my experience, there are very few IT factories which design layout and flow of operational processes. Or who design jobs and workflow within the operations environment, or which use MRP JIT and capacity planning to any extent in their own circumstances. Few operations functions apply quality planning, zero tolerance, failure prevention and recovery, and many other mature manufacturing techniques to themselves. And those IT factories that do this, are invariably the outsource providers. They do it because they have to. And this is one of the reasons why they interest businesses wanting better services from their in-house IT functions. Because businesses see a mirror of themselves in outsource providers. They look for companies with a profit motive, with a customer focus, with a desire to be contractually bound and with a professional factory outlook on their production services.

So while IT operations remains an essential pre-requisite to the successful use of information technology, it is precisely because it is so critical that it can't be left in the hands of the in-house staff, who don't adopt the boring and safe practices which were learned by manufacturers over the last 200 years.

Because keep in mind that one of the prime requisites of the business of IT is stable and efficient IT operations with almost no thought or input from themselves. IT operations is a background thing. If it comes to the foreground, it is in trouble.

Something that can't be outsourced is the interface between your business and its IT service provider. So even if your business has gone the outsource route, it still needs someone with sufficient knowledge of IT not to have the wool pulled over their eyes. And who better than in-house IT people?

I want to extend my domain thinking into the IT operations discipline, especially when it comes to running applications. What if we were to think of every application as an environment or domain? What are the elements of domain management? Firstly a domain has boundaries. The operational boundaries of an applications domain will include the users, their geographical spread, their movements. The domain will also have overlaps or interfaces to other domains. And within the domain we have to apply the 'POEM' principle. We need to plan, organise, execute and measure the application constituents. I often ask a Facilities Manager to show me his or her plans for say the organisation's 'Order Fulfilment' domain, only to be met with a blank look. Somehow the Facilities Manager doesn't see their role as planning the capacity, organic growth or shrinkage, or indeed the termination of the application domain. How long is the particular application's life cycle, when did it last have a major re-fit? These and many other questions often go unanswered. Where are the domain statistics which will allow proactive decisions to be made?

And yes, networks are a domain, as is security, or databases or as is processing power; the list goes on.

5.2.6 Strategy – alignment, vision, mission

What is strategy? There are a number of confusing definitions, and certainly when I ask the question in workshops and classes, I always get the time dimension. Some people think of business in three levels – operational (happening right now), tactical (happening in the next few months) and strategic (happening in the next few years).

I prefer the thinking of Ward and Griffiths[4] who free up our thinking to view strategy in present and future dimensions.

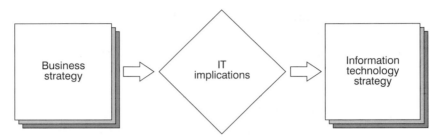

Figure 5.2 Traditional strategy view

> Strategy can be defined as an integrated set of actions aimed at increasing the long-term well being and strength of the enterprise relative to competitors.
>
> (Ward and Griffiths, 1996)

I suppose I like it because it focuses on 'an integrated set of actions,' which moves us away from the idea that strategy is a document. Certainly strategy is often documented, but just as often it isn't documented at all. It is merely enacted within a well-defined strategic framework in a strategically focused organisation[5]. This needs a supporting culture and a bunch of other prerequisites but it is happening more and more often these days.

So the question we need to ask is what is the strategic role of IT in their business? Well the traditional view of IT strategy looks as shown in Figure 5.2.

More contemporary approaches to strategy allow that the business strategy and the IT strategy should be built together. And e-business strategies often work in reverse, where the technology dictates where the business is going.

Whatever the approach, it seems to me that something is missing. It comes back to relationships again, but strategic IT involves three elements: firstly there is a need to be aligned with business initiatives – now and in the future. There is also a need to have an IT vision for the business, and to sell that vision to the business – or if you can't sell it, at least have open discussions about what you believe the future holds. Finally there is the 'mission' element of IT strategy. Your mission (should you choose to accept it) is the set of domains and activity areas in which you, as IT, operate. Defining your mission is an ongoing IT activity – if you are not examining your mission every three months, you are probably standing still. And as someone once said: 'the best way of sliding backward is to stand still.'

So strategic thinking in IT answers these three questions:

● where is the business going?

● what can we bring to the table?

● what are we doing now, and what should we be doing to intersect the future?

Of course this involves the integration of all your frameworks – architectural, organisational, future, and all other frameworks that you have at your disposal.

I also believe that there is great value to be derived from scenario thinking, best outlined in Peter Schwartz's '*Art of the Long View*' in which an ongoing conversation about the future is conducted within a specific framework. You look at what could happen given your present and past. But in our case, the frameworks that define your scenario thinking are both the seven domains, and the frameworks (future, architectural, etc.) that you have developed.

5.2.7 People are people too – the real power

When you come down to it, very few organisations seem to trust their people. Alan Weiss, author of a fun and cynical exposé on management stupidity called: *Our Emperors Have No Clothes*[6] says this about organisational trust:

> I've always wanted to write a pragmatic pop-psychology book with the title 'I'm OK, You Stink' because that's how most organisations operate.
>
> (Weiss, 1995)

He goes on to argue that people's behaviour is consistent with only one thing: the reward system. And if a reward system requires individuals to meet production quotas no matter what, then that's what they will do, no matter who they step on to do so.

It goes a little beyond just rewards and includes the whole system. If a system is set up to minimise individual contributions in favour of institutionalised methods, then the staff of an organisation will slowly withdraw their personal offerings from the system. I have (to my embarrassment) acted like this myself: I joined a growing company in the belief that I was expected to contribute new and radical ideas. I started off writing proposals and offering suggestions. My boss nodded, and thanked me for my contribution. And nothing happened. The time wasn't right, or some other evasion. Over a year, I withdrew my input to new initiatives, knowing it would be overruled, often in favour of the boss's ideas. I withdrew my services from that company soon afterwards.

I suppose most people want themselves and their contribution to be respected. Treating people with respect requires a deep understanding of what makes people tick, satisfying your best people first and foremost so that they come back in the morning. Thus begins the break-away from traditional management – a new manager is a servant.

The future IT in the new environment requires management to enlist the intellect, energy and enthusiasm of all the people who work in IT.

So how should we tap into the people – power in IT? There is much research that has gone into what motivates IT people.

Professor Tampoe[7], at Henley Management College, surprisingly found that they are not particularly motivated by money. Certainly they need to be earning enough, but they are motivated by three other factors: firstly, they need to have a degree of autonomy. Give them a task, and then let them use their intellect and skills to solve it. IT people don't need close management, mentoring, or nurturing. Secondly, they need to be given a 'do-able' task. Something which has boundaries and specified goals. Not for them the endless cycle of activity and meetings which seem to go nowhere. Thirdly, they need to have a say. They need to have their opinion heard and respected. And if they are motivated by money, then says Karl Erik Sveiby[8]:

> ... it should be recognized that money is usually a substitute for something more intangible, like prestige or independence.

> (Sveiby, 1997)

Of course money is important. But provided your remuneration system is fair, both internally and within the industry, then the prevailing concerns of your staff will be around the three issues highlighted by Tampoe.

So the big trick in running an IT function will be around how to give your people enough autonomy to use their skills, to define the task or project without over specifying it, but with sufficient detail to be do-able, and finally to set up feedback and 'conversation' mechanisms so that your people can be heard.

I'll deal with all this in a later chapter, but I need to say that the people dimension of re-inventing the IT department will be the most complex and difficult element of the process – but potentially the most rewarding.

5.2.8 Underpinning IT – finance and administration

I won't dwell on finance and administration for IT departments, although I should. The way you define your budget, present it

What you have to spend in order to increase business momentum
- Research
- Strategy
- New solutions

Momentum line
- -

What you have to spend in order to maintain business momentum
- Core production
- Upgrades
- Statutory requirements

Figure 5.3 The momentum line

and then effect it will strengthen or weaken your relationships within your organisation.

However, a useful mental tool for defining where the expenditure is to take place is the concept of the 'momentum line'. This is a budgetary line drawn on a time graph (see Figure 5.3).

Any expenditure below the line, involves maintaining the current momentum of the business. This does not mean that you let things run-down, rather that you will be spending money on upgrades or meeting legal requirements. So maintenance of momentum is more than keeping the current environment operational, it involves maintenance of the current environments at the velocity and mass that they currently have. Velocity (to get mildly scientific) involves the speed and direction of a business operation. So if a business operation is processing 'x' number (speed) of 'y' transactions (direction) that is its current 'velocity'. Its 'mass' involves how many units of business (workstations, departments, branches, etc.) are operational. So to bring a new branch online increases the IT 'mass' of the organisation. To replace an existing branches' workstations does not increase the 'mass'. The new branch would be budgeted 'above the line' while the replacement workstations would be budgeted 'below the line'. New systems where none has existed before are 'above the line' and upgrades are 'below the line'. Don't get too literal here, because you'll tie yourself in knots saying things like, 'this new upgrade adds 20% new functionality, therefore it is 20% above the line and 80% below'. This will drive you crazy. Rather look at things from a business view, and say, is this something the business has done before using IT or not? If not, then consider it above the line. Mostly this is a helpful model for business people, so that they can understand that this fancy new upgrade is doing nothing more than maintaining existing business momentum. It helps people focus on the genuinely new capacity-building IT expenditure. I did some work for a company that hadn't thought in these terms, and once IT expenditure was represented in these terms, it became brutally clear that although they were spending a fortune in cash, time and energy, most of that IT spend was below the momentum line. All the activity had the illusion of progress and growth, but in reality they were merely maintaining momentum. Sadly they didn't take radical action to increase their business momentum, and became a victim of a hostile buy-out by a smaller player in the field.

Largely speaking, the IT domain's budgets would fall into the following 'above' and 'below' the line representation (see Figure 5.4).

As you can see there is an element of IT solutions provision work 'below the line', which would denote upgrades and replacement of legacy systems with new technology. Just as there is some Core IT Production work 'above the line' as new branches are brought online, and new capacity is added to cater for business growth and new business activities. Architecture is a mixed bag, but hopefully strategy is largely 'above the line'. IT Leadership, if it is worth anything, should be largely above the line, although there are leadership elements which deal with maintaining business

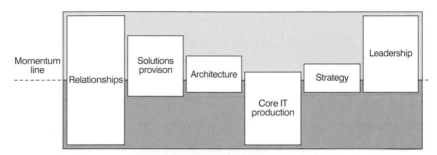

Figure 5.4 IT domains above and below the momentum line

momentum, for instance, convincing a reluctant user area to move off their ancient and unsupportable technology. Of course relationships cover the entire spectrum of activity.

5.3 Four-leafed clovers – lucky for some, but luck favours the astute

Charles Handy[9] described an organisational form which he called the 'Shamrock Organisation' which is structured in three 'Clover leaves': the first leaf is what Handy called the 'core' – employees who possess the competencies that make the company competitive. The job of the core is simple – do the business that makes the money. Non-core activities such as computing, training, administration, even engineering and manufacture, are the 'second leaf', and can be contracted out to suppliers who specialise in that service. Handy's third leaf is what he calls the 'flexible labour force'. While some of these people want to be independent and choose the temporary lifestyle, most are the result of downsizing, merging and restructuring. I also place consultants into this leaf – filling temporary need. US government statistics estimated in 1986 that 26% of workers were temporary or contingent. Handy predicted that this figure would rise to 50% by the turn of the century. Handy predicted with less certainty the rise of a 'fourth leaf' to

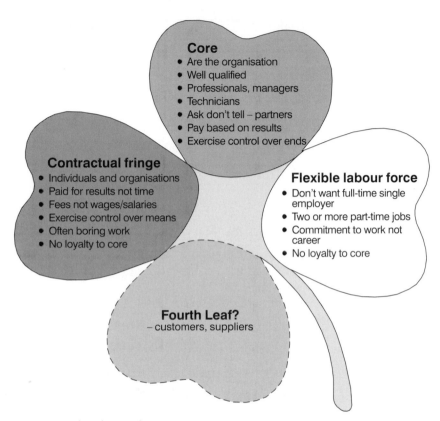

Figure 5.5 The Shamrock Organisation

his shamrock – that of the customer. Where the customer does a significant amount of work which was previously done by the company themselves. The example Handy uses is the cafeteria where customers perform the task of placing orders directly with the kitchen. Remembering that Handy predicted these things some 14 years ago, it is illuminating to see that networks and the Internet have allowed the creation of organisations where the fourth leaf is the largest.

The difficulty with the Shamrock Organisation is that each leaf requires a different management style. The core would be managed in a collegiate peer-to-peer manner, while the contractual fringe needs to be managed as an outsource environment. The flexible workforce is made up of individuals, each with their own needs and engagement assignment and conditions. Finally, the fourth leaf requires a win-win arrangement in which both parties see the benefits they are receiving.

Deciding who's in what leaf is equally difficult. It never fails — whenever I talk to an organisation about the Shamrock, everyone nods their head in agreement. But each person there assumes they are part of the core. They believe they will be controlling the ensemble. But in reality less than 20% of people in standard organisations will end up in the core. Neither will the consideration of implementing the Shamrock Organisation receive much political favour. I was involved with the fundamental automation of a government loan institution. Our team was tasked with designing the new 'computerised' organisation. (This was in 1998 — there are still institutions with green-screen batch driven computer systems.) So we sat one hot afternoon and posed the hypothetical question: 'how many people would this institution need if it was fully automated and if it aggressively adopted the Shamrock Organisation?' We came up with a final staff count of 50. Problem was that the institution had 1500 people in 26 branches around the country. We couldn't even broach that figure with the client. So we settled on a starting, kick-off number of 150 people figuring that a 90% cut was radical enough. This wasn't a total downsizing exercise. The automation could cut staff numbers in half, and the Shamrock Organisation would employ the rest in one of the shamrock's leaves. Through negotiation with the client we eventually settled on the 'non-shamrocked' organisation because the political fallout from cutting staff from 1500 to 150 could not be borne. Strangely, it was of course the computerisation that presaged the job-losses but the shamrock that received the cut.

I can't prescribe a Shamrock Organisation in a general way, but if the IT department chose to dispassionately apply the

Shamrock Organisation, it could (although I don't recommend it) reduce its core staff to 7 people – one for each domain.

Implementation ideas

1 What is the mission of IT in your organisation? This is not a trivial question. It will probably also be informed by the stakeholder analysis including a look at their expectations of IT. But add other mission elements, because following stakeholder expectations will only ever present a part of the picture – a large part, but never the complete picture.

2 Draw up your own domain diagram. Firstly take the above exercise and define what you need to be doing to fulfil that mission. Then list your domains. Then fill in the mission of each.

3 List the frameworks that you and the business need to think more clearly about IT and its role in the organisation.

References

1. White, T. (1995) Towards a Model for the Integration of New Technologies into Organizations. *Unpublished Master's Thesis.* University of the Witwatersrand

2. Lewis, J.D. (1995) *The Connected Corporation: How Leading Companies Win Through Customer-Supplier Alliances.* Free Press Publishers, NY

3. Moore, G. (1991) *Crossing the Chasm; Marketing and Selling Technology Products to Mainstream Customers.* Capstone Publishing Limited, Oxford.

4. Ward, J. and Griffiths, P. (1996) *Strategic Planning for Information Systems.* John Wiley & Sons, Chichester, UK

5. Gluck, F.W., Kaufmann, S.P. and Walleck, A.S. (1980) *Strategic Management for Competitive Advantage*, Harvard Business Review, July/August

6. Weiss, A. (1995) *Our Emperors Have No Clothes*. Career Press, NJ

7. Tampoe, M. (1993) Motivating knowledge workers: The challenge of the 1990s. *Long Range Planning*, Vol. 26, No. 3

8. Sveiby, K.E. (1997) *The New Organizational Wealth*. Berrett-Koehler, CA

9. Handy, C. (1989) *Age of Unreason*. Random House, London

6 | If we're so clever, why can't we think? – new way of thinking for IT

I was facilitating a workshop the other day, and the CEO of the mining company, who is very forward in his thinking, suggested that we needed to give all the people working in the company a new way to think. Not brainwashing of course, but more along the lines of the 'reframing' exercise that I introduced in Chapter 1. This particular mining company has an opportunity to do something that very few companies ever do: to start from scratch, but with major backing and little interference from their mother company – and a mandate to 'do it differently'. In my opinion they have embarked on the journey with all the right tools and attitudes: they want their people to go beyond the rules to where the common sense lies. They want guidelines rather than policies. They have set up real cross-boundary teams and are working within a set of well-considered values. They have a tight and inspiring vision. They believe that thinking is more important than imposing regulations.

I had been brought in to help their people, who largely come from a traditional mining background, to change their behaviours and thinking. But in this particular workshop there was an engineer who quietly shook his head when the CEO suggested that we help people think in a different way. 'Not possible', he said. 'You think the way you think. Certainly you may be able to work on what motivates me, but I was born with the way I think, and there's not a lot anyone can do about it.'

Which is a very 'engineering' view of things. I'll explain in a moment that there's not a lot wrong with an engineering view of life, after all it keeps aeroplanes in the air and bridges poised securely over precipices, but there are other ways of thinking that are equally valid.

6.1 If you find yourself in a hole, it's probably a good idea to stop digging

According to Mitroff and Linstone in their book *The Unbound Mind*[1] many people have a particular way of thinking. The authors call it technical thinking: a logic-based enquiry method which attempts to solve problems and find answers. Engineers, accountants and IT people are good at this form of thought. It's not merely good enough to get the right answer, but it is also essential to reach a conclusion and move on, with a minimum wastage of time and unnecessary discussion. Which in itself is an admirable, even desirable, thinking approach. Certainly so when lives depend on the reliability of an aeroplane or bridge.

Technical thinking is the sort of thinking driven into us at school. What's wrong with the following scene? Teacher asks the kids: 'what's two plus one plus five, class?' Immediately up go the hands, and the imperious eye of teacher picks out one and says: 'yes Johnny?' 'Eight' replies Johnny and sits down to the warm approbation of teacher, as she turns to the blackboard to continue the lesson.

What is wrong with that scene? Firstly, when the hands shot up, what was the issue? It was a case of publicly announcing that you knew the answer. But not only that, it also signified that you knew the answer before everyone else. So from grade one, we have been taught that the first to the answer is rewarded. (Why for instance do examinations have time limits? – Is this because we value quick answers? Because I thought that examinations were designed to test students' knowledge, more than their speed. I suspect that examinations have time periods to ease the logistical and administrative burden, rather than to test students.)

Another flaw in this teaching style is that teacher didn't ask who else had that answer. And more importantly, who had a different answer. Imagine if you will, teacher actually asking that question, and little Mary at the back of the class puts her hand up. Teacher now asks: 'what was your answer little Mary?' 'Fruit salad', replies Mary. If she survives the sniggers of her classmates, and gets to explain, she might have said: 'well my mom cut up two apples, one orange and five grapes, and we had fruit salad for breakfast'. Is that answer any less accurate than Johnny's? Not really, and it might have led to an interesting discussion on adding like with like. But throughout our traditional schooling, we are conditioned to think in a technical way, and why not?

This book is all about why technical thinking is not the only form of thinking which is appropriate today: Chapter 1 deals with the need to reframe IT's role in the organisation; Chapter 2 is directed at explaining that there are new world trends in economies, nations, businesses and people. Chapter 3 explains the new business bill of rights pertinent to IT, and IT's need to conform to that bill of rights or be bypassed, and Chapter 5 presents a case for new activities to govern the IT function. What better argument for a need to think differently?

Mitroff and Linstone also recognise two other types of mental process in our organisations: The first, they call 'organisational' thinking and the second is 'personal' thinking. 'Organisational' thinkers drive their 'technical' associates to distraction: they are concerned with the social environment, with agendas, and with abstract concepts of justice, fairness and reasonableness. They compromise and bargain and look for acceptable solutions rather than the 'right' answer. In IT there has been a dramatic growth in 'Change Management' over the last few years, reflecting our recognition that the 'soft' aspects of information technology are becoming more and more important in the success of any particular implementation. In fact, I hear that change management represents the major growth area in IT consulting globally. Change management deals with people's use of technology and with their response to technologies. It concerns itself with human behaviour, with the social environment, with agendas, and with abstract concepts of justice, fairness and reasonableness. Sound familiar?

Finally Mitroff and Linstone suggest that the third form of thinking is the 'personal' thinking mode. The 'personal' perspective is one which we are often unwilling to own up to. It is a constant background process that worries about personal power, prestige and security. It seeks to reduce ambiguity: 'I know that there will be an organisational reshuffle soon, but where do I fit in?' Personal thinking relies on experience and intuition. The personal perspective is probably the chief motivator in you reading this book: you may be asking yourself: 'how can I use this stuff at work (to allow me to succeed)?' Nothing wrong with that. But the personal perspective is such a driving force in thinking, that if you lose sight of it and of the fact that almost everyone's personal perspective thinking is different from yours but still needs to be considered, then you lose sight of a valuable management and political tool.

There is a place for all three modes of thought in management, depending on the problem at hand. You can't build motor cars and computers with organisational thinking, but you also can't build organisations with technical thinking. And if there is no personal benefit, you can't build anything.

As today's business environment becomes more complex and moves faster, a manager's success will depend on his or her ability to handle ambiguity. F. Scott Fitzgerald said: 'the test of a first-rate intelligence is the ability to hold two opposed ideas in the mind at the same time.' Many of our managers seem to be unable to hold two opposing ideas in the same organisation at the same time, let alone in their minds.

For example: empowerment does not mean 'handing over power to the masses.' Neither does having a 'non-financial' mind-set mean that profits become unimportant. Nor does having a multi-stakeholder focus mean that shareholders are irrelevant. Or that customer-centred companies compromise their margins in favour of bending over backwards to meet customer demands. But again and again, when new ideas are presented to managers, these ideas are seen to be threatening, because they conflict with the current dogma.

So if you find someone who presents ideas which conflict with your mindset, remember that it's just a mindset after all. Try unsetting it for a moment, and follow Stephen Covey's[2] advice. Say: 'good, you see things differently. Show me what you see, and I'll show you what I see.'

6.2 Five ways to be wrong and four ways to be right

If we're going to think about thinking, then Edward de Bono is the obvious source of material. I have taken much of the structure of this section from a book by de Bono called *Practical Thinking*[3]. In it, he talks about five levels of understanding, the five ways to be mistaken and four ways to be right. But he starts his thesis by questioning what being 'right' is. He asks: 'how is it that in an argument both sides are always right?' Both parties in an argument deem themselves to be right, and the other to be wrong. How can that be if there is an absolute rightness?

6.2.1 Five ways to be wrong

One of de Bono's ways of being wrong he calls the 'must-be mistake' and he subtitles it the 'arrogance mistake.' It is a mistake which acknowledges the rightness of the answer, without allowing further development. I used to tear my hair out when, in project proposals, my staff used to present me with only one option to consider. I would send them away and ask them for at least three options. They would return with three options loosely categorised as 'do nothing', 'our answer', and 'the ludicrous choice'. Their thinking was flawed by the 'must-be' mistake. Such mistakes shut out alternatives, stop evolution of ideas, and enforce traditional solutions.

De Bono also talks of the 'monorail mistake' which follows a single track to apply an inappropriate solution to a problem. Typically in organisations, such single-track thinking manifests itself in 'x=y' kind of formula. You know the type: 'high costs=retrench staff', 're-engineering=downsizing', 'Pilfering from the stationery cupboard=lock the cupboard and institute stationery request forms.' 'IT development=project'. While these answers to problems are easy to arrive at, they ignore all qualifying factors. (I devote a chapter to my thinking that IT development should not be accomplished through the 'project' mode of thinking – if this conflicts with your current mindset check yourself for thinking faults.) It is difficult to convince a person who has made a monorail mistake to consider other factors. Take the example described by Darien McWhirter in *'Managing People: Creating Team Based Organization'*,[4] of a bank in which a dozen secretaries had cheque writing authority. When it became clear that one, and only one, secretary was abusing the trust, two new employees were hired, a cheque request was created, the dozen secretaries were required to fill in triplicate forms, and cheque writing took two days. Rather than deal with the employee, an elaborate and expensive system was put in place. Imaging what that did to the feeling of trust in the bank. As one executive pointed out: 'so 2% of our employees are jerks.

Why have a system that says to the other 98%: "You're jerks?" Do your IT procedures follow the same thought process?

Another mistake in thinking is what de Bono calls the 'magnitude mistake'. I am guilty of this type of thinking when I cook. I reckon if one tablespoon of sugar is good then two tablespoons of sugar must be better. Or the kind of thinking that is currently going on in the firearm control debate in which many governments are proposing restricting the number of guns for self-defence to two or three per person. Opponents of this control accuse these governments of disarming the nation, and leaving them defenceless at the hands of criminals. I don't own a gun, but I don't understand how having two or three would leave me defenceless. Magnitude mistakes are often made by absolutists, those who only see right and wrong. Pointing out to them that 'two or three' does not equal 'none' is difficult. You may be accused of splitting hairs, when good thinking depends on the ability to split hairs if necessary.

Business people are also guilty of de Bono's 'misfit mistake' in which you see only sufficient elements of a problem to recognise it and apply a solution. Something is seen as familiar when in fact it turns out to be quite different. A new circumstance is judged by the old reality. A classic and oft-quoted case of this is IBM's inability to recognise the development of the personal computer as a threat to their mainframe sales. To their credit, once they had recognised the problem, their response kept them as the leading PC suppliers for a number of years. Another mistake is currently being made by many companies who think that e-business is merely old business done electronically. When they wake up, not only will they have lost the game, but they also won't even know what the game is anymore. Recognise this attitude in your organisation?

De Bono's final mistake is what he calls the 'miss-out' mistake. This is when you selectively choose information which supports your solution and leave out information which refutes it. But as

Aldous Huxley said: 'facts do not cease to exist because they are ignored.' This mistake is easy to spot when you can see the whole picture, but difficult to see when presented with only a partial picture. We often see politicians using this technique to promote their cause. Advertisers are good at this as well. When they tell you that their product has 'no added sugar,' what they avoid telling you is that the constituent ingredients are packed with sugar, or MSG or whatever. Often these mistakes arise from where one chooses to draw the boundaries around the problem: is unemployment due solely to the current economic policy of the government, or are there other factors to consider? Ask a politician, and see what he leaves out in his answer, depending on whose side he stands.

Let me wrap up the mistakes with a few quotes that will illuminate my view on 'mistakes:' Walter Lipman said: 'when all men think alike, no-one thinks very much'. So mistakes should be treated as a different thought pattern from which we can learn, rather than something to be rejected – remember the 'must-be' mistake.

Albert Einstein said: 'only two things are infinite, the universe and human stupidity, and I'm not sure about the former.' And whilst this sounds arrogant and dismissive, perhaps we should take another look at it. Who says stupidity is bad? Certainly not Edward de Bono, who believes that 'man may be smarter than animals only because he is stupider. The paradox is that man may be able to go much further in his thinking than animals only because his basic thinking is less precise.' Because man is less sure of things he has to reason, to think, to trust his gut.

I like mistakes. I like stupidity. I once asked my boss: 'why do you put up with Peter? He is a pain in the neck.' He answered: 'Yes he is. But he asks the stupid questions.'

Mahfouz Naguib said: 'you can tell whether a man is clever by his answers. You can tell whether a man is wise by his questions.'

6.2.2 Four ways to be right

We're told that: 'it's all in the mind.' And yet we are not taught how to think at school, or in most cases even at university. We are not told about how to see things from multiple perspectives, we are not taught how to draw mind-maps, nor is our education system geared towards training or rewarding more than two or three of the nine forms of intelligence. We are seldom expected to operate in real thinking teams. And we are not taught how to calm our minds, and to manage them for thinking tasks. Which probably explains why, once we get into business, we bemoan the fact that our people can't see the wood for the trees, never give us multiple options in their proposals, stick doggedly to outdated ideas, don't work in teams and generally resist changing their minds and behaviours.

Again I will be using Edward de Bono's book *Practical Thinking* to examine ways of being right in your thinking and the problem of arrogance in being right.

The first way of being right is what de Bono calls 'logical rightness.' He also calls it 'jigsaw puzzle' rightness. If all the pieces are there, and they fit together then chances are you're right. Although this is a sound way of thinking, I often used to use this brand of thinking in preparing budget presentations for my executives. All the pieces were there, and they all added up to the 'right' numbers, so my budgets were approved. However, I knew that in any one year, I would not be able to spend about 15% of my budget, because of developments in the business or in the industry. By the same token, I knew that about 15% of my spending during the year could also not have been budgeted for because of developments in the business or in the industry. So year after year, the budget added up, and year after year, my budget was 'right' when in fact, it was only ever a good approximation. And year after year I would have about 7.5 million to play with, without having to go through the authorisation process. Mind you, had I chosen to follow the 'right' route and put in a budget category called: 'money we won't spend because one of you chaps will change your mind about it during the year', or 'money we will spend, but I can't see where at the moment,' I bet my budget would be hurled out the door, closely followed by myself. De Bono draws our attention to these limitations in being logically right. He asks what we will do with funny shaped pieces of the jigsaw that just don't fit the solution? And what about choosing our own pieces to make the jigsaw look right?

The second way of being right is unpalatable to many executives. De Bono calls it 'emotional rightness.' Because the elements of a solution are 'good' then the solution itself is 'good'. Politicians often use this method. But then so do many business people. There surely can't be anything wrong with setting up a customer call centre, can there? And what about all the 'good' words in your vision?: 'to be the leading supplier of quality wing-nuts to our chosen market.' Nothing wrong with that vision statement surely? And what could possibly be wrong with having a knowledge management or e-business strategy and system? And indeed in many cases this is the right thing for an organisation to be doing. De Bono also allows that gut feeling plays an important part in emotional rightness. In fact most problem-solving methods are based on gut feeling. The advertising industry almost exclusively depends on decisions based on emotional rightness. Very few people read ingredients lists, test drive every car, see every showhouse. Almost all of us make our decisions based on our emotional reaction to information. Funny how this mode of decision-making has to be kept in the background in the boardroom.

A third way of being right is called 'unique rightness'. If all the facts fit only one answer then that is the right answer. As all the facts fitted Sir Isaac Newton's theories before Albert Einstein offered alternatives. Or as De Bono describes: if a red-haired man is seen robbing a bank, and a week later a red-haired man uses marked banknotes stolen in the robbery to buy goods, then he must be the robber. Of course the real robber could have used a red wig and made a point of paying over money to a red haired man. But in general Occam's Razor applies to this form of rightness. Occam's Razor states that if there are two right explanations for a problem, then the simplest one should hold true. De Bono is very negative about this form of rightness and he postulates de Bono's second law:

> Proof is often no more than lack of imagination in providing an alternate explanation. Or in its fiercer form: Certainty arises from a feeble imagination.

> (De Bono, 1992)

Finally there is 'recognition rightness.' This is really what most of life is about. If we spent our time constantly diagnosing situations we'd never get anything done. Imagine having to learn that 'steam'='boiling water' before recognising that you might scald yourself. Or having to learn that a red traffic light means 'stop' every time you encounter one. Or having to learn the hard way that falling sales will lead to closing the business. Recognition rightness leads to action.

There are three features of recognition rightness worth discussing. Firstly most of our recognition is immediate and all recognition is learned. Secondly, if we don't recognise something, we have to break it down into smaller parts that we do recognise, and problem-solve from there. Thirdly, recognition is based on the need to have enough features which match up to your solution, and no more. Once you have enough facts to recognise a solution, you stop looking. Perhaps you recognise the limitations in every one of these three features to see that each is linked to one of the ways of being wrong.

I won't dot all the t's and cross all the i's for you. Perhaps this is an opportunity to apply the five ways of being wrong and the four ways of being right to your re-inventing your IT function in your organisation. Take some time. Explore ideas. Keep exploring after you have the answer. J.R.R. Tolkein said: 'not all who wander are lost.'

Of course being right can lead to arrogance. De Bono again:

> The arrogance of righteousness is probably the most dangerous fault of human thinking.
>
> (De Bono, 1992)

Arrogance is based on two types of thinking; firstly the 'unique rightness' type of thinking in which the facts fit my answer, so it is the only answer. And secondly on the 'logical rightness' thinking in which all the facts fit together to form an elegant solution. And the very elegance of the solution leads to the arrogance.

De Bono conducted an experiment with 1000 students, in which they had to explain a particularly puzzling event. Of the 1000 students only three did not venture an explanation. And only one out of ten who did submit an explanation, suggested that there could be an alternative answer to the one they had offered. So almost everyone believed they had an explanation, and 90% of those believed that their explanation was right.

Finally De Bono equates arrogance with stupidity:

> The most characteristic feature of stupidity is not an inability or lack of knowledge but the certainty with which ideas are held.
>
> (De Bono, 1992)

So I suppose the question is this: how certain are you that your thinking on IT is the right thinking? Or is there room for different ideas and actions?

6.3 Active and passive thinking styles – the road to responsibility

Finally in this chapter on thinking I would like to explore a revelation that came to me some years ago:

What's wrong with this letter? 'We apologize for the poor service: in connection with the downtime of e-mail services over the last two days, we are pleased to announce that the service has been restored and e-mail communication may be resumed. Please note that due to backup problems, e-mails that were received during the e-mail downtime period have not been saved, and these have been lost. There was also a regrettable corruption of data on the e-mail server and the last three week's e-mail in-box contents have been deleted. We apologise for any inconvenience.'

Apart from the fact that I didn't understand this (I took it from a real communication from our techies), you get the feeling that they haven't really apologised, and neither have they accepted responsibility for the mistakes they made. Also, how much effort do you think they have made at making sure their problem never occurs again?

How do you get these impressions? As far as the support team is concerned, they have responded to your complaint, and rectified an e-mail downtime experience. As far as you're concerned, it's time to start looking for different e-mail support options.

One of the key problems is that the letter is written in the passive voice. An 'active-voiced' letter would say the following: 'we apologise for our poor service. We have restored the e-mail service which we did not have available for two days. You may use your e-mail system again. Please note that we did not back up any incoming e-mails during the downtime period, and consequently we did not save any e-mail messages which arrived over that period. We also corrupted the data on the e-mail server and deleted the last three week's e-mail in-box contents. We apologize for any inconvenience.'

The active voice assigns responsibility to actions. And in this case points out the incompetence of the support team. And responsibility sits very uncomfortably if you don't take action. So an adjunct to this letter should be something like: 'in taking responsibility for the inconvenience we have caused you, we recognise that our backup procedures need significant re-examination, and we have taken steps to do so to ensure that this never happens again. Also we have scheduled our technicians on training in e-mail management and promise that our service will not deteriorate to this level again.' Painful stuff, but do you think that the users of this e-mail service will give it one (and only one) more chance?

I had exactly this chain of events occur to me some years back. Our support manager brought a passive-voiced letter for my approval, which I would have approved had I not just read something about active- and passive-voiced communications and responsibility. I asked her to re-write the letter in active-voice. The response from our users reinforced my determination to use active-voice in my business communications. Our users said: 'gosh that's the first time you IT people have been honest with us in years. Congratulations. Keep it up.'

Most office memo's are written in the passive voice – is it just office etiquette or is it a reluctance to take responsibility? What is your response to these two examples? 'As a result of poor performance, there will be a right-sizing exercise in the next few months.' Or; 'we have performed badly, and we are looking at ways to improve this performance. We may need to downsize soon.' Apart from being simpler, the second statement accepts responsibility.

The use of the passive voice in memo's, announcements and letters allows the writer to avoid apportioning blame: 'our programmers missed the deadline', leaves us in no doubt about who did what. 'The deadline was missed by our programmers', looks innocuous enough, but we can remove the object of the sentence, and so remove the apportionment of responsibility: 'the deadline was missed', says nothing about who did it.

Many experts believe that the use of language in organisations is a key lever of behavioural change. We programme ourselves and our organisations with words. The more we use certain words and phrases, the more likely they will come to pass. So if you allow your IT function and yourself to speak in the passive-voice, you can expect your company and employees not to take responsibility for their actions.

Try the passive-voice test on your reports and memo's. Turn them into active-voice.

6.4 Thinking and the new IT mindset

'What earthly use is an examination of thinking styles in IT?' you might ask. Well the rules have changed completely. And those people who are able to examine ideas and the way these ideas were constructed, and their own thinking styles will be better positioned to see their truth in the chaotic milieu that defines their working environment. And to me the 'truth' is, if the rules have changed, then surely our behaviours should change. There's a trite little homily that sticks in my mind that says that the true sign of insanity is a person who continues to do the same thing again and again, and yet expects different results. The opposite of this homily suggests that: 'if you want things to be different, you have to do something different.' And to do something different, you need to think differently.

Let me summarise this thinking discussion so far, before we look at how to apply thinking in an IT environment:

Three types of thinking:

- technical – logic is the only way of being right;

- organisational – people are important and imprecise, progress is important even without an answer;

- personal – what's in it for me?

Five ways of being wrong

- must-be mistakes – this is right, there is no other answer;

- monorail mistakes – 'x=y' or 'reengineering=downsizing';

- magnitude mistakes – one=everyone, if it's a little right, it's all right;

- misfit mistakes – if it looks like this, then it is this. New circumstances/old reality;

- miss-out mistake – selective hearing, don't look at facts which don't fit the answer.

Four ways of being right

- logical rightness – if all the pieces of the jigsaw fit, then it is right;

- emotional rightness – if it is 'good' then it is right;

- unique rightness – if there is only one answer, the answer is right;

- recognition rightness – learned recognition of leads to action – 'see then do'.

Active and passive voice thinking

- passive voice allow you to absolve yourself;

- active voice acknowledges responsibility and demands action.

Having re-read this list of thinking styles and modes, I am struck by the pessimistic tone of the thinking styles. I have talked about ways of being wrong, and of avoiding responsibility, and even the ways of being right seem to be wrong. Funnily enough, having internalised most of these insights (although I slip regularly), I don't feel negative about them. Rather I use the insights as a screen or template against which I try to weed out my own closed-mindedness, and to recognise thinking styles in others, so that I may help them think differently for different situations.

So I would like to use this thinking filter to allow ourselves to examine IT within the new economy. Keep in mind that these are just ideas. Ideas should not threaten anyone. After all they have no material substance. But as Charles Handy[5] says:

> In the long perspective of history it may seem that the really influential people in the last 100 years were not Hitler or Churchill, Stalin or Gorbachev, but Freud, Marx and Einstein, men who changed nothing except the way we think, but that changed everything.
>
> (Handy, 1995)

So let's play with some ideas. Perhaps we can change everything by changing the way we think.

6.5 Thinking about IT – some ideas to play with

I am going to propose some ideas about IT as 'facts', not because they necessarily *are* facts, but more because I am trying to be positive and 'active-voiced' about them. Try them on. See if they fit. If they don't fit, run them through the filter of thinking styles that I laid out above, and check your mindset. If they still don't fit, that's fine. You are allowed to differ, that's where growth comes from, but know why you differ.

6.5.1 Sir Isaac Newton and information technology

Isaac Newton developed numerous universal laws that governed how scientists saw the universe for nearly 300 years. The universe was predictable and 'law-abiding' and the scientific paradigm worked well within these laws. Then along came a number of thinkers, most notably Albert Einstein, Max Planck and Werner Heisenberg, who recognised that scientists had been responsible for three classic thinking mistakes: the must-be mistake, or 'Isaac Newton solved this 300 years ago, and it has held true for that long therefore it must be right.' The magnitude mistake which believed that discrepancies which were calculated at the very large scale (i.e., light speed) and the very small (i.e., sub-atomic particles) were of little importance and were probably due to rounding errors. Finally and most importantly, the miss-out mistake which allowed scientists to ignore these discrepancies because they didn't fit with accepted laws.

Einstein concluded that energy is matter and vice versa, Planck deduced that atoms were not static bits of matter but were pulsating bundles of energy and Heisenberg concluded quite alarmingly that electrons can either be matter or energy depending on how you choose to look. We are still exploring the ramifications of these three science-changing conclusions. Business is starting to discover that at the speed of light, or electronic speed, it is less important to count on matter or physical things, and more important to count on intelligence and imagination. This is a similar mindset change to business thinking, as was Albert Einstein's proposal to the scientific world, and will have as profound a change on the business world as Einstein's thinking had on science. (The accountants have only just started to wonder how we can count intellectual assets into the value of an organisation.) More interestingly (and here the technical thinkers are going to have to loosen up a little), it seems that humans behave very differently depending on how we choose to look at them. If we prefer to see them as work-capable units, intrinsically out to take what they can get, then we will structure our companies and policies in a particular way. Or if you choose to see people as the repositories of intelligence and imagination, who are willing and able to bring this intelligence to bear on your behalf if you set things up for them to do so, then your organisation and policies will be different again. And in both cases people behave according to your expectations. (Again accountants are battling to come to grips with the concept of people as an asset.) Oh by the way, in 1992 Jorgenson and Fraumeni[6] determined that the value of human capital is ten times greater than former calculations, totally eclipsing other kinds of investment.

What does the above have to do with IT? Everything.

If the new way of doing business is at light speed, your organisation will be expecting to be connected to their suppliers, customers, investors, community, researchers and the world in general. What have you done to be ready when the time comes? This doesn't mean shoving e-business down their throats either. It means building your relationship with your organisation so that they turn to you first when they want e-solutions and it means being ready to say 'yes' when they do.

When it comes to the new way of seeing people, you can change the way you manage your own IT people right now. Read the later chapter on 'Organising IT' first though, because it's not as easy as I am suggesting here. But you should also be aware of the contribution that IT will be expected to make to the organisation if they choose to enlist the intellect and imagination of their people. They will expect knowledge creating and supporting systems, modelling systems, and enough flexibility in all systems so that when someone comes up with a viable, and exciting business idea IT is seen as an enabler rather than a disabler of the idea.

6.5.2 Systems thinking is greater than the sum of the parts

There is a growing school of thought that accepts that you can't solve a problem solely by breaking it down into its constituent parts, examining the parts and solving the problem in the faulty unit, then putting it all back together to make a working system again. Peter Senge[7] regards the ultimate discipline for managers to master, to be the ability to see everything as part of a system rather than a discrete element. His view of systems thinking requires you to view the unit on its own as well as part of the system to which it belongs. Not only that, but you should view systems at two levels at least – the primary level (that which you can see) and the secondary level (that which causes what you can see).

This seems to be complicated so let us go back to the example of the e-mail server failure that I apologised for earlier in this chapter. Apparently the e-mail service was rendered defunct through some incident (perhaps a virus, or the disk space ran out of capacity, or any other reason). The support people tried to solve the e-mail problem, but forgot to capture incoming e-mails for later distribution. In their efforts to fix the problem they also managed to trash the files containing everyone's inbox contents. Finally, they didn't have sufficient backups to restore things back to just prior to the failure. Sigh. This sounds terribly ham-handed of them, but I've seen a similar train of events in almost every serious IT problem that I've encountered. They viewed the problem on its own: 'something's wrong with the e-mail server. Therefore fix the server.' Which on its own was not a bad course of action to take. A systems view would say: 'yes, let's fix the server, but before we do that, what system is it a part of?' And I'm not just talking about computer systems here either. People, backup processes, incoming and outgoing messages are all part of the e-mail system. Systems thinking may have led our hapless support personnel to wonder about what will happen to incoming mail, and about what to do with the people who use the e-mail on a regular basis. This is the 'seen' system. But the real power of systems thinking comes when you look at what causes what we can see of the system. There's something wrong with the e-mail server. What caused that? What allowed that cause to happen in the first place? What caused us to neglect the incoming mails? How do we fix the cause rather than the problem? And so on.

If systems thinking seems like a lot of work, it is. But I can defend it from a personal perspective because through the application of systems thinking, my department managed to cut the number of priority one problems in IT from 22 per month to one every two months. Don't applaud, anyone can do the same if they take systems thinking seriously.

6.5.3 Determinism versus uncertainty and ambiguity

Another mindset shift for IT is the change from deterministic thinking to ambiguous thinking. Determinism is a little like de Bono's monorail thinking, but extends the concept a whole lot further. Determinism suggests that you can determine the answer to any problem. Do you recognise a technical mindset here? One problem equals one solution. Ambiguity thinking accepts that conditions change so fast and are so complex that there is no way of having one answer to one problem, at least not for very long. Today's answers limit tomorrow's actions. Working with uncertainty requires of us a 'satisficing' perspective, which asks: 'do we have enough to satisfy the problem and to proceed?' Because tomorrow we may have more information and need to change the path we're on.

Dealing with uncertainty and ambiguity in IT is difficult, and doesn't make you any friends amongst the engineers and accountants either. You proceed in the direction of a desired outcome, satisfying the criteria of as many problems and issues that you can see without feeling the need to solve every problem right now, and also without closing any doors to the future if you can help it. Wishy-washy it may be, but that's the way to progress in a fast-moving, chaotic world. I offer a practical approach to this form of thinking in Chapter 11 on IT solutions provision. I start my thinking on IT development from a viewpoint that there is no way that you or your users can determine up-front what they want from a system. The environment, business conditions and their minds are changing too fast to specify a set of requirements 18 months ahead of delivery of the system. And it is very liberating, although very difficult, to get people (both users and IT development people) to accept that things change and therefore a 'satisficing' standpoint will serve the development environment better in the longer term.

6.5.4 Guidance versus control – the essential difficulty

Most of us react badly to tight control. Whether it is the housing authority telling you what you can or can't build on your property, or the beach guard telling you where you can or can't swim, or your spouse telling you what you can or cannot eat (or wear). We react with resentment and rebellion to some degree. And yet many organisations feel very comfortable telling you how to behave, when to work, where to smoke, and how to do your job. (I once worked for a company that put a lot of pressure on me to upgrade my motor-car because mine was too modest for the image they wanted to project.) Yes I know organisations believe they have the right to issue instructions and apply controls because they pay you. Perhaps you also believe they have that right.

The world has changed. There is a sweeping democratisation of the workplace. Largely this is due to the information revolution and the move in general of workers towards being service providers, rather than manufacturing or industrial workers. The difference between service provision and industrial work is profound. Industrial work is largely repetitive and predictable, where service provision is significantly less recurrent and predictable. Why? Because service involves dealing face-to-face with customers, and customers are becoming more discriminating in their demands on products and services. Customers can afford to be harder to please because there is so much choice, that they can get equivalent services from another supplier without particular effort on their part.

When people serve other people they need to use their wits and intelligence to structure the service so that it conforms to increasingly particular customer needs. And if the organisation has bound its people too tightly in controls, rules and regulations, it will lose customers, followed fairly soon by disgruntled staff. If you want to provide service, you have to engage the brains of your staff. If you want to engage the brains of your people, then you can't control them.

But all is not lost. Companies are discovering that they get much better results from people if they guide them to use their intellect within wide parameters. This involves using guidelines instead of policies, of setting up frameworks and templates to be used as resources by staff, rather than requiring them to comply with rules and stringent methodologies. All of this to be glued together with a tight and driving vision, with a cogent value system, and with a clear mission.

The impact on IT here is great. Because guidelines rather than policies, templates rather than methodologies, vision and values rather than 'do what I say', must surely strike dread in the heart of IT architects and developers. 'How are we to have any standards if people are free to do whatever they want?' might be the lament of architects. Developers might also mutter darkly to themselves as they envision a runaway project heading for the cliff-edge. By now you should recognise two mistakes, the monorail mistake and the magnitude mistake. Having guidelines and frameworks does not mean having nothing (magnitude mistake) and not having policies and standards does not mean chaos if there is another answer (monorail mistake). I will deal with standards and architectures and with development methodologies in later chapters, but this appetiser is to get you thinking: why do you need standards if everyone buys in to the need to do things in a certain way? And why do you need a methodology if users and IT people are operating within a well thought-out and structured template?

6.6 Why not? – thinking like a renegade

Renegade thinking works deliberately against the flow of ideas. And sometimes while everyone else is actually struggling against the flow, renegade thinking turns round and sees where the flow takes them. Renegade thinkers are rebels, but are not destructive in their rebellion. They are also not dogmatic – remember the monorail mistake where everyone else is wrong and I am right. Renegade thinkers believe in the value of ideas, and if they can have a contrary idea, then anyone else can have an idea which differs from theirs.

Ultimately, I suppose my credo is: 'why not?'

If someone says to me that this can't be done that way, my first response is 'why not?' If the answer is something like: 'because that's the way it's done,' or 'because we've always done it this way,' then the field is wide open for some searching questions and some renegade thinking.

Of course informed renegade thinking leads you down fewer unproductive paths, but I am also aware that many of the world's major inventions have come from people outside, or at the edge of an industry, who did not know enough to know that things couldn't be done that way. They just did it, and the industry was startled to have their deeply held beliefs so thoroughly dashed. The first flying machine was built by the Wright brothers, owners of a bicycle shop in Dayton. Samuel

Pierpoint Langley on the other hand was backed by the Smithsonian Institute, Congress and the US Army to build the first aeroplane. Langley was a scientist, had teams of assistants, and failed outright to build anything that did more than fall off the end of a ramp into the Potomac River[8]. (The Smithsonian Institute backed Langley to such an extent that they refused to acknowledge the Wright brother's accomplishment for almost 40 years.)

I would be delighted if you read something that I suggest you can't do and ask yourself: 'why not?' Run your thinking through the various filters. And come up with startling ideas. And then when you get into implementation mode, and you strike a hitch or a problem, keep asking yourself 'why not?'

Implementation ideas

1 Apply the five ways of being wrong and the four ways of being right to your re-inventing your IT function in your organisation. Take the time to examine the 'sacred cows' in IT. The first one could easily be: 'should there be a separate IT department?' and 'what are the boundaries of IT?'

2 Look to how you can tap into the thinking power of all your people. They will expect knowledge creating and supporting systems, modelling systems, and enough flexibility in all systems so that when someone comes up with a viable, and exciting business idea, IT is seen as an enabler rather than a disabler of the idea.

3 What is the impact of 'light-speed' business? What are the possibilities? This is not just e-business, but might also be 'e-IT'. What IT domains can be run from somewhere else in the world?

4 Examine your organisation for passive-voiced communication and the attendant abdication of responsibility.

References

1. Mitroff and Linstone (1993) *The Unbounded Mind*. Oxford University Press, Oxford
2. Covey, S. (1989) *Seven Habits of Highly Effective People*. Fireside Books
3. De Bono, E. (1992) *Practical Thinking*. Penguin, USA
4. McWhirter, D. *'Managing People: Creating Team Based Organization.'*
5. Handy, C. (1995) *Beyond Certainty*. Hutchinson
6. Jorgenson, D.W. and Fraumeni B. *Investment in Education and US Economic Growth*. Harvard Institute of Economic Research (1992) *HIER Discussion Paper* No. 1573, (April)
7. Senge, P.M. (1990) *The Fifth Discipline*. Doubleday
8. Bryson, B. (1994) *Made in America*. Martin, Secker & Warburgh

7 The soft stuff is hard – the new business/IT relationship

In the past, and perhaps even now, the relationship between an organisation and its IT function was defined largely by technology. IT's retreat into technology is entirely understandable. IT was required to focus on communal services and systems for the business, often drawing further away from the business as the technology became more demanding, and frankly more *friendly* than users. On the other hand, easy to use PC application packages available from your nearest 'corner-store' haven't made the relationship between IT and business any easier to sustain. Most of these PC applications are simple to operate, have little security and the crudest networking capability if any. This might lead the average business person to believe that IT is easy. When in fact we know that the complexity of IT is seldom within a system, and is more often found outside the system, in the architecture, in the interfacing, in the multi-user accessibility functions, in the security and firewalling, and in the upgrading and general maintenance (backups, etc.). No wonder IT and business people don't see eye to eye, in many cases not seeing each other for weeks at a time.

The bad news is that the relationship between IT and the business is one of the primary determinants of success for IT. We have to make an effort. Many CIOs have set up 'user-liaison' positions only to be disappointed with their failure[1]. Some business units have set up the opposite IT liaison function to face similar disappointment.

7.1 Organisational relationships

I looked up 'relationships' in a book on psychology in the working environment[2] and was a little taken aback to find that the section on relationships was located in the chapter entitled: 'Work, Stress and Psychological Well-being'. But on reflection I saw that relationships and stress are indeed related:

> Other people – and our varied encounters with them – can be a major source of both stress and support. At work, especially, dealings with bosses, peers and subordinates can dramatically affect the way we feel at the end of the day . . . Learning to live with other people is one of the most stressful aspects of life.
>
> (Arnold et al., 1998)

I cannot disagree that relationships are stressful. Certainly I found dealing with difficult users one of the toughest elements of my job as CIO. More so, when they were in some degree right in the position they were taking – often I could not provide what they wanted, and could not explain in words of one syllable why. Which is why it is important to embark on a structured relationship building programme with key business people. If you rely on often adversarial contacts to create a working relationship you will not succeed in a mutually respectful and functional association.

You may see your relationship task as managing relations between the IT function and your business as depicted in Figure 7.1.

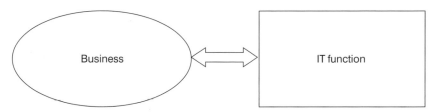

Figure 7.1 The simple IT function/business relationship

Or perhaps the above relationship might look more like that depicted in Figure 7.2.

But of course relationship management today is much more complex and requires that you manage the jumble of relationships depicted in Figure 7.3.

You definitely need to manage relationships between IT and the business, but it's a little more complex than that: for example, our company's e-connections open up a whole new relationship dimension. I once asked a CIO of a very large bank how much time he spent with the bank's customers. He reckoned he spent about 30% of his time talking to bank customers, and that the percentage was growing. Finally you should not ignore the relationship between yourself as an employer, and your staff

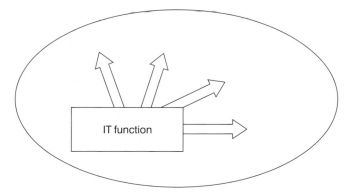

Figure 7.2 IT within a business – a one-way street

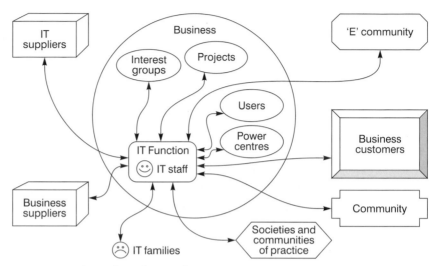

Figure 7.3 Relationships that need managing in IT

and their families. Modern thinking is showing that you cannot separate the individual from their environment. And their family is an important part of their environment.

In summary then, you need to pay attention to the following relationships:

● the supply chain – both IT's and the company's – possible strategic alliances;

● customers of your organisation, including the prospective customers of your organisation;

● your staff and their families – see staff as part of a unit;

● communities within your business – the executive, power centres (groups or individuals who have some interest in IT and have the power to make their interests compelling), users of different IT services, and project groups who are working to achieve a specific goal – either with you or in spite of you;

● the community – if IT is an enabler, its power to enable within the community is clear, and you should give some thought to using this power. (I know that having set up a computer school for underprivileged kids using obsolete computers reclaimed from the business, the IT function became the flagship of our company's community involvement programme.)

Later I offer some concrete relationship management ideas which might get you on the road to managing all the above relationships with greater purpose and advantage for yourself.

7.2 Partnerships

I like words. And when a word strikes me as interesting, I try to find out a little more about it. Take 'partnership' for instance. The word is probably derived from the Middle-English word 'parcener' who is one of two or more persons sharing an inheritance – a joint heir. Which has a message for us, because we are joint heirs of the fortunes of the company, yet some people seem not to see the need to build a relationship with others in our business. Among the many partnership-related words in my thesaurus I found the words which support my view of the IT-business partnership: association, alliance, community, trust, compact, affiliation. Probably the most important word in this selection is 'trust.' A significant amount of relationship-building activity is really trust-building activity. And trust works both ways. Trust depends on confidence in the other's ability to deliver on promises. IT has a long way to go on the trust stakes.

Jordan Lewis[3] deals with strategic partnering between customers and suppliers, and it is instructive to look at his list of customer traits that make for poor partnerships. His criteria for poor customer relations are on the left of Table 7.1, and my interpretation of the IT perspective is on the right of the table

Table 7.1
Second-rate
customers –
and IT
interpretations

		Bad customers	**IT 'customers'**
	1	Negotiate on price alone	Is your performance primarily defined by cost? I worked with an IT function whose entire performance base was founded on the fact that they cost 1.5% of turnover, while the CEO had read that 1% of turnover was the standard. Never mind that the CEO was looking at the wrong industry for his standard.
	2	Do not keep promises	Are you first in line for budget cuts?
	3	Don't make long term commitments	How long is your strategic horizon? Can you get a five-year commitment on an architectural direction? 'Short-termism' is often linked to point 1 above.
	4	Have weak teamwork across their own functions	Are you constantly battling with different power-groups that play you as a pawn in their games? Do you have conflicting requirements from different power groups? If they can't get their acts together, why should you do it for them? (By the way you should! But it requires master relationship management.)
	5	Use adversarial relationships in their dealings with you	How many tense meetings do you attend with the business? Are they on your side? Or do they want to play a part in the solution? Or is it all up to you? There's a good approach to this situation outlined in Fisher and Ury's book: *Getting to Yes*[4], which suggests that you delve beyond the positions that people take, to find their interest in the situation.
	6	Are 'punishment' focused, not solutions driven when there are supply problems	Do your business 'customers' criticise your function unfairly without a thought for solving the problem? This is related to point 8, but really it is an education issue.

Table 7.1
(continued)

	Bad customers	**IT 'customers'**
7	Insist on detailed contracts with little room for change or manoeuvre	Do you have a Service Level Agreement? If so, is it the law, with no variations allowed, no matter what the circumstances. Alternatively, if you do not have a formal SLA, do your 'customers' seem to have their own one in their heads, without telling you what the rules are?
8	Have very little interest in suppliers – especially in their benefits from the relationship	I once had a severe critic in the business who publicly lambasted me for some perceived flaw in my IT function. When I asked him what he suggested I do, the wretch said: 'it's not my job to solve your problems for you'. I still haven't thought of a snappy retort, and that was 10 years ago.
9	Are not open to supplier suggestions	How well received are your suggestions and initiatives in the business? A CEO once asked me: 'are you trying to tell me how to run my business?' To which I replied (but more diplomatically): 'yes'. I luckily had a relationship in which I could explain that IT has a significant role to play in determining business practices, and the CEO adopted an accommodation perspective.
10	Are unwilling to share information	This relates less to the sharing of information when you ask them, as in the development of a systems environment. Rather it should be seen in the light of whether the business proactively shares information with IT. Or do you have to find out about business developments after they have occurred?
11	Do not share management responsibility for the relationship	This links to points 5 and 8, in which the business regards the IT-Business relationship as your problem.

Table 7.1
(continued)

	Bad customers	IT 'customers'
12	Have little active support from their top executives	I eventually left an organisation whose CEO said: 'for heaven's sake, keep IT as far away from me as possible.' I might try harder to get close to the CEO now that I am older and wiser. The proper response would be to draw a relationship diagram for the CEO, and to work on his surrounding group. There are always ways.
13	Have a reputation of frustrating other suppliers	This doesn't directly apply. But does your business often look elsewhere for their IT services? If so, regard this as a warning signal on both your relationship and your service.

Now this litany of woe might not hold true in every case, but just one of these traits represents a partnership in some form of trouble. How healthy is your partnership with your 'customers?' Each of these areas suggests specific actions. All of them apply to relationship management.

Of course relationships are definitely not all your problem. Eric Berne[5] was a psychologist who in 1964 identified the games that people play in order to get what they want. And some of the games various business people play are directly related to keeping the spotlight off themselves. One of the many games Berne describes is the 'now I've got you, you son of a bitch' game, in which one party waits in ambush for the other to make a mistake, no matter how small. Then, from on-high adopts an attitude of avenging righteousness often completely out of proportion to the mistake. The other party obligingly co-operates by playing the 'why does this always happen to me?' game or the 'kick me' game or the 'wooden leg' (I can't help it, I've got a wooden leg) game. There are reasons for each party playing their games, which are the subject of Berne's book. It seems to me that the 'now I've got you, you son of a bitch'

(NIGYSOB) game is quite often played by users and IT, respectively. Berne recommends that the way to counter game playing people, is not to even enter into the game in the first place. So when someone plays the 'NIGYSOB' game, the correct response would be to admit the mistake (using active not passive voice) and move on together to resolving the problem.

7.2.1 Teams – a new set of relationships

Teams are set up between business and IT people to tackle projects and problems and represent their own particular set of relationship problems. In the preface of a book entitled: *Why Teams Don't Work*, by Harvey Robbins and Mike Finley[6] they say this about teams:

> (Teams) not only founder, they shudder and convulse. They fall victim to . . . confusions about objectives, indifferent leadership, and poor communication. No team is ever far from betrayal, from the outside and the inside, and this creates a tension few consider exquisite. Teams are hard work, mentally and emotionally.
>
> (Robbins and Finley, 1997)

7.3 Why there's no such thing as an internal customer

I used to think there were three types of customer: 'Big C', 'Middle C' and 'Little c' customers. 'Little c' customers were team mates and department associates. 'Middle C' customers were other functions within your organisation who you supplied with goods or services, and 'Big C' customers were those external customers who bought stuff from your organisation. I have seen the error of my ways: there is only one customer – the person or organisation who pays for goods or services. There is no such thing as an internal customer. If you do not believe that, just try shopping somewhere else when you are unhappy with the quality of service from your HR, Finance, Marketing, Engineering or whatever department. Alternatively consider that your business associates are largely unable to go elsewhere for their IT services if you prove to be inadequate.

A true customer–supplier relationship has a number of factors which are particular to it. But the most telling one in connection with the IT-business relationship is that both parties are able to fire each other: the customer can look elsewhere for their services, and the supplier can withdraw their services from the customer if he or she becomes uneconomical to service. Usually this is not possible in in-house business-IT relationships.

Besides which, to my mind, a real customer is a special thing and deserves all the care, nurturing and attention that you can give him or her. Your internal customers should be rightly termed 'partners,' 'associates,' 'team members,' or any other name, but 'customer' should be reserved for the real thing.

John Guaspari, named one of the 'new quality gurus' by Quality Digest has this to say about customers:

> Let's be clear about another definition. When I talk about customers, what I mean is customers, people who pay money for goods and/or services. What I'm not talking about here is the so-called 'internal customer.' For the record, the concept of the internal customer is a useful one insofar as it can help people to look beyond the ends of their noses and recognise that they are part of a larger work process. . . . Of course, the folks in the Systems department need to ensure that what they do serves the needs of their colleagues throughout the rest of the organisation, but wouldn't it be better still if all that Systems work were done – consciously and explicitly – as a means of maximising the level of value delivered to (real) customers? Wouldn't that challenge the folks in Systems more, and more deeply?[7]

(Guaspari, 2000)

I looked up the origin of the word 'customer,' fully expecting it to be related to the Latin word 'custodia,' a guard, a custodian. Therefore, a customer would be someone cared for, watched over. I was wrong. The word 'customer' comes from the Latin word 'consuetudo,' meaning custom or habit. This puts a different slant on your organisation's customers. They are people who are habituated to your company. Those whose habits include spending their money in your direction. Your knowledge of their habits must then surely be critical to satisfying their needs. But once your customers have established a habit of buying from you, you must become a custodian over their satisfaction.

Real customers are pivotal to the company's livelihood. The emphasis is moving from short-term, arms-length relationships with customers, to long-term, attentive rapport.

Almost everything that goes into a customer-centred culture should be guided by improving service to customers. Improving the fit between their requirements and your product. Improving your knowledge about them, and about yourselves. Profit will follow. James Collins and Jerry Porras studied enduring and visionary companies, and in their book: *Built to Last*[8] they report that: 'contrary to business school doctrine, "maximizing share-holder wealth" or "profit maximization" is not the driving force in visionary companies. They pursue a cluster of objectives, of which making money is only one, and not necessarily a primary one. These companies understand that the customer, and only the customer, is responsible for their income. Paradoxically, these companies make more money than their profit-driven counterparts.'

I was once called by a particularly difficult user who made his usual string of unreasonable demands. When I said that we couldn't do what he wanted, he retorted: 'may I point out to you that I am your customer?' to which I replied: 'no John, you are not. Partner, associate, colleague you are, but customer you are not.' Which so surprised him that we embarked on a discussion about why I believed I had no internal customers, and the conversation switched to our working together to meet both of our external customer's needs. I would like to report that this one exchange converted John into a friend of IT, but alas only on TV does such simple human interaction occur. John continued to badger IT, until the miracle happened. John came to work in my department. Now the difficult thing was to control John's vitriol as he dealt with sensitive users. Nobody ever said it was easy.

So we've established that you should reserve the word customer for 'external' customers only. This chapter is about managing relationships between your department and the business, but spare a thought for your position in an organisation that is, or becomes customer-focused.

7.3.1 What does a customer-focused in-house function look like?

What would IT have to do if they were to adopt an (external) customer-centred direction unequivocally?

The implications of having a customer-centric IT culture are significant. Be aware that I choose to use the word 'culture' rather than 'system,' for IT is more than technology, or implemented processes – IT is about the way the business operates.

One implication of electing to have a customer-centred IT culture involves the technical staff who put the technological support environment together. When did they last meet and deal with a customer? Or are they true back-room people? If they are, you will need to see that someone who does deal with customers guides their efforts. Your average technical person may be inclined to design and build inwardly focused IT solutions. It will take active vigilance to direct the underlying technologies outwards.

Paying attention to the needs of customers takes effort and directed activity. In a survey conducted by Koch and Godden[9] into how managers spend their time, they found that from a sample of 434 corporate managers, the average amount of time dealing with customers was less than 5%. This statistic may seem to be biased, especially as it is reported in their book: *Managing without Managers*, where they have a case to prove. However, the authors do make an observation that: 'customer obsession is incompatible with most forms of traditional management and control,' and I can't disagree with that. If you want your IT staff and managers to pay attention to customers, you will probably need to make it imperative for them to do so. Include customer focus in their measurement and reward package.

Probably the most important implication of having a customer-focused IT culture is to do with boundaries. Those often artificial barriers that you set up to keep distance between yourselves and your organisation's customers and suppliers. A customer-centric IT culture demands active dismantling of barriers. Why can't your customers check on the status of their order? Or your suppliers check on your production schedules? But of course there is a quid pro quo. You need to know about your customers and suppliers. What are their expectations, their requirements, how will they use your product?

Often the busiest people in the organisation are customer-focused. Or perhaps the customer-focused people are the busiest. This has implications for both the building of your IT culture, and for the sustainability of the culture. I have personal experience of a knowledge system, which on paper appeared to be the answer to a global organisation's knowledge sharing needs about customers. Trouble is, the people who used it most, who followed the threads and updated their conversations on a daily basis came to be known as the permanent committee attendees. 'Real' people, involved with the day to day running of the business, and who deal directly with customers, were too busy to be bothered with the system and the circular discussions. So when building an IT culture, you need to pay attention to those people who haven't the time to spend using the expensive IT system. How do you make any IT systems easy for them to use? How do you make their jobs easier? How can you structure your performance management system so that it rewards the *use* of customer knowledge systems?

This brings up the issue of organisation. Not of your company, but of the knowledge about the customer which is useful to the concern. The concept of self-organisation is important: this is when feedback creates automatic change within the systems. Both the customer knowledge that you use and the way in which you use it should be capable of changing, based on feedback from your customers and those people who deal with them. One of the major issues facing Information Technology managers today is the subject of legacy computer systems. Indeed the Y2K problem was in broad terms a legacy problem. When your systems become too large, deep rooted and cumbersome to allow your business to change quickly, you have an unwelcome inheritance. Don't let your customer knowledge suffer the legacy trap. If you wish to avoid it telling you about what your customers wanted three years ago, you need to pay attention to the concept of self-organisation.

An issue worth considering is that of front-line access. How many of the organisation's staff who deal with customers have access to your decision-making and knowledge-management systems? Or are they the preserve of management? Because we have seen how much managers deal with customers. Allowing 'front-line' workers access to these systems needs structure. They need to know what customers are saying about the organisation and service. They need to be able to check on a specific customer's requirements and history. The more your staff knows about their customers, the better they are able to create that intimate rapport with them.

Another matter to be considered when focusing your IT culture around the customer, is the question: 'who's the enemy?' Strangely, some companies, and many IT practitioners don't have an idea of who the company competes with for its customers. Who's the enemy? If we're going to focus on customers, who do we have to beat? Who took the last 10 sales from us? Who do our customers turn to when they move on? Why? Focusing on customers should not preclude the other side of the equation: who else is focusing on our customers? Your customer-centric IT culture and systems should, by definition, also look your competition in the eyes.

How do you know your customer targeted IT activities are working? It would probably be a good idea to ask your customers. And while you're asking them, let them help you compile your customer profiles. This may involve regular customer meetings, or surveys, or more adventurously, letting your customers gain access to your systems. But if you and your company are not getting regular feedback from your customers, and you are not changing as a result of this knowledge, you can fully expect your IT culture to slip into oblivion.

7.4 People as partners – a fundamental mindset shift

There was a writer named Michael Pollan, who excavated a pond in front of the studio window of his house set in the woodlands of Connecticut[10]. Very soon, the pond magically filled, and various forms of life came to stay. The quantity and diversity of life that took up residence amazed him, and he waxed enthusiastically lyrical in his articles for *The New York Times.* But as summer developed, the pond emptied, and all the new occupants packed their bags and left. In autumn the pond filled again and the cycle of life returned. Pollan tried to keep the pond full every summer, but nothing worked. Eventually someone explained that because his house was located on glacial till, his pond was in essence a 'window on a seasonal underground river,' which would dry out every summer and fill every winter. The term for this type of feature is a 'vernal pool,' and they are very important elements in the survival of frogs. Because the pool dries out every summer, fish cannot take up residence, which gives the frogs an ideal breading ground. Once Pollan had re-framed his view of his 'leaky pond' he saw it not as a failed project but as a highly successful and important addition to the local ecology. Pollan stopped trying to water-proof his pond, and was content. It's funny that frogs have come up twice in respect of re-examining our view on the world. But perhaps if you find something you don't understand or dislike, it's time to look at your perspective, and not at the object of your displeasure.

I have painted something of a bleak picture of relationships in business, and so they will remain until we undergo the mind-shift necessary if we are to see relationships as the foundation of all IT efforts:

First let's look at 'relationships' and reframe them. In organisations there are five levels of relationship:

- between individuals;
- within teams;
- to the organisation's purpose;
- with other organisations and with the community;
- with the environment.

When the environment is unstable, then the relationships which work within that environment must necessarily adapt. Businesses are complex and getting more so, and where complexity dominates, relationships become the most important element of business.

> In a non-linear, dynamic world, everything exists only in relation to everything else, and the interactions among agents in the system lead to complex, unpredictable outcomes. In this world, interactions, or relationships, . . . are the organising principle[11].

Relationships are the answer. The rest is mechanics. Manage your relationships and you are already ahead. Ignore your relationships, and ignore your future.

7.5 The new IT relationship

It's easy to proclaim a string of 'should-do's.' But putting relationships into action is a lot harder to do than that. But the most important part of relationships is recognising them as being important, and doing something positive about that. I offer some tools to manage relationships between IT departments and the business, but because of the complexity and fluidity of the business environment, it really must be left to you to take your own route.

7.5.1 Map them, track them, manage them – be purposeful

There are various ways of mapping relationships. Probably the most obvious is the organisation chart. Organisation charts map authority and responsibility. Or should do. Sometimes organisation charts map ineffectuality, but perhaps that's a little too cynical. It's what you do with an organisation chart that makes the difference. Look for gaps in IT's influence. Why do they exist? Look for pressure points. Look for influences.

A sample organisational mapping may look like the simple one represented in Figure 7.4. This is obviously simplified, but it works as a checklist and as a discussion agenda for the IT management team in their relationship planning.

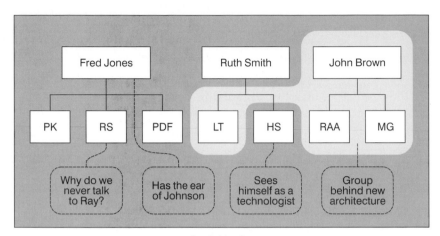

Figure 7.4 Mapping organisational relationships

Another form of relationship mapping works well when considered in the context of a particular issue or problem. For instance say you have to convince the marketing department to move off their existing application dependence, towards an architecturally preferred solution, you might map the relationships as lines with different values as in Figure 7.5.

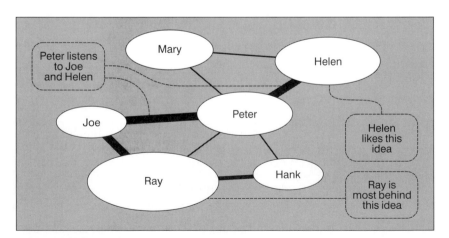

Figure 7.5 Mapping strength of relationships

In this diagram, it is important to get Peter behind the idea. But he is undecided. However, it would be constructive to talk to Helen and Ray, because even though Ray doesn't have a strong relationship with Peter, he can use his relationship with Joe, and Joe's with Peter, to swing things.

There are many other forms of mapping of relationships that you can use. I have used circles to represent key people and filled the circles appropriate to the 'percentage' of IT friendliness that I believed these people had. Then it was simply a case of using the IT friendly people to work on the less friendly.

There is another technique that I have used, which I borrowed and adapted from one of those 'sell your way to fabulous fortunes!' books many years ago. Basically you track your key customers (or in our case stakeholders or associates, but not customers) on the following table:

Table 7.1: Tracking key IT stakeholders

Stakeholder	Description	IT needs	Issues/ concerns	Status	Next actions	Comments

Feel free to add or subtract column headings, as long as you find it useful. I often put in 'expectations' of IT as a column. However, there is only one proviso for this type of table: you must use it. Especially the actions part. You might also wish to track the visits you or your people make to stakeholders. I personally find that a little too mechanistic, but you might benefit from it.

7.5.2 Power in the organisation – treading the artful path through politics

I read a definition of organisational politics once which said something like, 'politics is the art of making people owe you one'. Perhaps. Certainly favours represent an element of politics, but so does avoidance of responsibility and conflict, as does the gathering of organisational power to you. Politics in organisations is real. It appears that whenever more than two people work together, then you have politics. I can't offer extensive advice on politics, mostly because I appear to be very bad at playing the office political game. I can offer an insight into personal power based on the original definitions of power by French, Etzioni and McClelland in 1959[12], that I find useful when I try to work out: 'what's going on here?'

I have refined my definitions of organisational power over the years, and I have developed a view of seven types of power I have found useful. Power is neither good nor bad in and of itself. It is the use of power that gives it its value (positive or negative). My definition of power involves getting others to do things for you. I propose seven types of power, but you can add or subtract as you wish. As long as your categories of power help you understand the human dynamics and allow you to function better in your organisational relationships.

Positional power: this is the type of power that people enjoy because of their position. The obvious people with positional power are of course managers, but there are less obvious positions that bestow power on people. Secretaries are an example, as are those intensely annoying civil servants who have the power to use their clerical position to keep you waiting for ever.

Invested power: this is different from positional power in that we invest power in the individual concerned because of our perspective in relation to that person. Culture plays an important role here. We might regard any CEO as way above our stratum and invest in them some kind of omniscience, whether it is true or not. Many people find themselves intimidated by medical people, and invest in them powers beyond those they really have. Invested power is related to our conditioning.

Relational power: it's who you know that counts. Secretaries normally have great relational powers and they often use them. Friends or relatives have relational power.

Coercive power: if someone can get you fired or into trouble because of their power, and they choose to let you know about this power they hold, they are using coercive power. This form of power is both organisationally and privately bestowed. Often the organisation places the right to hire and fire in the hands of someone. How they use that power is the issue. Alternatively, if I know you said nasty things about the boss's wife, I could choose to use that power coercively.

Expert Power: what people know gives people power. The technologist who can get your PC on the road again has power. Salespeople dread the hidden expert, who advises buyers but never appears himself. They call these experts 'gatekeepers.' The Internet is making more and more experts, and this rise in expert power is driving significant unseen and unplanned for organisational shifts and trends.

Respect power: this is a form of invested power, but it derives from a person truly deserving esteem and admiration. Leaders have this power, and sometimes even though people may not understand the leader's chosen direction, they will follow because they respect that leader.

Results power: it seems that people who get results are relatively untouchable. No one may like the person, or they may not follow all the rules, yet they enjoy a privileged position in the organisation.

Power is neither positive nor negative, but it is real. It is how people decide to use it (or whether they choose to use it at all), that gives the power its value. Indeed if someone chooses not to use their coercive power, if they never take advantage of the secrets they know, their relational and respect power is likely to grow.

A simple example on analysing power may clarify things a little. I was once making good progress with my relationship with a senior manager of a business unit. Suddenly it seemed to be going sour. When I investigated further, I found the manager was close to one of his people who regarded herself as an IT expert. She saw her expert power waning as a result of the talks I was having with her manager, and was maligning the IT function at every possible opportunity. Some of the mud was beginning to stick. I offered her a job in IT, which she refused, but we mutually agreed that she was to get much closer to IT and to get involved in our IT trend work and architectural analyses. Once she felt her 'expert' status was recognised by the IT department, she backed off and in fact became one of our chief promoters. All this through recognising expert power which was being threatened.

Implementation ideas

1 Table 7.1 details a number of customer-supplier relationship problems and what the IT interpretation of those problems is. Go through the table and ask the questions of your department. The issues you identify will position you to plan some relationship fixing activities.

2 Conduct a stakeholder analysis. Identify stakeholders in IT, describe them, discover their motives and expectations.

3 Draw some relationship maps. Relate a map to a specific relationship problem that you have and use it to identify actions that you can follow to resolve the issue.

4 Become an 'external customer' focused IT function by following the suggestions earlier in the chapter.

5 Find out how much knowledge your organisation has about its customers, and use the technology at your fingertips to build and use that knowledge.

References

1. Cole-Gomolski, B. and Hoffman, T. (1998) Bridge Over Troubled Waters. *Computerworld*, March 23
2. Arnold, J., Cooper, C.L. and Robertson, I.T. (1998) *Work Psychology – Understanding Human Behaviour in the Workplace*. Financial Times – Pitman, London
3. Lewis, J.D. (1995) *The Connected Corporation: How Leading Companies Win Through Customer-Supplier Alliances*. Free Press Publishers, NY
4. Fisher, R. and Ury, W. (1981) *Getting to Yes*. Random House
5. Berne, E. (1964) *Games People Play: The Psychology of Human Relationships*. Penguin Books, London
6. Robbins, H. and Finley, M. (1997) *Why Teams Don't Work*. Orion Publishing, London
7. Guaspari, J. (2000) *The Value Effect*. Berrett-Koehler Publishers, San Francisco, CA
8. Collins, J.C. and Porras, J.I. (1994) *Built to Last – Successful Habits of Visionary Companies*. HarperBusiness NY
9. Koch, R. and Godden, I. (1996) *Managing Without Management*. Nicholas Brealey Publishing
10. Lewin, R. and Regine, B. (1999) *The Soul at Work – Unleashing the Power of Complexity Science for Business Success*. Orion Business Publishers
11. Lewin, R. and Regine, B. (1999) *The Soul at Work – Unleashing the Power of Complexity Science for Business Success*. Orion Business Publishers
12. Young, R. and Mould, K. (1994) *Managing Information Systems Professionals*. Butterworths

8 Building on quicksand? – the IT cornerstone – architecture

When I wrote the title to this chapter, I wondered if a chapter on architecture was even necessary. Surely every IT department has an enterprise architecture? But only today, as I worked in a large finance company helping them implement a Decision Support project, I had my assumption dashed. Not only do they not have an enterprise architecture, but they also seem to miss the point of having one. They can't see that their current IT projects which are worth some $20 million will be sub-optimised at best, and discarded as unworkable at worst. Finally, they do not even calculate the ongoing costs of having their staff leave one system in order to get to another system and live much of their working lives 'between systems.' They have some four systems, each with their own data-mart and each with their own GUI, and each with their own reporting tools. Yes the systems talk to each other through some fervent interface design, which had they had an architecture, would be largely unnecessary. Not having an architecture is a little like presenting your business with one of those 'connect the dots' puzzles. However, in this case each dot costs a fortune and more dots are going to be added. (Some of these expensive dots won't actually fit the bigger picture.) Now you expect either your technical staff, or worse the business users, to draw the lines between these dots. It is just not acceptable business practice anymore.

Why would an IT function not have an architecture by now?

- perhaps the CIO is too focused on the operation of the function and has never had the time to put one together. Without an architecture, the infrastructure must have grown in a relatively casual way;

- perhaps someone had or has an architecture in his or her head. But of course it is useless as a communication tool unless that someone does the communication. And if that person leaves, then clearly value is lost;

- perhaps the IT function is *too* focused on technology, which seems paradoxical because if your focus is on technology, then surely you would focus on how it all fits together? But it seems to be more of a issue of technical scale – what interests the technical mind may be the technology at a lower level than the model of how it fits together (now and in the future);

- perhaps there's analysis paralysis – certainly if you take a zero-based approach to architecture, then you have an enormous amount of analysis to do before you can propose an informed, robust and integrated architectural solution. But there are many architectural solutions on the market (with attendant implementers) and there are equally many methodologies available if you want a home-grown solution;

- perhaps the function has an architecture but it is shelf-ware – reports and paperwork that has ceased to be consulted. Here we have an application problem. At a Gartner Group Convention in 2000, it was estimated that 50% of architectural projects fail. Failure to apply an architecture is still failure;

- perhaps there's an arrogance problem – 'We don't need an architecture, we know what we are doing.

Completing an architecture is a step-by-step progression, that starts with a commitment to spend the time. Then you need to set yourself an architectural goal (I'll discuss the reasons for having an architecture later). I think Forrest Gump said, 'If you're going to do something, try to have a reason for doing it.' Then you need to locate an architect, and you're rolling.

Let me say now, and clearly, I am not an IT architect, nor do I even understand the various architectures particularly well. Which means that I only feel qualified in discussing the management effects and the outcomes that occur as a result of having an architecture. There are many technical references to architectures if you want to pursue the IT architecture route further. I confess I have never endured beyond Chapter 1 of these texts, that and looking at the pictures. What I can say with some force, is that any CIO of a moderate or sizeable IT function who does not have a resident architect and an enterprise architecture should be dismissed. Forceful enough? I come back to my finance company. Their CIO is already squandering millions in wasted time and built-in inefficiencies based on poor performance of IT investments and on time wasted by both IT and general staff in connecting the dots. And he is setting his company up to 'micturate money against the mural': (there is a translation of this phrase but it's impolite). Basically his company will be wasting a significant amount of its future IT expenditure – and the bad news is, they won't even know it because technical talk can bamboozle their executives.

8.1 What is an architecture? – a non-technical position

I will say this again – I am not a technical person, so this will not be a technical discussion. Rather I will talk from a management perspective.

There are many things that can be called an architecture. It often depends on the level of detail and complexity that you are examining. Hardware has an architecture, as do operating systems, transfer protocols and standards, as well as applications vendors. There are of course also data and information architectures as well. Much of the level that I picture is at an IT function level and at a business level – these are commonly called the IT architecture and the Enterprise architecture.

In summary, you have three primary architectural levels:

● foundation level architectures, which define how the units are structured. These units are combined to form the IT infrastructure. There are levels within this level from microscopic architectures to application software architectures;

● business level architectures also have levels depending on chosen organisational and process boundaries. Thus you may have an architecture for the supply chain process, the customer service process, etc., which if you are wise all fit into the enterprise architecture – the overarching architecture that covers all that the company does in IT. You could go beyond IT in your architectural deliberations (I know a number of companies with architectures around which they organise their people, how they sell, and so on), but I'll stay with IT for the moment – it's complicated enough thank you;

● information architectures include how the data and processes are structured in order to carry out the work of the business.

I looked up the term architecture in the dictionary, and apart from the expected building-related definitions they had this to say about architecture: 'the conceptual structure and logical organisation of a computer or computer-based system[1].' That works for me. The emphasis for me would be on the words: 'conceptual', 'logical', 'structure' and 'organisation'. I would also include in my definition an addendum as follows: '. . . that allows communication of complex ideas in a simple format'. Now the techies need their complexity, and I don't deny that, but an architecture is not useful if it cannot be communicated easily to both technical and non-technical minds. An architecture becomes shelf-ware if the communication element is missing.

Pictorially your average enterprise architecture is depicted as follows:

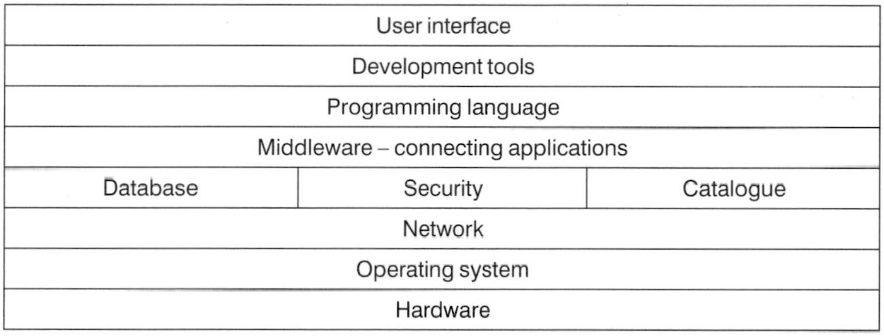

User interface		
Development tools		
Programming language		
Middleware – connecting applications		
Database	Security	Catalogue
Network		
Operating system		
Hardware		

Figure 8.1 Typical IT enterprise architecture

It's a bit like the song that goes: 'The knee-bone's connected to the thigh-bone, the thigh-bone's connected to the hip-bone, the hip-bone's connected to the network . . .' and so on. Perhaps there's room for someone to do an 'architectural' song along the same lines. OK perhaps not.

The issue is as much the spaces between the boxes as the boxes themselves. Essentially your architecture is a sophisticated shopping-list. It defines what will fit into your infrastructure and what will not. The trick in designing an architecture is to close as few doors as possible. And here is an obvious caveat: if you use a hardware or software vendor to design your architecture, you can be fairly sure that they will specify their product, and as sure that they will close a number of doors on their opposition – it makes good business sense to most of them. So use an independent architect.

The other trick is for your architecture to be seen as a friend, pointing the way and allowing as much as possible, rather than as 'the enemy' guarding the portals of IT, forbidding entry and ease of movement. This friendly view should also be presented to techies as well as to business people.

Communication of the architecture is important. I often use the term blueprint rather than architecture. I have used the concept of building blocks, and sometimes even bring building blocks into meetings to illustrate the point. I also try not to use technical terms with business people. The more you communicate your architecture and its friendliness and benefits, the more people will consult it and you when making IT decisions. You will actually need two architectures – one for the technologists and one for the business, and both are equally important.

8.2 Why architect?

There is a wonderful cartoon strip in which a little boy decides he is going to start 'verbing.' He explains this is the act of turning nouns into verbs, for example access, impact, parent all used to be nouns. Now you 'access' an application, and this application 'impacts' the sales-force. And 'parenting' may be what you do when you aren't 'accessing' and 'impacting'. So allow me to verb a bit: why architect (v) indeed? And of course the action of putting an architecture together is called architecting. My spell-check hates this!

Back to the subject. You need an architecture because the forces of technology will pull your IT infrastructure apart if you don't model, plan and execute a logical connection of all these technologies. Remember Moore's Law, Gilder's Law, and Metcalfe's Law? Specifically technology pulls at the stability of your infrastructure in the following ways:

- old technology is not forward compatible. Which means that when you design new technology, how can you design interfaces to something that hasn't yet been conceived? And more and more new technology is hitting the streets, so how do you cater for it all?

- solution technologies (those that offer a complete solution have their own architectures, as well as completely stand-alone functionality – data-warehouses, reporting tools, development languages and the like). Vendors have to do this to provide a total solution, but without an architecture how will you know which report writer or development tools you will use out of the many you have installed?

- business-to-business connections are making standards and common platforms more difficult to achieve;

- users have more power and are developing their own IT solutions. The first you hear of it is when you get the e-mail which asks you to connect their dinosaur software to your space-age infrastructure (or vice versa);

- associated with user power is unit autonomy, and each business unit develops their own solutions. The problem is customers of your company in one city expect the same service in other cities or countries.

How will you achieve that if you have different systems? But do all systems need to be the same, or can you have a set of systems with total autonomy?

8.3 Objectives of architecting

There's very little point in building an architecture if you don't know why you're doing it. Your architecture will fail. Because architecture is more than a model on a piece of paper – it is a discussion instrument that grows and changes with changing circumstances. It generates arguments and disagreements as well as agreement. It requires divergent thinkers to commit to effort and technologies that they may not wholly support. So it has to be robust. And if there is no strong *raison d'être* for your architecture, it will crumble at the first opposition. So have a *real* business reason or reasons for generating an architecture. Reasons which will carry the day when arguments cause people to lose the way – that's when you will need to come back to the underlying reason.

Here are some general reasons why CIOs build architectures:

- maximize interoperability: probably the prime reason to have an architecture is to ensure, as far as possible, that applications can transfer data and transactions between themselves in real-time mode. So that one application can 'see' the others in the company;

- not falling between the cracks: my IT architect associate used to talk about vertical and horizontal integration. Vertical integration involved using 'best-of class' software, and using your technologists to link different interfaces. Horizontal integration is where you choose a suite of application solutions that already have interfaces, and communicate easily with each other. What is important is that in vertical architectures staff and users spend more time 'between' applications setting up interfaces and manipulating data from one application format to another. In horizontal architectures staff spend more time inside the applications using them more deeply, because the interface problem is sorted out by the vendor. (The average ratio of network technicians per workstation was 1:100. Because of horizontal integration I only needed 1:500 network technicians per workstation.) However, horizontal architectures have a drawback in that the individual products within the system are seldom the best-of-class solutions that are available as stand-alone products;

- maximize transportability: applications need to be able to 'float' on their supporting operating systems and hardware, because these will change at times when you wish your application to remain constant;

- reduce redundancy: you would like as far as possible not to own several applications that perform different core work, but that duplicate the same thing when it comes to reports, data storage, etc. Or if they all do have similar supporting tools, you need to know which one will be best to use;

- facilitate buying decisions: architectures allow you to narrow the field of view when looking for new technology. Some applications serve the purpose of no more than a sophisticated IT shopping list. Which, if that's the reason for its existence, is fine;

- purchasing economies: a defined architectural choice, that everyone in the company adheres to, can allow you to approach vendors from a position of strength. If everyone in the company has agreed to use XYZ product, then your user population for that product is greater and volume discounts and support agreements are attainable;

- knowledge focus: this was one of the primary reasons that I used my architecture when I was a CIO. It helped focus the minds of my technical people. We had focused training. There was no wandering off to 'interesting' but useless seminars and product launches. Finally we could allow our technical people to get deep, quality knowledge about specific tools, which improved development quality and time;

- communication: this is the second main reason I used an architecture. Two architectures actually – one for the technical people and one for the users. Both were the same but used different language. When general business people accepted the architecture, things went a lot smoother;

- crowd-control: there are two main 'crowds' in your organisation – technologists who want to be up there with the latest IT developments, and business people who want an instant solution to their IT related problem. I once had a deputation of engineers walk into my office wanting to know why we weren't going forward with their spreadsheet software, upon which they had developed many engineering solutions. After showing them our architecture and how everything fitted and communicated following the new route, they calmed down and even became enthusiastic, and we could get on with problem-solving on how to convert their engineering applications to the new technology. Your architectural model should show people how things fit together and also how they fit with the future;

- span of influence: knowing what is 'out there' is always useful, especially if it is in your company. Being able to influence what you know can be facilitated with a well crafted architecture;

- stability within chaotic technological growth: making sense of the technical advances that seem to be bombarding us and our stable infrastructures is a primary use of an architectural model;

- time – keep up with business cycles: there is another important reason to have a current working architecture – reducing time to deliver IT solutions. Business cycles are significantly shorter than IT development cycles. You should do anything you can to speed up IT decisions and to get on with delivering IT solutions.

8.4 Managing IT architecture processes

I can't pretend to help you put together a technical architecture, but I can tell you how to manage the process.

8.4.1 The role of the architect

Architecture is a full-time job. It is one of the few things that should never be outsourced. The architect needs to work not only in IT but in the business as well. They have the following major role elements:

- scan the technology on a continuous basis and keep current with developments and future technologies. Identify potentially useful technologies. Take a position on all technologies;

- design an IT architecture at all levels;

- develop architectural models for communicating the architecture to both technologists and lay people;

- keep the business informed on important technological developments and trends – targeting particular audiences for particular messages;

- communicate architectural models, designs, concepts, ideas and standards;

- prepare position papers and thirty second messages – see later sections in this chapter;

- answer user and technological queries on technologies on an ongoing basis.

As you can see, this is not a case of prepare an architecture and revisit it once a year. The architect needs to be current, and accessible to both IT and business people. He or she must be able to communicate well. An architect who is so introspective and introverted as to be unapproachable is useless to you. As is an architect who buries herself so deep in research that he or she delivers nothing. They must produce models, position papers, presentations and designs on an ongoing basis.

8.4.2 Manage the process, insist on deliverables, focus on outcomes

Managing architects can be difficult. You may find yourself sucked into the deep technology or skating across the top of it, depending on your personal approach to technology. Also, there is a tendency to be so busy keeping up with trends and developments, that architects deliver very little. (I have come across the, 'I can't deliver anything right now because there is a new release of (XYZ) that will change everything. We need to wait 3 months,' syndrome quite often.) The trick is to manage the process, as in: 'show me what you are busy with right now, or this week.' You need to insist on deliverables – understandable ones at that. Position papers give you a steady flow of deliverables to monitor. Finally focus on the results of having an architect. If nothing changes, dismiss the architect. Their job is to effect changes in mindsets in the IT department and in the organisation as a whole. Make them responsible for proving their effectiveness.

8.4.3 The bottom line – architecture is nothing if you don't deliver

The final criterion of success of an architecture must be an evaluation of your architectural goals against your actual deliverables. It is pointless having goals if you don't have measures for those goals. Again if you have the measures, then you must work out how to monitor the measures. Finally, if monitoring the measures isn't converted into some kind of outcome, you will have wasted your time and money on architecture. Architecting is not an academic activity. It has real business goals, and operates in a real business environment. And if it doesn't produce real deliverables, then don't bother.

8.5 Communicating your architecture

I have said that an architecture is a communication tool. As such, it must fulfil some communication criteria. Show me a technical architecture and I'll show you a spaghetti junction. Real business people cannot be expected to understand architecture. But they do understand something a lot more familiar, which many of them grew up with: plastic building blocks. Use simple, common concepts to explain the technology. If you can't do it, get a communications expert in who can.

8.5.1 Simple language – two architectural views

If your architecture is to be more than a technical model (which it should be), then you will need to develop at least two views of your architecture, one for the technical people and one for the general business person. They should be views of the same thing, so that when the general user wants to get more technical, you can switch.

Think of it in building architectural terms – when an architect wants to present his building design in toto to the sponsors and non-technical people, he builds a miniature of the building and then presents that. The next level is architectural plans and drawings and the final level, the bill of materials if you like, is for the quantity surveyor – detailing materials to be used. So your IT architecture could follow similar lines. Even go as far, if you want as getting building blocks and labelling them.

8.5.2 The 30 second message

I used to walk into our architect's office and say to him: 'your 30 second message on transponders please' (or whatever). He would sit for 10 seconds, then say something like: 'hasn't crossed the chasm. Good speculative prospect, especially in our warehouses. But if it's to be mainstream, wait 18 months.' Now this sounds like code, and indeed it is, but given the pressures on my time, and his, it worked very well. Let me translate. I knew that his 30 second messages were supported by deep research. That's what I paid him for. I also knew that I could trust his thinking. The translation goes like this: I told him that

I or someone in the business was thinking about using transponders somewhere – very often I would tell him where, if I knew (but my message also fitted into 30 seconds). The 30 second message depends on having a common language that takes a lot more than 30 seconds to develop. We would sit for hours discussing concepts and ideas until we had a shared meaning. In this particular 30 second message, when my colleague said, 'hasn't crossed the chasm', he was referring to a book by Geoffrey Moore entitled *Crossing the chasm*[2]. He was telling me that transponder technology was relatively immature in that it was a hot new technology that cannot be easily translated into business benefits. The technologists love it, but its practical application in the business world is limited. Also standards are a problem – there are no accepted standards at the moment that we can rely on into the future. Finally the product itself may eventually fail, not because it doesn't work, but because alternative solutions may yet win the acceptance of business in general. All that in four words. But provided we had both read the book, understood its message and discussed its meaning and application in our organisation, four words was all that was necessary. I won't translate the rest of his 30 second message because, again he was referring to models, ideas and shared concepts that would take quite some time to explain.

Thirty second messages are also possible between IT and the business, but as you can see, your relationship, communication, and shared understanding of various models and concepts must be quite advanced. An alternative to 30 second messages is what I called position papers.

8.5.3 Position papers

I used to be approached by colleagues who would say something like: 'I've just come across a printer that is really cheap and seems to have really amazing functionality – can you check it out for me? Because I want to buy 10 for my department. Let's face it, the standard printer you people insist we use is so expensive that I would only be able to afford six, where here I can have 10.' This wouldn't necessarily be a difficult situation, if you hadn't had someone yesterday extolling the virtues of another printer, and yet someone else asking why we can't go the paperless-office route. There is too much technology out there with too many entrances into your business. So most CIOs end up being driven into the role of martinet – a strict disciplinarian who can't afford to allow themselves to be questioned.

There is another way, but it requires some work to set up. Your architect's role, apart from developing architectures and staying concurrent with technology so that he or she can deliver 30 second messages, is to prepare position papers on architectural decisions and on technologies. You need to develop a template for your organisation that encompasses common models and ideas in your organisation. I must stress that you use what works for you and your company in the political, cultural and strategic context. Figure 8.2 is a sample position paper.

We found it useful to describe the big picture – what was happening in this particular technology area in the world. Then we also found it *very* useful to define how we measure performance of the technology. Typically when a user read this, the light dawned that we weren't merely considering purchase price and functionality as sole criteria of performance.

We then also had our organisation's position on the technology – for instance we would say something like 'skipping (XYZ) release of this software'. Our rationale would be 'the release after (XYZ) includes laptop functionality that will allow our sales-force to link directly to the database'. Obviously we would go into detail if needed. The technology would always be plotted on a technology adoption curve, as well as using the future/strategic matrix. This helped use sensitise business people to strategic factors as well as technology life cycles.

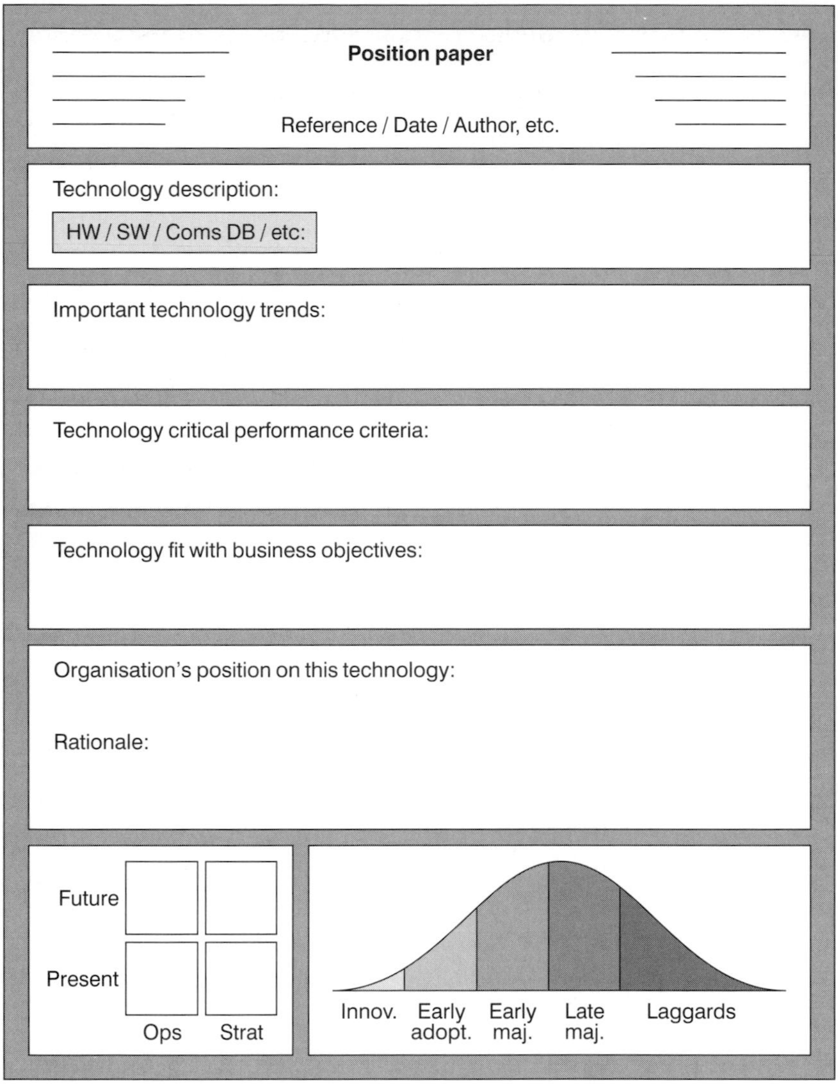

Figure 8.2 Sample position paper

Don't get too complicated (don't let your architect develop the position paper template, rather use key users to identify what they want answered when asking about a technology).

8.5.4 Creative communication – maps, mice and murals

Use wall posters, make maps, to be interesting about your architecture. I once used a cartoonist, a chap who drew these incredibly 'crowded' posters with funny little people getting up to strange things, to draw an organisation's architecture. This takes some effort, because you still have to be relatively true to the technological solution. Our final poster was presented as a building site, with little men and women on scaffolding, ladders and cranes, putting the architecture together (and in one instance demolishing an old bit of architecture). The poster was accepted so well it ended up in most user's offices. There's nothing better that you could ask for than to have your IT architecture on the wall of most of your users.

I have also used mouse-pads to get messages across. In this case it was critical keystrokes in a particular system that we transferred onto a mouse-pad, with the number of our call-centre. This was for in-house users. There's no reason why you should not adopt a professional marketing approach within your organisation.

I have also had a number of big monitors installed in the reception of an IT department. On these screens, the department communicates their statistics, organisational changes, architectural message, and anything else worth saying. There is a danger here. Be current. There is nothing worse than a message that has been loaded and forgotten. Messages are so old that users can see cobwebs growing in the corners. The only message you give then is that IT is asleep.

What is the GUI of your architecture? The graphical user interface of an architecture is essentially the way users see your architecture. If they see it as a series of endless technical reports, you have failed in your mission to communicate. If it is in fact a GUI, perhaps linked HTML pages on your intranet web site allowing drill-down through the architectural models then you are well on the way to effective communication. (You don't have an intranet web-site? Well it's not too late now.)

Other communication ideas could include screen-savers, or how about automatically uploaded screen-savers sending messages to any networked computer?

Intranet web sites, downloadable presentations and videos, or any other method of communication are worth investigating. Be radical, or if you can't be radical, call in the advertising experts and pay them to be radical for you.

8.5.5 IT architects – user-friendly techies?

When you communicate, make sure that your message is simple and understandable. One problem here is that your technologists and architects find it difficult to be simple and understandable. It's the nature of the beast. So you may need a translator, who can take complex messages and simplify them. The technologists need to be consulted on the final message and while they will invariably say that the message is oversimplified – as long as the message is understandable by the layman and isn't misleading or patently incorrect, then you are on the right track.

However of all the technical people in IT, your architect does need to have good communication skills. They need to talk to a lot of people within the business, and they need to be convincing. They need to give presentations, have one-on-one meetings, and simplify difficult concepts. If your architect can't do this, you'll lose credibility with your users.

Implementation ideas

1 If you don't have an architect, now's the time to get one. Use the role description in this chapter to define a job, advertise and recruit. There may be a closet architect sitting inside your

organisation already. The caution must be around delivery. Manage outputs or your architect could end up with true propeller-head status.

2 Decide which models you need to put into the position paper and into the 30 second message. They may be 'Boston Boxes' or graphs or any manner of model that makes sense to you in explaining why you have or have not chosen a technology.

3 Assemble a few knowledgeable users and construct a position paper.

References

1. *The Concise Oxford Dictionary* (Ninth Edition) (1997) Oxford University Press, Oxford
2. Moore, G. (1991) *Crossing the Chasm; Marketing and Selling Technology Products to Mainstream Customers*. Capstone Publishing Limited, Oxford

9 The 'Canute' effect – bringing new technologies in

I have had a number of CIOs bemoan the fact that they are unable to control their business partners from bringing new technologies to them as the latest silver bullet solution for their specific problem. No amount of explaining seems to get through to their users that the technology is either not stable enough to be relied on, or the technology does not fit the chosen architecture, or cheap solutions are often poorly supported or bug-ridden, or the company that supports the technology is on its way out, or any number of reasons for the technology being inappropriate. Or more ominously, someone in the business introduces a new technology without telling you. The first you hear of it is when they try to connect to the network, or can't get their regular programmes to run, or can't get support from the supplier. I call these 'undercover' technologies.

'It's like trying to hold back the tide', the CIOs say, referring to the story of King Canute who tried to do just that.

Apparently King Canute believed himself to be so powerful that he was able to stop the tide from coming in. Being a man to put his money where his mouth was, he had his throne positioned at low tide, and then set about stopping the tide from advancing. Evidently Canute hadn't had a good education because he would have known that tides have very little to do with water, and everything to do with the spinning of the earth and the gravitational pull of the moon. Alas, Canute was not only vain, he was proud as well, and when it appeared that the tide would advance irrespective of Canute's wishes, he stubbornly refused to move. And so it was that Canute was drowned by the thing that he was trying to control.

Your average high school scholar could have told Canute the facts of life, or in his case death. But far more intelligent people seem to have great difficulty trying to stop the influx of new technologies coming into their organisations. Perhaps it is because like Canute they have not realised the factors driving the increasing flood of technological novelties into their organisations.

There was actually a King Canute. He was the King of England, Denmark and Norway from 1016 to 1035. He died at Shaftesbury in England. He was a brutal king at first but later changed to reigning with wisdom and temperance. He was 39 when he died, so he must have been a mere 20 years old when he ascended to the throne, having invaded and conquered England with his father when he was only 17. No hanging around the shopping malls for Canute. He was the subject of many fables and legends, of which the one above endures. (Given that Shaftesbury where he died, is more than 40 kilometers from the nearest bit of beach, it is patently a myth.)

I have researched the issue of bringing new technologies into organisations extensively, and this chapter represents my own findings.

Two factors underpin the influx of new technologies into organisations: firstly, people are frantically trying to find a solution to a problem, and the regular mainstream way is not the solution. Very often it has very little to do with you or your department's abilities, and is more to do with your company's policies and budget. Secondly it sounds a little far-fetched but non-conformist technology influx is linked to the quality of relationships in organisations. The quality of relationships themselves is also linked to geographical spread, as well as the structure of the organisation.

Most problems that CIOs have with integration of new technologies are with people and behaviours external to the IS department. 'Undercover' technologies and user 'experts' provide the most management headaches. Lack of understanding of, or support for, IT initiatives also troubled many managers I interviewed. One CIO reported a 40 million dollar project that had no user sponsor. Apparently the original sponsor had left the organisation as the political risks associated with being linked to the project were too great. Most user managers felt that the project was necessary and 'probably a good thing' but none would specifically come out in support of it. Therefore the IS department was pressing ahead without specific user executive support. The project failed in the end. Another CIO reported having a number of PhD users, who had no problem in initiating a project, and when they got into trouble (which they always did), calling on IS to rescue them. He estimated that half a million dollars had been wasted in the previous year in this way.

Internal IS team composition and roles were significant management problems as well. One manager, who had been a CIO, but had recently become an external consultant, was vitriolic in his condemnation of the change resistance and protectionism that he found within the IS departments. He now targets the users expressly because 'IS personnel protect their existing skills and are therefore closed to new technology.'

I prefer to see non-conforming technology influx as a call for help, and as a relationship building exercise. The problem is most of us don't have the time we need to spend educating the miscreant and for building a relationship with them.

Even if you can keep track of these new technologies the process of integrating mainstream technologies and undercover technologies seems to be a complex and never ending task.

9.1 Dealing with undercover technologies

The problem is not an easy or quick one to solve. It depends on the building of an environment of trust in which it wouldn't enter into people's thinking not to consult IT in the matter of new technologies. There are three linked actions you should take:

9.1.1 Relationship

Firstly I come back to my standard refrain – if trust exists between IT and the users of IT, then the problem of undercover technologies will be significantly reduced.

9.1.2 Position papers

I discuss position papers at some length in the chapter on architecture (Chapter 8). Position papers go a long way towards helping users come to terms with existing technologies and with being open when wanting to introduce an undercover technology.

9.1.3 Open architecture

Another way of dealing with undercover technologies is to ensure that your architecture can accommodate as much variety as possible. That way you will be less reproachful when you do discover such technologies and so will support a trusting relationship with your users.

9.2 A new technologies integration process

A few years ago I developed a model that allowed me to discuss technology introduction and focus on the process of introducing the technology.

9.2.1 Environment

The processes described in the model function within an environment which dictates which process operates, what inputs are required, and how the outputs should be treated.

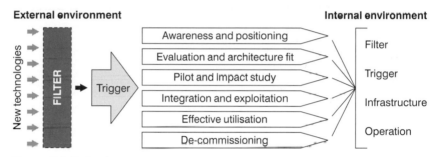

Figure 9.1 Technology integration environment

Filters

An efficient organisation should be able to filter a steady stream of new technologies, so that it does not extend its resources beyond acceptable limits. Filters such as the company strategy, the IT strategy, the IT architecture, and the principles by which a company operates, should all serve to exclude many technologies from even being examined. And that's the important bit – excluding unsuitable technologies from taking up too much time.

Alignment of all employees to these mechanisms would imply that a company looks only at those new technologies which contribute to the strategy, fit the architecture, and adhere to the principles and values of the company. Conversely, a company which is expending too much energy evaluating or piloting new technologies should look to the efficacy of its filters.

Triggers

Once a new technology has been filtered, a process is triggered.

A number of circumstances may trigger a process. The obvious triggers would derive from the business environment. These triggers are adequately described by Porter's Five Forces model. Other obvious triggers are IT trends, and the company's reaction to that trend. New technology vendors often act as triggers. Legal requirements may trigger new technology integration processes.

These triggers all suggest that an efficient filter is operating. However, where a company does not have an efficient filter, or has no filter at all, other triggers can be envisaged:

- unforeseen: for various reasons the new technology may not have been anticipated;

- bad planning: the planning process did not anticipate the triggering of a process to integrate a new technology;

- undercover: where a company's filters and staff alignment are dysfunctional a new technology may be discovered to have been introduced without strategic or architectural approval or awareness;

- positional: an individual may be able to operate outside the filter because of his/her position. This may be good or bad, depending on the person's alignment to the greater company goals and principles.

9.2.2 Processes

The model assumes that six processes operate in the integration of new technologies:

Process	Objectives	Possible outcomes
Awareness and positioning (A&P)	To become aware of a technology which fits the company strategies, and to take a position on how and when the technology will be used.	High level evaluation of filtered technologies. Information and position papers. Information paper. Trigger E&F process.
Product evaluation and architectural fit (E&F)	To understand the technical functionality, and to assess how the technology will fit with the current infrastructure to narrow the product decision range.	Short list chosen and tested. Evaluation paper. Supplier evaluation. Decision analysis. Trigger P&I process.
Pilot and impact study (P&I)	The technology is proven in a business environment. The organisation learns the implications of introducing the new tool.	Working prototype operation. Implications report. Support plan. Preliminary exploitation plan. Trigger I&E process.
Integration and exploitation (I&E)	The technology is put into the business in a planned way to achieve maximum payback.	Exploitation plan. Roll-out plan. Trigger EU process.
Effective utilisation (EU)	Mature technology management principles are applied. Performance and capacity are measured and managed.	Performance monitoring. Capacity review and plan. Fit for purpose review. Trigger DCom process.
De-commissioning (DCom)	The technology is completely removed from the business environment	Removal plan. Impact study. Removal audit.

I found this useful when discussing any new technology with either IT people or users. The architect's job was made up of the first two processes. A brief description of each process follows.

Awareness and positioning (A&P) process

The A&P process operates at a high level, evaluating new technologies which may be of use to the company. The aim is to match technology trends, company strategy and company readiness so that the company can take a position on the technology and can communicate that position to interested parties. It should be accepted that the majority of position papers would reject technologies. The awareness and positioning process exist to provide focus. The output of the A&P process is position papers.

The risks are low, as no major expense is incurred in the A&P process. The rewards are potentially high, not only because new technologies may be identified which significantly change the business, but also because the process should prevent the company from purchasing technologies which do not add significant benefits.

Evaluation and architectural fit (E&F) process

The technological field is evaluated to ascertain which products are most likely to serve the company's needs. A short list of products is evaluated for its functionality versus business need, and for its fit with the current company infrastructure. The final product list is prepared. The E&F process concerns itself with choosing the right product.

The objective of the E&F process is to narrow the available technology choices to those that suit the business best and that fit the architecture. This is a risk reducing process. Inherent risk is low as the technology is being evaluated, without being purchased or installed.

Pilot and impact study (P&I) process

The technology is applied to a limited business environment with the intention of learning how the functions serve the business need, how the technology integrates with the existing environment, and how the technology impacts on business operations and personnel. The ultimate aim of the process is to have chosen one technology product, *and to have assessed the impact that this technology will have on the business as a whole.*

The prime purpose of the P&I process is to solve a business problem and to assess the impacts and risks of implementing the technology. The innovation is implemented in a limited way, so the costs are kept down. Risks increase if the potential of a good new idea to proliferate throughout the organisation in an uncontrolled way is not managed sensitively. The start-up cost relative to the benefit is high. Rewards are localised.

Integration and exploitation (I&E) process

This involves a substantial change in risk, reward, operating principles and in the roles played by the change personnel. The driving force in the Pilot & Impact process was the idea champion, working on a business problem of importance to him or herself. This problem may now be resolved, and the driving force is dissipated, or disappears altogether.

The I&E process is mostly drudgery. But the business payback is arguably the greatest. (This assumes that the company is resolved to utilise its technologies fully, rather than have a series of pilot sites where technology champions exist.)

Effective utilisation (EU) process

Mature technology management principles are applied. Performance is monitored, and capacity management techniques are used. The focus moves from step change to incremental improvement. Production reliability and stability are paramount. Tracking the performance and capacity utilisation provides an indicator for when the de-commissioning process should be considered.

The business purpose for which the technology was implemented should periodically be reviewed, to assess if the technology is no longer 'fit for purpose'.

De-commissioning (DCom) process

In my experience this is one of the least considered processes in technology adoption. The removal of an old technology reduces support and maintenance costs, and simplifies the business environment. An old technology is one that has lost fit with the business, or with the installed infrastructure. The DCom process aims to effect the complete removal of the technology from the business environment. There may be resistance to the removal, and this circumstance should be managed.

By far the greatest number of problems experienced by CIOs I discussed this model with, were in two of the first three processes: 'awareness and positioning', and 'pilot and impact study'.

9.2.3 Implementing new technologies – issues and problems

Most CIOs that I surveyed felt that there should be more business involvement in the early stages of technology adoption, and that adoption should be based on a business rather than a technical case. But equally most were at a loss about how to get that early involvement. I suggest relationship management will resolve this one, but it won't be easy.

CIOs felt that the planning for implementation should not commence until the impact study had been performed. The impact study should include the impact of the new technology on:

business process, people (jobs and roles), other technology, and company resources.

Only then should the further implementation of the new technology be contemplated.

The early stages of technology adoption represent a problem, because of lack of business involvement, because of resistance to change within the IS department, and because it appears that to investigate the technology and the impacts that the technology will have, is difficult, time consuming and slow. This lack of detailed analysis up front may lead to problems in later processes.

Internal IT function participation problems (team composition, resistance to change), and external participation problems (weak sponsors, user 'experts', and the behaviour of department heads) were cited as causing significant management issues when integrating new technologies. The negative action of participants on the processes was ascribed to politics, 'power-plays', protection of the status quo, and lack of understanding of the benefits to be derived from the new technology. In companies which were small enough to have contact with most users, there tended not to be participant issues.

The internal composition of the team also seems to be important: there is considerable difficulty in getting IT R&D people to produce written material, or to take a position (other than *'wait, there is something better being released in August'*). Most of the CIOs that I talked to agreed that R&D people should not be allowed to operate outside the 'awareness and positioning' or 'evaluation and fit' processes, and that they should be forced to take written positions.

Most CIOs regarded the relationship between their department and the rest of the company as being critical to the success of integration processes. Only 20% of the CIOs I worked with believed that they had good relationships with their business partners. And these few CIOs did not have problems integrating new technologies into their organisations.

Talking about new technologies and relationships one CIO said:

> Managers will often try to solve a business problem by throwing technology at it. Then when the problem remains they can blame the technology. Worst of all, an adversarial relationship builds up between the users and the technology.

Another CIO believed that the culture of the organisation was critical to the successful bringing of new technologies into their business:

> If a company has a culture which allow mistakes, and which learns from their mistakes, and is very open in communication, there can be few problems with the integration of new technologies.

This CIO went on to state that he:

> . . . never has a problem with 'undercover' technologies, because it would be unthinkable to managers not to communicate with IT function the minute they started looking at a new idea.

The tolerance of mistakes seems to be important: one company expected that when their staff made mistakes, they would communicate their learning. Most companies I surveyed did not easily tolerate mistakes, and so much new technology was introduced without ISD knowledge, that the CIOs concerned were unsure of how many new technologies were 'out there'.

The more open and tolerant a company, the fewer integration problems are experienced. On the other hand the more autocratic and bureaucratic a company, the more problems are experienced.

When it comes to communication, three factors may be linked: IS/company relationship, culture of the organisation and physical dispersion and size of the company are all interpreted as being enablers or disablers of good communication within the company. CIOs who had positive relationships, positive cultures, and were not too large or dispersed, had fewer integration problems.

9.3 Last words on implementing new technologies

Many, many gurus and advisors tell a similar parable to this one: there once was a fish named Flippy, who joined his friends and family every day in swimming against the current of a large river. The daily struggles kept everyone busy, and even allowed them to find out who was the 'best swimmer against the current'. They had awards and everything. One day a startling and subversive thought came to Flippy. 'What if he no longer swam against the current, but swam with it instead?' He discussed his idea with his friends and as could be expected, they thought he was insane. He would be swept away, lost forever, and besides which, swimming against the current was what fish did! It was absurd to think that swimming with the current would be in any way satisfying. What would Flippy do for a living, if he didn't swim against the current? His parents refused to even enter into the discussion and forbade him to think such thoughts. But the thought gnawed at him, until one day, he bade his friends and family farewell and started to swim with the current. Things were hectic for a while, but soon Flippy discovered that he didn't actually have to do anything. The current took him along without effort. And Flippy was content.

Avoiding the obvious conclusion that eventually Flippy gets swept out to sea, there are some analogies worth examining.

Coming back to Canute and trying to stop the unstoppable, and to Flippy swimming against the current, it does make sense to explore how IT can swim with the current of new technologies, rather than struggling against them.

Again I come back to my usual refrain – it's all in the relationship. But there's something else that I've only recently begun to explore with new technological adoption – complex adaptive systems and self-organisation.

9.3.1 Self-organisation and new technologies

Ideally one should recognise that the relationship between new technologies and your organisation is a complex system, with significant interaction between the various new technologies and their agents and the employees in your organisation. To create an adaptive system from this complex environment is an ideal objective, because that's when the constant need for stern interventions will be avoided.

Essentially, you should be looking to see how you and the entire organisation can 'go with the flow' when it comes to new technologies, while maintaining some headway. I used to be a canoeist, and in a rapid the trick was always to be paddling with the flow of water, maintaining a momentum which was faster than the surrounding water. This is what should guide you when you look for a driving purpose in the adoption of new technologies. Some fractal rules that come to mind with respect to new technologies are:

- say yes – establish a culture in IT that looks at how you can say yes to new technologies without compromising the mainstream stability and capacity. If this means that you buy some PC package as a prototype or that you set up a 'laboratory' to test the technology, that's what 'say yes' is likely to mean. Why do scientists perform experiments in a laboratory? Because it's safer and easier to test theories, chemicals, drugs and technologies in an enclosed environment where the results are clearly distinguishable from the mass of real world phenomena. And so your 'IT laboratory' should be set up in the same vein: make it an enclosed environment where the results are clearly demonstrable;

- pre-empt new technologies – maintain a momentum which is faster than the outside world. This means not only staying up to speed with the developments, but with the help of your architect, you need to be the source on information on new technologies for your organisation. Ever given any thought to an in-house IT magazine? Match the world in their information flow;

- guide and mentor your non-IT leaders – the objective of this fractal rule is to allow you to make your organisation's leadership IT savvy and successful. Be seen as the mentor to be approached when new technologies confuse non-IT leaders.

The environment in which all this happens is obviously driven by two overriding factors – relationships and architecture. Going with the flow of new technologies, and maintaining a positive momentum will be impossible if you don't have the relationships in which there is mutual trust and access, and in which you don't have a clear and living architecture.

Implementation ideas

1 Draw a relationship map of your organisation with the intent of examining who brings new technologies into the organisation. Where should new technologies arise? And where do they? Can you help those who should be bringing new technologies in, while communicating with those who bring in undercover technologies?

2 Set up your own in-house techno-geek magazine. Choose technologies with architectural fit and steal the march on external magazines – after all you know your audience better than they do. But make the magazine light.

3 Set up a computer shop inside your organisation. Who says external vendors are the only ones with access to your organisation's staff? Whether you use real money or an authorised expenditure process is up to you and your culture. But certainly with your buying power you can offer technologies for home use at discounted prices.

4 Perhaps you could combine your shop with a laboratory where new technological ideas are tested. Or even go the whole hog and add an Internet Café.

10 Rules about rules – standards, methods, tools

I was paging through a textbook on *Management Information Systems*[1] and found this advice:

> Typically an IS organisation develops and follows procedures for the operation of information systems. Using standard procedures promotes quality and minimises the chances of errors and fraud. It helps both end users and IS specialists know what is expected of them in operating procedures and system quality. In addition, documentation of the systems and software design and the operation of the system must be developed and kept up-to-date. Documentation is invaluable in the maintenance of a system as needed improvements are made.
>
> (O'Brien, 1999)

I seem to have lived on a different planet from the author. I agree with his sentiments and perfect-world outlook. But in my experience it just doesn't happen that way. Actually the textbook is good. It's in its fourth edition. People buy it – students of course. But when these students enter the real world they find a free-for-all with the 'standards and procedures' things to be avoided, evaded and ignored in the interests of getting the job done. Remember user requirements and project plans? They may make provision for the development of standards and procedures, but they can't be serious. Certainly the developers who read this specification have every *intention* of documenting the system *this time round*. But when the deadlines get tight, the first thing to be deferred into the misty future is 'documentation.' Mind you, no-one is ever going to read this stuff anyway. I have seen very good documentation, standards, and procedures. It's a pity because it is out of date.

Before I continue, did you know that 74% of statistics are made up on the spot? (Including that one.) The next statistics come from my heart rather than from comprehensive research.

If we had to keep our documentation up-to-date as the textbook suggests, probably 35% of IT's time (made that statistic up too!) would be spent documenting. I really don't know what the statistics are (and I would suggest that the person who bothered to measure these statistics probably has a dull social life indeed), but I do know that nothing like the amount of documentation or keeping to standards advocated by the textbooks, is actually done.

I once called in my IT department project managers (who by some quirk of statistics happened to all be women), and told all of them that from this day forth, our department would have no development standards. Because after all, no-one was keeping to them anyway. I was surprised and secretly pleased when they objected. 'How could we do without standards?' they cried. 'Simple,' I said, 'we've done without them for years, so why stop now?' We eventually came to a compromise: the project managers would decide on the minimum standards which were still appropriate to the current conditions. This they did, and cut our development standards from around 20 to six.

Standards have to earn their living, or die a quiet death.

10.1 What is a standard?

There are two domains in which standards are used – in the industry in general and in the organisation. There is a commercial paradox in industrial standards. Vendors want standards to allow their product to work in the wider world, but they also don't want standards because then their customers are locked-in to using their suite of standardised products. This is why industry standards debates are heated and often acrimonious – vendors are fighting in a Jekyll and Hyde way for market share.

This chapter deals with internal or organisational standards. There are three primary reasons[2] for imposing standards inside an organisation:

- co-ordination standards are created to allow large teams to work in the same way. Everyone can see their value, most try to follow them, but when these standards are imposed from Head Offices on regions and branches, compliance with these standards is erratic at best;

- control standards are designed to make the workings of the developers visible (and thus controllable) to project and IT management staff. But as Friedman[3] says:

Although these standards received considerable attention from the theorists and were widely implemented in many organizations to some degree or other, there is little evidence to suggest that they had more than a slight impact of the problems of systems development at the time.

(Friedman)

- life-cycle standards are designed to allow others to work on the programming code at some later date in the life of the system. Of course, because there are very many ways of resolving the same user requirement, often dependent on the personality of the programmer, and it was in an attempt to inhibit individuality in programmes that these standards were introduced. Properly implemented, these standards made the organisation less dependent on individuals to upgrade and maintain their code.

10.1.1 Why have standards?

So if all this is so difficult, why bother with standards at all? I know the textbooks are right. We do need to develop quality solutions, that are maintainable over time and that allow integration between systems. The ideal of having standards is less of the problem than is the way in which standards are applied. My mental model for standards looks like this:

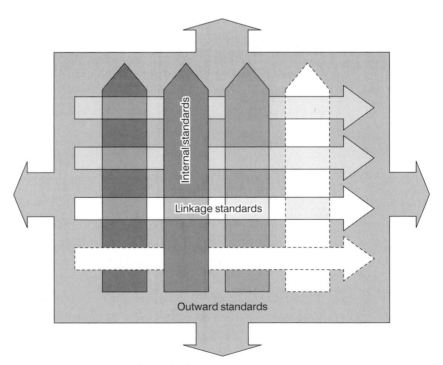

Figure 10.1 Overview of standards

Internal standards

I see a need for standards within systems to allow internal integrity in two areas. Firstly – consistency – allowing many people to work on the same elements of the system at the same time. This is more important as we start to work from various locations, countries or even times. Secondly – continuity – allowing others to maintain the system at some later date in the manner to which it has become accustomed.

Linkage standards

These make sense if one of your solutions is to talk to others, and to talk to your infrastructure.

Outward standards

Normally these would be handled by the vendor, but if your solutions are going to talk to the outside world, then you had better know what standards and protocols are out there, and then you should conform. Be aware of the technology adoption life-cycle of the technology that you are using or intending to use. I have spoken about Moore's[4] concept of 'crossing the chasm.' Technologies that have not crossed the chasm in general exhibit divergent standards, and the standards debate rages in the industry. If the standards debate hasn't even started, the technology is still in the innovation phase and should signal cautious action from your point of view. Once the technology 'crosses the chasm' then its acceptance and application in the wider world is growing. The battle of the standards intensifies briefly as customers place vendors under pressure to stabilise and integrate the technology. So a diverging standards debate signifies a technology that has less of a certain future than one in which the standard is set.

10.2 Setting, applying and monitoring standards

10.2.1 Minimalists should set standards

My experience of standard setters is that they are either bored out of their skulls or are a special type of person who actually enjoys this stuff. Beware of both types. The bored standard setter tends to do a haphazard job, and the enthusiast overdoes things.

The way through the setting of standards is so obvious that no-one seems to follow it: know *why* you need the standard. This is a simple and mildly demanding task. You need to get the people who use the technology or develop the solutions together and ask:

● why do we need internal standards in this company? (You'll have to respond to those who look at you as if you had asked why the sky is blue.);

● what are the minimum set of internal standards we would need to meet the requirements defined above? (Emphasise the minimum. When they get warmed up many technologists want to standardise everything.);

● if we had this minimum set of internal standards how would we sell the need for them.

Then you do the same for linkage and outward standards. Then the team has fun slashing all the unnecessary standards that have crept into the organisation.

Allow minimal thinking to guide you when it comes to standards.

10.2.2 Practitioners should (want to) apply the standards

If the people responsible for doing the work don't uphold the standards, then the standard cannot succeed. To quote the poet Yeats:

Things fall apart; the centre cannot hold;

Mere anarchy is loosed upon the world

(Yeats)

This is a little more significant than saying the workers should work according to the rules. Practitioners apply standards because they see the need to do so. There are so many alternative ways of getting IT work done that bypassing a standard is relatively easy. Therefore all efforts should be made in convincing the practitioners and then allowing self-enforcement to take over.

10.2.3 Sceptics should monitor standards

A person who doubts the need for a standard should be the person to monitor the use and effectiveness of the standard. In this way you entrench the minimalist approach. Your sceptic would be constantly questioning the need for the standard, and more importantly, if he or she has accepted the need, then they will be inclined to be dogmatic about the use of the standard.

10.3 Perspectives on standards

Perhaps there is one 'truth' regarding standards. However, I suspect that there is a spectrum of opinion ranging from the anarchist – 'no standards are ever necessary', through to the dictator – 'everything is controllable, according to my standard', viewpoints. I subscribe to a more left-of-centre perspective. Some standards are necessary, but that they have to earn their way. There are too many unnecessary standards.

10.3.1 The cat in the monastery – the need to expel old standards

Many years ago, there was a monastery in which the abbot owned a cat. The problem was that when the monks gathered to pray, the cat would weave in and out amongst them rubbing and purring. Eventually the monks complained to the abbot, who hit upon this solution: during communal prayer time, the cat was to be locked in a comfortable cage near the abbot so it wouldn't get lonely. The solution worked and everyone was pleased. After some years the abbot died. Because the cat lived on, it continued to be locked in the cage during communal prayers. When many years later the cat died, the monks went out to get another, because the standard was to lock a cat in a cage during communal prayers. This has happened to many of our standards.

In another real example (only the names and places have been changed to protect the incompetent), I did some work for a railway company in 1999. One of their managers told me this tale. Each locomotive marshalling yard was required to fill in a daily situation report. In 1993 this particular manager noticed that one of the situation reports from a coastal city marshalling yard included the statistic: 'number of whales in the harbour.' Interested to see why this statistic was needed the manager traced its origins. It appeared that in 1956 an inland general manager wanted to take his family on holiday, and show his kids the whaling station that still operated in the harbour. He was also keen for them to see it when a whaling ship had brought its catch into harbour. So he requested that this statistic be added to the situation report, so that he would know when to take his family to the coast. It took until 1993 for that statistic to be questioned and discarded. The whaling station closed in 1964, but 30 years later the railway company was still reporting away.

It seems to be really hard for companies to stop doing things. As Peter Drucker says:

> A company should be able to eliminate its waste. The human body does it automatically. In the corporate 'body,' there is enormous resistance[5].
>
> (Drucker, 2000)

The image conjures up some bizarre thoughts, but surely you must pay a lot of attention to the initiation of standards. Once a standard has found its way into the corporate lexicon, it seems to slip into the unseen 'way we do things around here' category, never to surface again unless someone searches it out. To follow Drucker's metaphor, you need to give your company a standards enema. Crude I know, but perhaps it's necessary – you decide.

There should be a clear *and visible* reason why a standard exists. If that reason is lost, then eject the standard.

10.3.2 'Use my standard, curse you!'

A standard should be sold not imposed – very few standards can be imposed. History shows us that successful standards are those that are adopted willingly by the practitioner, or alternatively there is no other way of doing things. Many industry standards are unpalatable to the vendors who comply with them, but if they want to do business, then they have to use them. I have dealt with the need for a minimalist approach to standards. The approach should also take into account those 'standards' which are unnecessary because if you examine them, there's really no other way of doing things. Which leaves us with those standards that are adopted willingly.

How do you encourage the willing use of a standard? The traditional answer would be 'communicate'. I agree, but it is the way you communicate that's important. You are aiming for a soft sell here. You need to be restrained and subtly persuasive rather than dominating. Yes, you can try the dominating route, but every force in the emerging business world is against you succeeding. So you need to sell. And selling means planning your sales strategy, looking at why your target would want to 'buy' your standard. What are the benefits of having the standard? If there are none for the individual, then you have some serious selling ahead. Perhaps a little market research is necessary as well: What are people doing now? How would they feel about this standard? What problems do they experience that this standard might resolve? And so on. Of course any sales campaign also measures the success of the sales strategy, so you need to have feedback loops, and to survey the acceptance of the standard.

If there are problems, imagine what a sales force might do – they would certainly not storm up to their customer and shout into their face: 'BUY MY PRODUCT, CURSE YOU!' Which is the equivalent of what many managers do with the memos they send out saying something like: 'it has come to my attention that staff are not following the 5-minute tea break policy. Henceforth staff will be required to sign the register at reception when going on their break and when returning from it. Staff who are found to abuse their tea-break privileges will be required to explain their actions to myself. Thank you for your co-operation.' Does this sound harsh? It is based on a very similar memo that was sent out by a partner at a consultancy I worked for, but the subject was more important, which makes the tone inappropriate – the lack of additions to the knowledge management system. The response was of course negative. So you need to sell standards. People have many ways of avoiding, evading and ignoring standards they don't believe in.

Selling standards sounds like hard work. It is. Which is another reason for having a minimum number of standards. Each needs its own sales strategy and monitoring process.

10.3.3 Standards and boredom

The step between rigour and rigor-mortis is a small one. It seems that the purpose of many organisations' standards is to bore everyone to death. Thick files of closely typed print, punctuated by the odd incredibly complex table or diagram. (This brings new meaning to the phrase 'bulk standard'.) No wonder standards don't get accepted. The practitioners died of boredom a long time ago. (Or as a friend of mine says: 'how can you possibly bore people with standards if they don't even read them in the first place?')

You have some of the most innovative brains working for you right now. They call themselves programmers or business analysts or project managers. And yet you dull their senses with your grey, tedious, tiresome, stale, dry standard documentation. Who then is responsible for their ennui?

Where are the colours, the intranet sites, the animations, the diagrams, the 'standards for beginners', the *interesting* communications? Have you designed a GUI (graphical user interface) for standards?

You need to make standards interesting if you want to sell them. Get your people to help you structure the standards interface, or manuals, or magazine.

10.4 Trade-offs and education

There are of course trade-offs in the standards debate, as with any debate.

The nature of the human beast seems to be to resist control. Any standard, no matter how well sold or structured or how necessary, will have its detractors. You need to have the debate with these people, listen to their views and accommodate good ideas as far as possible. But ultimately there is a need to get on with it. If the majority of people have 'bought in' to the standard, implement it. But don't stop selling to the detractors. However, make sure that your systems do not reward people for applying non-standard solutions. It seem that most people get away with not changing because the organisation's reward systems (salary, reward schemes, etc.) continue to compensate non-conforming behaviour. If this sounds a little harsh, it is. But ultimately standards, if designed and implemented correctly, should facilitate a positive outcome for the organisation. If the organisation pays for people's time and energy (see Chapter 14 because you pay for a whole lot more than time and energy) then the organisation has a right to expect that energy to be aligned. Standards aim to create alignment.

Some people resist standards because they don't know the context in which standards are applied. Often these people are outside the IT department. Then the relationship and your education/information efforts are more important than ever. Most people, when they understand why something is done, will align themselves appropriately.

The final words on standards must be:

- have a real reason for having a standard;

- keep standards to a minimum;

- sell standards, don't impose them;

- give standards a friendly face – make them easily accessible;

- educate and communicate standards.

Implementation ideas

1 Call your developers and project managers together and tell them you are rescinding all standards forthwith. I hope you get the same reaction I had. But if everyone nods and heads

off into the sunset, then you know you have a real problem on your hands.

2 Find your minimalists who will set the new standards, the practitioners who will apply them and the sceptics who will monitor their use.

3 Develop a sales plan for each standard. There had better be a few or you will be inundated with work. Buy a book on selling and apply it to your standards.

4 Produce a standards magazine for the wider organisational audience. Be interesting and colourful. Use analogies, cartoons, diagrams and competitions to keep people's interest.

References

1. O'Brien, J.A. (1999) *Management Information Systems: Managing Information Technology in the Internetworked Enterprise (4th edn.)*; Irwin/McGraw-Hill
2. Friedman, A.L. (1999) *Computer Systems Development: History, Organization and Implementation*. John Wiley & Sons, Chichester
3. Friedman, A.L. (1999) *Computer Systems Development: History, Organization and Implementation*. Wiley, Chichester.
4. Moore, G. (1991) *Crossing the Chasm; Marketing and Selling Technology Products to Mainstream Customers*. Capstone Publishing Limited, Oxford
5. Drucker, P.F. (2000) Sage Advice; Interview with Peter Drucker. *Business 2.0 Magazine*, October 2000, (SA Edition)

Running the race – providing business solutions from IT

It is a race. Against time, against the changing business environment, against internal business changes, against solutions providers, against changing technologies, and against the impatience of people to get on with the job.

I don't have the total solution, and much of my thinking in this area is admittedly untested. So I offer these ideas as just that: ideas. If you like them, try them. *'Caveat emptor'* and all that, but suspend judgement for a moment as we reframe the provision of IT solutions.

I have deliberately not called this chapter 'IT Development'. I also didn't call it 'Providing IT solutions'. Because I want to break down the illusory barrier that somehow IT is responsible for developing systems or providing technology. It is of course, but if that's the whole gamut of your, or the business' thinking, then it's time to change the rules. IT departments are responsible for helping the business solve their problems from an IT perspective. It remains a business problem, and IT provides the expertise, experience, methods and manpower to drive that perspective. But if the business throws their problem over the wall into the IT department, and then go to the exit hatch and wait for the solution to pop out the other end, we're in trouble. The focus must shift to 'business', and must also shift to 'solutions'. Read the advertising brochures of any technology supplier, and they will emphasise that they provide complete solutions. This is a tad arrogant, unless they intend building the kind of relationship with the business that will allow them to suggest changes to the organisation's strategy, goals, operational processes, organisation, performance systems and reward systems. Vendors would have to be very trusted before the average business person will buy into that. And who is better positioned to provide such solutions but the in-house IT department, which has focused on its relationships and built trust?

A complete solution relies on resolving the problem or filling the need, and as such requires significant attention in the build up to the problem statement and more importantly after the remedy is implemented. Providing a complete solution is wider and deeper than a project, wider because it should cross boundaries outside of the project domain, and deeper because it starts before the project, and ends (if ever) after the project is wrapped up. No external vendor can provide that very easily.

11.1 Delivery of solutions and outcomes

There is a difference between an output and an outcome. An output is what many IT development functions work towards. Admittedly they are looking for a positive output, but their boundaries confine their thinking. An output is deliverable, the *product* of a process. Call it a system or an architecture, or a plan, or a technology implementation. An outcome is the result or visible effect that occurs as a result of having delivered the output. It necessitates meeting the objectives of the project. Many CIOs have said to me that meeting the business objectives of the business is outside their mandate. I mentioned in Chapter 1 the need for IT to stop behaving like librarians, who check books in and out but never read them. If IT is to become part of the solution, then they must get involved in business problems. Leave traditional development to someone else. It is IT's job to ensure the outcome of an objective from an

IT perspective. An inordinate number of financial people make it to the top of organisations. That is less because they have their fingers on the financial pulse, and more because they don't set themselves a financial boundary. Some do, and they become the scorekeepers of the organisation (and I've never seen a scorekeeper graduating to the position of coach). But many financial people do not impose a financial boundary on themselves, rather they help the business solve problems from a financial perspective. See the analogy? IT people should help the business solve their problems from an IT standpoint. IT is not what you do, it is merely the perspective you bring to doing business. (If we were to keep to the scorekeeper metaphor for bounded financial people, then bounded IT people would be the locker room attendants, checking the real players' gear in and out, and making sure that they can get out there and play. Maybe they would also do laundry – it depends on their self-image.)

Outcomes are visible. In a previous book[1] I developed the concept of 'outcome space'. This is a list of benefits derived from having the solution. And IT's job doesn't stop until these benefits have been achieved. If you want to get on the board of the company, this is the space in which you must operate. I was startled the other day, to come across a multimillion dollar IT project in which no-one knew the benefits. When I asked the IT people, they said: 'Oh, that's in the specification document, or the business case somewhere?' So I asked the business sponsor, and he could think of a few of the major benefits like: 'focus on strategic issues' and the like. When I asked what this focus on strategic issues would look like, remembering that outcomes are visible, he couldn't really say. This is a company spending millions, and it doesn't have a clear idea on what that spend will bring them. In this case I blame the consultants who had a 'solution' and sold the problem to the company.

An outcome space lists the benefits and defines the visible behaviours that are expected in a business environment. In doing so you do not necessarily confine yourself to one solution. There are often many ways of achieving the outcome, some of which may not involve IT. ('We want a customer relationship system' is not an outcome, benefit or behaviour.) So the objective of the CIO is not just to bring an IT perspective to the business issue, but to focus on the outcome. It will mean stepping in other people's patches, but provided you've done your relationship work, have tact, and are acting in the best interests of the outcome, you are on fairly solid ground.

Defining an outcome space also allows you to accommodate change during the 'project' because if you filter every potential change through the outcome space you will know whether that change conforms to the desired benefits.

11.2 Intersecting with the business 'bill of rights'

Keep in mind the business bill of rights when considering solutions. Particular aspects of the bill of rights which relate to the IT perspective in the solution are flexibility, operating in the same time-frame, technological leadership and guidance, alignment with business objectives and the right of the business to change their requirements.

How then is one to satisfy this bill of rights and still maintain some kind of discipline and forward motion from an IT perspective? An answer lies in a concept developed by Profs. Dan Remenyi, Mike Sherwood-Smith and myself called Active Benefits Realisation or ABR[2]. The basic idea behind ABR employs the concepts of co-evolution, outcome space, and formative evaluation.

Co-evolution is really just the acceptance by the business and IT that they are in this together, and that through interacting with each other new answers to issues, needs and problems will evolve.

The outcome space is the picture of what will have changed once the envisaged deliverable has been implemented. It is a picture, rather than a thick document. If you can put it on a poster or chart on the wall, so much the better. We also suggested the notion of a benefit 'stream', to highlight the fact that benefits are not delivered on day one, but flow into the organisation over time as new behaviours and processes take hold.

Finally the concept of formative evaluation links co-evolution and the outcome space. It is the *formal* act of getting all the interested parties together, probably every three months but more often if needs be, and examining the outcome space and the current activities directed at getting to that space. People are allowed to bring new ideas to the table and test them against the outcome space. The name 'formative evaluation' suggests that you can form new activities based on your evaluation of the existing activities and the outcome space. Also you can stop, or change existing activities if they are no longer heading in the right direction. A number of people have argued that this kind of apparently free-wheeling approach will lead to scope-creep at best, and anything from analysis-paralysis to anarchy at worst and certainly will create a budgetary explosion as things drift out of control. Of course this is monorail thinking at its best. The ABR process is structured but allows change. When we started thinking our way through the process, we started on the premise: 'What if change were inevitable, and was allowed?' ABR was the result. A summary diagram of ABR looks is presented in Figure 11.1.

When we developed the ABR process we were at pains to point out that it is not a methodology. Rather it is a framework or mind-set which allows you to accommodate change in the provision of business solutions from IT. It looks a little complicated, but really it is fairly straightforward: you have a set of initial conditions. Don't sweat specifying the detail here, because you can get into analysis-paralysis very easily. What is

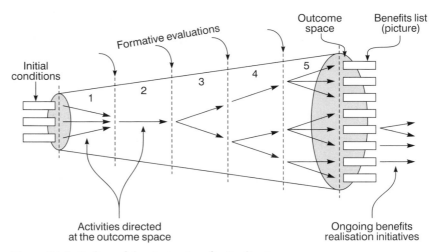

Figure 11.1 Outline of the Active Benefits Realisation process

important to sweat is the outcome space and the benefits list. Then you specify a set of activities that will move you in the direction of the outcome space. As you can see from the first period there are three activities directed at resolving some issues, perhaps an examination of the data architecture, a look at the business conditions and a look at customer perceptions. In period two, it is decided to consolidate the activities into one, to develop a common approach to getting to the outcome space. Period three sees two activities which move us forward to the outcome space, and so on. Also note that there are four activities that continue after 'reaching' the outcome space.

It is important to see ABR as an agenda and framework for progressing towards a desired outcome. Activities and decisions must be tracked. The formative evaluation sessions also have a specific structure. They require that a set of stakeholders in the outcome space are defined and briefed. A set of criteria is determined which will allow stakeholders to evaluate activities in the light of the outcome space benefits. These criteria may be financial, business processes and conditions, and technical in nature. (A technical criterion will definitely involve satisfying architectural requirements.) A review of activities takes place according to the criteria. Trade-offs may be made in terms of cost, functionality, time and skills with respect to current activities. New activities are formed if necessary and some activities may be stopped. And the next activity cycle begins.

ABR and formative evaluation represent a way to progress towards and beyond a set of objectives in a co-evolutionary, actively learning and changing environment. It is a powerful tool in the provision of solutions from an IT perspective.

11.3 The Russians are coming – the new solution providers

You no doubt have seen those Russian-dolls, where you open up the large doll to find a smaller one inside? Open that one, and there is a yet smaller one inside, and so on. This is the model to follow when considering solutions provision. The business sees the outer doll, provided by IT, but there is no reason why inside that doll you can't have external providers of services to your business. The move towards outsourcing is an obvious example. As will be the current trend towards 'Applications Service Providers'. As will be distributed data storage. K.B. Chandrasekhar, founder of the Application Service Provider company 'Jamcrackers' when interviewed by *Business 2.0* magazine said:

> My vision is that in five years, people will not be running any applications inside their business[3].

> (Chandrasekhar, 2000)

And one of his customers, Tushar Trivedi, Chief Technology Officer of ChannelAutomation who runs seven of his core applications on Jamcracker, agrees:

We have no applications in-house, we only have a local-area network to share files and we may get rid of that ... I'm working with limited funds here, so this is perfect; we have no capital expenditures and no payroll expenses for IT staff, but we still have the applications we need.

But the issue here, is to be the outer Russian doll, as is Trivedi. This doesn't mean that you bar vendors of the 'inner doll' services from ever seeing the business, but if in-house IT is to maintain purpose in the business it should represent the business view with an IT perspective. This places IT departments at the interface between vendors or self-styled solutions providers and the business. And who better to translate business needs, strategy and culture into IT service?

The provision of business solutions from an IT perspective takes on a totally new role in the new in-house IT function.

Firstly, in-house solutions providers must have the relationship with the business to firstly understand their needs, strategies, and culture. Indeed the nature of the relationship with the business must be such that they co-evolve these needs, strategies and cultures with the business, providing the IT perspective. The nature of the relationship also must be that IT can work with the business to change its strategy, goals, operational processes, organisation, performance systems and reward systems.

Secondly, in-house solutions providers must be business analysts. They need to be able to take a business need and translate it into technological requirements.

They need to be investigators. I was once looking for a hospital management system, and we had the consultants develop a short-list of seven potential suppliers from an initial list of about 400. A team of three people then flew around the world to visit these suppliers and see their product and company. Eventually they returned triumphant from the USA bearing the product that best fit our company's requirements. It was an expensive investigation, but it was worth it. Or so we thought. What our world-tripping trio didn't know was that the source code was undocumented, and was chaotically muddled at best. What they also didn't find out was that the vendor had recently lost its core development team members, who had set up their own business, as well as losing a key contract that would have funded further development. What they also didn't know was that the remaining project management skills left at the vendor couldn't have managed a kiddies' birthday party, let alone a multi-million dollar product. Finally they didn't find out that the company was in severe financial straits, and that ours was the last-ditch sale that they pulled out all stops for. To be fair, they weren't briefed to find this stuff out (my fault), and they weren't qualified to do so. As a result we ended up suing the vendor for the source code, and supported it ourselves. I have since left that company (no, not over this fiasco), and to my knowledge it is implemented in about 60 hospitals, and it is entirely supported locally. So in-house solutions providers need to be serious investigators. Due diligence investigations should also be a prerequisite investigation of any major IT acquisition.

Thirdly, in-house solutions providers must manage the inner dolls. Yes, set up the partnerships with vendors, but as the IT representative of the business it is essential that you get into the 'POEM' paradigm. You need to 'plan, organise, execute, and monitor' at great length and depth, the activities of the inner doll solutions providers. Why? Because your company and external vendors have different agendas and missions. While providing 'excellent customer service' may be the stated mission of a vendor, they will only remain in business if they make a profit from their customers, and your company also needs to make profits. Therefore there is an emphatic need to manage each inner doll vendor. You need to manage their performance from your organisation's perspective and you need to manage the integration of different service providers into a seamless outer doll experience. This takes time and effort.

Finally, in-house solution providers need to supply IT leadership. They need to offer an 'architected' view of information technology and of the organisation. They offer a company biased opinion on IT, and the need to offer proactive suggestions and solutions for business issues – the emphasis is on proactive.

You will notice that I have missed out the obvious functions of 'development' and 'maintenance' from this list of activities for in-house IT solutions providers. Because I'm not sure they should be doing any in-house development. Yes, I've heard the arguments that, 'we are different' and 'we need specialist solutions', but in today's world of object application architectures and Applications Service Providers, and Internet enabled applications, the need to have your own developers is diminishing. I know that should you choose to do so, you can outsource and buy in all the IT solutions that your company requires. So having an in-house development capability is a choice that should be consciously made in the light of your company's needs and in the light of what is available externally. Having an in-house development capability is not a foregone conclusion.

11.4 No projects

I don't think there should be any IT projects.

This topic always raises healthy discussion with whoever I talk to.

Various definitions of the term 'project' can be found, but they always go something like this: 'a project is a planned undertaking that has a start and an end, and has specific measurable objectives which must be met within acceptable time and budget constraints.' You can find many definitions, but projects are always planned, are time and budget bound and have specific objectives. These distinctions are made in order to separate project work from other managerial assignments and ongoing work. Why? Why do we need to differentiate between a project and 'normal' work? Does normal work not have to be planned and have measurable objectives? So the issue might be the start and end date. Which is strange because I have seldom seen a project come in on time or budget.

Perhaps projects are an issue of containment. We need to define boundaries (time, budget, and scope) around a piece of work so that it can be managed and manageable. Noble sentiments, but I would suggest that these boundaries keep more out than keep things in. Project boundaries become walls between 'normal' activities and 'special' work. And very little gets to cross the boundary. Getting business resources allocated to IT projects remains a serious problem for project managers. I once had a salary system project in which the Human Resources department allocated a newly started payroll clerk as their key user because everyone else was busy doing 'normal' work. I suggested to the HR Manager that a 'newly started payroll clerk' kind of system might not be what he wanted, and having seen the light he allocated his deputy for 50% of his time. A few projects get users allocated full-time to the project, which sounds like the ideal situation. But the boundary wall still exists. Having been yanked out of their 'normal' duties they become something else to the rest of the business. So it seems to me that project boundaries establish walls between 'normal work' and 'special work.'

The Active Benefits Realisation approach suggests that you be very clear on the outcome, and that you manage progress through Formative Evaluation. One of the actively managed elements of the outcome space is of course cost. This means that every time a formative evaluation is performed, the financial implications of starting new activities is considered. And a trade-off process is attended to with some rigour. Scope, time and budget issues are energetically tracked during the ABR and formative evaluation process, in a spirit of honest appraisal. The feared 'scope-creep' is kept in the open. Unlike many projects I have worked on in which the project team camouflages overruns by scrimping on quality issues such as testing and documentation. They do this because the project ethos of containment means that once the objective is set and the budget approved nothing may cross those boundaries without variance orders, signoffs, and probable embarrassment of the project members.

Surely a healthier approach is to define an environment in which related activities will take place. These activities are both 'normal' and 'project-like.' Normally an environment would be defined with a business process at its core, and would be inclusive of all people and activities that occupy that environmental space. That way, it seems to me that the barriers that build up in a project environment would be less likely to form.

Defining a business environment is not easy, because if any environment is worthwhile, it interfaces with so much else in the business, that its boundaries are hard to find. And they probably should be found, if only to maintain some manageable control over scope and cost views. Perhaps we need to rename the environment to a 'habitat' and define what lives inside the habitat and what lives outside.

If 'environments' rather than 'projects' were the accepted view of business activities they could be tracked over time, and yes, the period in which the 'project' activities occurred would represent a time of increased activity and cost to that environment. I have had a number of discussions with project managers on this concept, and their reactions have been mixed. The most alarming response was from a man who ran project management courses. He flatly opposed the environment concept, called me a dangerous nut-case (expletives deleted) and wouldn't talk to me again. Which is understandable and acceptable, because he probably saw my suggestion as targeting his expert power. I fully expect such reactions to continue. Yesterday, I was at the presentation of a consortium of companies proposing a solution to a large company for the total overhaul of their systems environment. There was no way that the solutions providers could start talking about a non-project environment and habitats. The ideas would have been mis-understood completely. So the notion of projects, budgets and implementation plans must necessarily remain. But I also got the sense that already the 'wall' was being erected. Perhaps this is the nature of nascent relationships, but I had the distinct feeling that the potential client was asking 'What will you do for us?' almost as if they would be interested bystanders in the project.

Projects will be around for a long time to come, but I would suggest that if you could start to see things in business environment and interconnected systemic terms, some of the traditional project problems may start to be resolved. Perhaps the first step towards environmental thinking is to start talking about the 'project system' rather than just projects.

11.5 Providing solutions when the goal-posts keep changing

Imagine if change was allowed. Imagine if our sense of the final solution adapted as we moved along in time. Active Benefit Realisation, Formative Evaluation and 'projects as environmen-tal systems' are some tools and mindsets we can use to accommodate constantly changing goals. Aiming at outcomes rather than outputs focuses on a more stable target. Let the outputs change, as long as continuous attention is paid to outcomes.

There is another tool you can apply to the solutions provision domain, and that is the application of complexity theory. You will need three elements of complex adaptive systems to start on the complex adaptive journey:

- a compelling purpose;

- a few rules;

- a nurturing environment.

You are aiming to create a self-organising solutions environment that maintains continuous focus on the business outcomes, and that delivers a stream of benefits over time.

In any given solutions environment you need to define the outcome space with some diligence and precision, because this will become the compelling purpose for the environment. You will then need to apply the tools of Active Benefit Realisation and Formative Evaluation in that solutions environment to move the environment constantly in the direction of the outcome space. You will also have to take the stakeholder issue seriously, identifying them and genuinely including them in the solutions team. Finally you need to nurture the environment, provide the tools needed for delivery of solutions, identify the habitat factors for the solution environment, and constantly minister to their well-being.

If this sounds like a laughably soft and fuzzy approach to IT development, you will find it otherwise. It requires a strong focus on people, on models, on communication, on monitoring change and on making inexorable progress towards the outcome space. It requires leadership and courage, because there will be many times in which you will question your chosen path and many detractors will intensify your uneasiness. Others who have tried and succeeded have gone through the same self-doubt. But in the end they trusted the kernel of knowledge inside them that believed that there had to be a different way.

And there has to be a different way of providing IT-based solutions or in-house IT is destined for the dump.

11.6 No development methodology

You will notice that I haven't recommended either a development methodology or a development method. This is deliberate and is a challenge to you. If you are looking for a methodology, I'm afraid that I cannot offer one with any confidence. That is because in my many years running an IT function, and in my subsequent work with other IT functions I have not found a methodology that caters for change other than the rapid application methodologies. Why are these methodologies so dry? Real people have to use them. If there was a methodology that I would support, I imagine it would be some sort of RAD approach in order to fit in with the Active Benefits Realisation and Formative Evaluation concepts.

Were I to choose a development tool, it would have to be object oriented. The idea of flexibility and quick delivery appeals to me.

Implementation ideas

1 Try Active Benefits Realisation and Formative Evaluation. Select a small project with an IT-friendly user. Go through the ideas with them and agree to try the path. Develop the outcome space and progress from there. It won't be easy. Feel free to adopt the approach as you see fit. But keep to the spirit of the process – change is inevitable and allowed.

2 Spend some time defining an environment. Pick an area of the business that you can assess where all the IT and other activity takes place. Then develop metrics for that environment. Cost, activity, resources are all metrics that will apply.

References

1. Remenyi, D.S.J., Sherwood-Smith, M. and White, T. (1997) *Maximising IT Benefits: A Process Approach*. Wiley
2. Remenyi, D.S.J., Sherwood-Smith, M. and White, T. (1997) *Maximising IT Benefits: A Process Approach*. Wiley, Chichester
3. Chandrasekhar, K.B. (2000) Jam on It. *Business 2.0 Magazine*; October 2000, (SA Edition)

12 The home fires – core production

I was appointed as Facilities Manager for a University as an experiment. The University had tried promoting from within, but without significant success, because they constantly came up against the 'Peter Principle.' Dr Laurence Peter proposed that employees are promoted to their level of incompetence and stick there. The University found that when they promoted their Operations Managers or their Network Manager into the post of Facilities Manager, they tended not to be either effective or happy there, and soon left. So the experiment was to bring in someone who didn't necessarily know anything about computing, but who had a track record of management. And so I became a Facilities Manager more or less without having been inside a machine-room before. This brought an outsider's perspective to the installation, and I must admit gave me many sleepless and uncertain nights. The learning curve was steep, but the experiment seemed to work, as we brought some order to the minutia of running a 24 hour 365 day per year operation.

The experience was tough, but it did teach me the value of bringing a newcomer's perspective into established processes. In this chapter, I am taking an opportunity to look at the traditional Facilities Section of the in-house IT department through different eyes.

'Facilities' includes the running and maintenance of the processors, networks, applications, and infrastructure. The installation of new IT infrastructure is included, as is backup, security, and contingency planning. Some installations incorporate the call-centre or IT help-desk into Facilities. Some also encompass the training and 'user services' elements of running the IT installation as well. It really is a choice, and one that must be made, as to what fits inside the production environment. Ultimately the question of outsourcing will arise, if it hasn't already, and it would be appropriate to have thought through the consequences and dependencies of obtaining the services of specialist providers of services to support your core IT production environment.

I would prefer to move away from the term 'Facilities' if possible. The word is redolent with meaning, and often not positive meaning. So for want of a better word I have settled on Core IT Production, in the hope of communicating that this is a core domain for IT and that it involves more than merely operating the equipment. (In the interests of shorter text, but at the expense of introducing another acronym to the world dare I call Core IT Production 'CIP'?)

The CIP domain produces 'stable capacity' to conduct business through information technology. This sounds a little too 'textbook' perfect for me, but let us explore the idea further. If you were to have a 'stability' production process then you need measures against which to define that stability. Those measures include availability, integrity and durability. Availability means that the systems are capable of being used where and when the business requires them. Integrity means that when the system is available it has internal integrity from moment to moment, and that its functions and data are trusted. Finally durability implies that the entire system is hard wearing and robust. Each of these measurement criteria has significant implications for CIP. But add the issue of 'capacity' to the equation, and matters become more complicated. Performance now, and into the future, and the planning and installation of technologies (both hard and soft) are central issues. A final capacity element that often gets overlooked is the evaluation of technologies prior to being

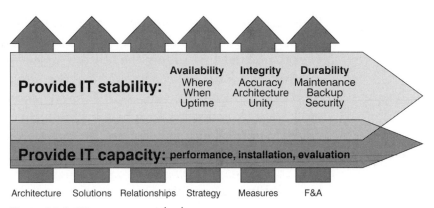

Figure 12.1 CIP processes and sub-processes

'fitted' into the production environment. Include in this evaluation element of 'capacity' the scanning for new technologies which will ease the CIP processing burden.

So the general itemisation of the CIP functional area would be divided into the processes and sub-processes presented in Figure 12.1.

12.1 The core IT production domain

The CIP domain is largely concerned with 'below the momentum line' activities. There are some activities that are concerned with increasing the organisation's momentum, but in general CIP is concerned with maintaining the current IT environmental stability and capacity.

In Figure 12.1 it is immediately obvious that to organise around these interlinked processes would require some rethinking of the traditional 'Operations, Networks, Technical Services and Data Management' functions that we have become used to. In fact it may be instructive to stay away from dividing CIP functions by areas of technological expertise on the assumption that technologies are converging, and while the technical detail might differ considerably, the CIP treatment of that technological area remains largely the same. This may be a significant mindset shift for many Facilities Managers – stop thinking about functions by technology and start thinking about the provision of IT stability and capacity whatever the technology.

12.1.1 Provide IT stability

Let stability be the guide. This means you need to benchmark IT environments against some universal measure. There are many benchmarking and measurement tools available, and certainly your IT environments should conform to world class standards, but the ultimate benchmark has to be what your user thinks. So step one must be to ask your users. Ask them about the availability, consistency and durability of the IT environments they use. You might be tempted to make IT distinctions and ask questions like, 'is the network available when you need it?' but resist the temptation. Ask the questions from a user perspective. Better still, get a few users to design your questions for you. I imagine their innocent blending of disparate technologies into one user view will be instructive. You might find they mix the telephone service with e-mail. You might find they have no concept of networks at all, which if you think about it is good. Don't be tempted to change this view radically, but do test it on a sample of other users first. Guide users, develop their knowledge but don't instruct them on 'the way things are in IT.'

Availability

Step one in the availability equation is to make IT capacity available where the work is done. This is a geographical question, and has to largely relate to network reach. Another consideration in the 'where' element of IT availability relates to workplace availability – if your sales staff are in the field almost all the time, that's where you make IT available. There are hostile working environments like mines, factories and remote backcountry. So if you consider the 'where' element of the availability sub-process, you will start to factor mobile support into your services. That's expensive though, especially if your organisation covers a wide geographical spread, so some serious thought for remote support needs to be considered.

Availability has to include times that the technology is accessible to the organisation. This has to depend on the business mission and vision. Availability is expensive if the organisation wishes access to systems outside of extended office hours, because it means doubling up on nearly every component of the IT environment. By the way, it's probably a good idea to have your users decide on access times, and to communicate these to the user base in general. It's not IT's role to communicate a business decision.

Availability must also include up-time status during the scheduled available hours. There is a simple benchmark here – the IT environment must be 100% available during access hours. Simple but expensive. However, there is no reason why you can't shoot for this goal. The closer you get to this goal, the more money will have to be spent on pre-emptive tools (error monitors, multiple network connections to one point, electricity generators, etc.) and the more difficult it becomes to justify the expenditure. No business likes to spend money on ensuring an increasingly diminishing risk of failure is catered for. So there is always a trade off. I have seen a vendor who spent significant capital on pre-emptive hardware and software, but their reasoning was sound, because they were running an outsource help-desk facility. They also took a leap of insight that seems to elude others: they realised that every piece of equipment connected to their network was . . . connected to their network. Not just a piece of gear that they had to service, but some intelligent equipment that had self-diagnostic capabilities, or that could be remotely tested and fixed. They staffed their help-desk with one call-taker, three technical boffins and a number of field technicians. This complement served six major companies. By the same token, I have seen a similar service needing 15 call-takers, and an army of technicians to support a similar user base. The difference is that the former help-desk service decided to avoid problems in the first place. They polled every network-connected device hourly and acted on every error message. Generally, the first users knew of a problem was when a technician made an appointment to replace some still to fail component after hours. The latter help-desk believed their mission was to solve problems efficiently and effectively, but their basic premise was flawed.

If the purpose of the CIP function revolves around stability rather than quick recovery from instability, then surely the mission for the function must be one of pre-empting failure.

Integrity

Trust in systems stems from the accuracy of data and consequently in 'accuracy' of outputs. The old GIGO (Garbage In – Garbage Out) rule still applies, and an organisation I once worked with had taken the credo to such lengths that their layers of verification in the various data capture systems meant that customers were forced to wait and the systems were made unusable. As a result, there was a very real need for throughput in servicing customers which the technical people resolved by switching off the verification routines. Needless to say, years later, they are unable to implement management information systems without a major effort at cleaning up the data environment. There is a tension between being totally right, and between getting work done. Considerable attention needs to be paid to the balance. Similarly if the algorithms are used by the system. Obviously GIGO is not the only factor affecting trust and accuracy in systems. Late updates, in-system data manipulation either manual or automatic, version control, unclear documentation and confused or untrained users all can contribute to dissatisfaction with the quality of data. Responsibility for data accuracy has to be shared, and if you find yourself at the end of 'an IT problem,' it's time to get back to relationships. Because IT should of course not own data, which suggests that the business owns data. And ownership implies responsibility. Your relationship work should answer the question: who is responsible for the authenticity, rigour, and correctness of information, and how will errors be handled?

Architecture addresses the integrity issue. Do systems talk to each other and in the same language? If not, architectural glitch or compromise may be signalled. CIP has a significant architectural feedback responsibility, informing architects (if they don't already know, and they should) of usage and integrity issues.

Finally I talk about 'unity' as being an integrity issue. Do the various IT applications represent a single unified solution? CIP contributes to this unity by ensuring that operational procedures conform to a common convention.

Durability

The robustness of applications depends to a large degree on the CIP function, once it has accepted the application into production. This begs the question of where the responsibility for maintaining application systems lies. Maintenance is a CIP responsibility. This goes against the traditional view that the 'Development' section maintains its systems. I have tried the approach of having the maintenance responsibility within the CIP environment with considerable success. Because the drivers of 'maintenance' are different from those of 'development.' Development is about extracting requirements from the business and translating those into a solution. Maintenance is about stability and efficiency. Having maintenance in CIP introduces new dynamics into the IT environment. Maintenance needs to accept systems into production. This is a laborious and often acrimonious activity, as the maintenance people refuse to accept poorly documented and error prone applications. I look upon it as an internal quality imposition, but I have had to intervene on occasion if the maintenance people insisted on a totally problem-free system. The trick is to set acceptable failure levels prior to system hand-over. Maintenance people are also concerned with performance, and track and react to performance statistics. Perhaps the trick in CIP and maintenance is to pay for stability and capacity rather than to pay for fixing things once they go wrong.

Durability obviously also includes the obvious elements of backups and contingency planning. But CIP needs to make this more than a ritual. I remember a story that was doing the rounds when I was a Facilities Manager, of the person who was responsible for taking the backup tapes to an off-site location across town every day. He was given taxi fare for the round trip, but true to human nature, he kept the fare money and travelled by underground train instead, placing the tapes at his feet on these trips. Of course the central electrical rail under the carriage wiped the tapes clean on every trip. When the disaster finally arrived, his company had no backups whatsoever. Try a dry run on your backups or disaster recovery plan. I guarantee you will find glitches. I tried exactly that, one cold winter's day. I had let my boss know, as well as our auditors that on this day, we would be testing our contingency plan. I then phoned my Facilities Manager at five in the morning and told him that there had been a gas explosion. The operations room was out of bounds, and that he was to bring up the company's entire IT infrastructure from our hot site for which we paid a monthly fee. Of course operations continued as usual from our main site, so I told him that the day's duty operators had been wiped out in the explosion. We learned a lot. We learned that it is all very well having a hot backup site, but if they don't have the operations manuals then they may as well not bother. (When the backup team phoned the real operators asking for an access code they were told: 'clear off, we're dead'.) We learned that it is good to lock the cases containing the backup tapes, but if you keep the keys in the operations room, you're going to have to buy a bolt-cutter to get into the backup tape boxes. We learned that suppliers don't keep backup manuals either. We eventually succeeded in recovering our systems in 18 hours.

So the lesson is that it's fine to have elaborate backup and contingency plans, but all of that is worthless if you don't test your durability.

12.1.2 Provide IT capacity

Performance now, and into the future, and the planning and installation of technologies (both hard and soft) are central issues. A final capacity element that often gets overlooked is the evaluation of technologies prior to being 'fitted' into the production environment. Include in this evaluation an element of 'capacity' and the scanning for new technologies which will ease the CIP processing burden.

The obvious performance criteria are those defined by your users. But it can never be as simple as that, because like all people if given an option, users will ask for the best – instant response times on systems which are permanently available. So now that we've established the principle, it is time to negotiate. Things fall back on the usual relationship circumstance. If your relationships are good ones then performance criteria will be agreed in a climate of mutual agreement and compromise. And if they are bad, then the negotiations aren't necessarily going to be more difficult, but any performance glitches will be cast in high profile for all to see. IT performance is a difficult subject and requires specialist attention. Which makes me wonder if there shouldn't be a capacity and performance specialist working in CIP? I haven't tried the idea, but it may have merit.

This person would understand performance principles standards and methods, and would analyse performance from different perspectives, particularly the user's, and offer solutions to performance problems. He or she would prepare business cases for additional capacity if this were needed. In retrospect, I would hope that your IT performance is good enough not to need such a specialist. But if your organisation depends on the performance of its IT, then there may be grounds for such a position.

Capacity represents a key part of the performance equation. Of course it is a little like those cartoon characters you see on the television who try to stop a leak in the dyke with their finger, only to have another appear somewhere else. In goes a toe. Another leak appears – you get the picture. It seemed to me that no sooner had my technical people convinced me to upgrade our network servers than they were back looking to upgrade the network lines. Once that was done, then additional processing power was needed elsewhere. The interdependencies in IT are such that any capacity plan must necessarily take the whole system into consideration. So the task of capacity planners has to be translating capacity requirements into something that general business people can understand, and something that shows as much as is known 'up front'. Surprise the person holding the purse strings and his hand will reflexively clench around those purse strings.

Capacity planning is only one of the tasks required in providing IT capacity. Monitoring capacity usage and projecting it into the future is as important. As is translating business capacity growth into IT capacity requirements. On the surface, this seems easy, but given the number of brand new systems that require an instant upgrade immediately after installation, it can't be that easy can it? Or is there something else happening? Perhaps capacity is a political issue? Or is it to do with the relationship? It would be worthwhile doing a relationship analysis whenever any IT capacity is planned, because it may lead you to identifying some political or cultural problem prior to presenting the capacity plan, and independent lobbying and discussion can often get around such roadblocks.

I suspect that why most capacity projections are toned down, or why most projects blow their budgets for that matter, relates to what I call the 'builder's quote' syndrome. Imagine that you want to build a wall at the bottom of your garden. You get various builders to quote, and because you are a wily home-owner, you give the job to the second lowest bid, knowing that the lowest bidder was probably cutting corners to get your custom. Of course, they are all cutting corners except possibly the highest quote which may be realistic. (Unfortunately, that builder never gets any work and so quickly goes out of business.) Now you might be both wily and tough, and hold the builder to his quoted figure, but the shortcuts will be there, in the less than adequate foundations, or the amount of cement in the mortar, or in the fact that he is running two jobs simultaneously to make ends meet, or that the builder puts his newly trained apprentices onto the job so that they can learn at your expense. In order for you to be on top of this situation would require you to be present all day and to have experience in brick-laying and quantity surveying, and any number of building skills. But you aren't the expert, or you would have done it yourself.

The same happens with projects and with capacity projections. The 'experts' know how much things will really cost, and know also that the business will probably not buy in, so they shave costs, cut corners, allocate cheaper resources, . . . sound familiar? And because they are the IT experts and the business is not, they tend to get away with it. The tragedy is that if the IT 'experts' were brutally honest, then they wouldn't get the job, along with their out-of-work builder mates. Capacity planners get around the problem by going for small upgrades often, rather than putting all the cards on the table for everyone to see.

Installation is also part of the capacity mélange. The provision of capacity to run business operations requires CIP to install the infrastructure that they will support. This requires the usual architectural input and technical planning, installation teams as well as good people management skills, but I want to concentrate on two areas not usually considered to be the ambit of IT or CIP. This is workplace design and ergonomics. Who better to design a workplace than the people who understand the capabilities of the technology? Workflow relates to the processes being automated and should have been dealt with by the solutions provision team (if not, there's another opportunity for the in-house IT function), but actual workplace design is another thing. These are special skills which will add value to the offering of CIPS.

12.2 No Service Level Agreements – internally we work together

I have had the misfortune of writing several Service Level Agreements. I say misfortune, because firstly I am not a detail person, secondly, the SLA is hardly in my opinion a welcomed bit of work, and thirdly they don't work. So why bother?

There is the story of an American negotiating team in China, who had concluded negotiations for a mutually beneficial joint venture in China. At the end of negotiations, the Americans got up from the table, shook hands all round, and said: 'we'll just get our lawyers to draft this agreement, and we'll get back to you soon'. The Chinese businessmen did not understand, because in their culture anything that was agreed was binding and didn't need reams of documentation to enforce it. There is also the view that says, the day you have to refer to the contract is the day the agreement is in trouble. Finally the words of Sam Goldwyn, American film producer: 'a verbal contract isn't worth the paper it is written on' provides a counterpoint to my anti-contract sentiments. Mind you, we shouldn't take Mr. Goldwyn too seriously, he also said: 'anyone who goes to a psychologist should have his head examined,' and '. . . they're always biting the hand of the goose that lays the golden egg[1].'

My basic standpoint is one of form versus function. Just because you have the outer appearances of something (form) does not mean that you have that thing (function). An example would be a customer services department. Many companies have them, but do they really have good customer service? Or because you have a Service Level Agreement does not mean your will get better, or even acceptable service? My suggestion is to focus on the function of SLAs and be less rigorous about the form, or the document or the signatures. My second perspective on SLAs develops from a deep-seated belief that when internal functions move towards a contractual slant to their relationship, then symbiosis and synergistic benefits are threatened. Mutual respect and trust suffer, and the relationship moves one step closer to antagonism. Many disagree with me on both these views, and that is their prerogative, but if I was to reframe the relationship between IT and the business, I would exclude Service Level Agreements from the frame.

I have to come back to my continued insistence on relationships. That most intimate of relationship is indeed bound by contract, but look at what causes people to get out and examine the contract – divorce. The relationship between CIP and the business should not be bound by a contract-like document. By mutual agreement certainly, but not by that dry, useless document called a Service Level Agreement. If you disagree, feel free to write down the reasons why an SLA is necessary. Then take the opportunity to reframe each of those reasons. I imagine you might come up with the following:

● clarity – everyone knows what is expected of both IT and of the users. Apart from the obvious comment that SLAs are invariably obtuse at best by their very nature in trying to cover all eventualities, I imagine a poster announcing availabilities, or user responsibilities will probably achieve a better effect;

- completeness – the whole IT service is encapsulated in one document. Personally I found that trying to capture everything that IT does on paper is exhausting and doomed to failure. (Besides which if you want to keep pace with both technological and business you will never be able to document the forward momentum of IT.) The complex nature of business is that you will never achieve completeness in documenting IT services, so you should probably try for agreement on various models of IT service and fit growth into each model;

- standards – the SLA will enforce an IT standard throughout the organisation. Right! Read the section on standards (chapter 10) to see why I don't think standards *enforce* anything. My view of standards is that they should be mutually agreed and 'sold' to those people who have to apply them. I don't see an SLA adding to this process in any way;

- cost – the SLA defines the cost, whether it be 'funny-money' transfer or merely internal departmental accounting, the cost per unit of service provided is clearly detailed. Of course the SLA doesn't actually measure the costs or manage them. Insofar as the SLA details cost elements for inclusion in the document, the process is useful, but in my experience we usually extracted these cost elements from some other accounting package. Keeping integrity between the accounting package and the SLA is always a difficulty. I would rather see management of costs as an ongoing activity and agreement around these costs as a continuous relationship management topic;

- quality – quality is defined as conformance to customer requirements and the SLA documents these requirements.

But requirements change, or should do so if the business is continuously meeting their changing customer requirements. How then is the SLA going to track these changes?

The idea behind SLAs is a good one. But the practical application seems to fall short of the idea. So I would rather suggest the following relationship-based approach:

- set up relationships with key IT users;

- propose various models of IT service based on what can be delivered, and what the requirements are. Models such as the 24×7×365 or the 18×6×350 models for availability;

- map each service to users (use models again);

- get agreement in principle for each service against each of these models;

- then don't document anything! Rather launch a marketing campaign to users and to IT staff alike communicating the agreement as it applies in each area;

- update as necessary;

- there is no reason why you should not document all the agreements in rough so that you can track agreements and possible conflicts, but this is not for public consumption, and usually takes the form of a spreadsheet or table which is constantly updated and referred to;

- whatever you do, don't get signatures.

If my thinking sounds a little radical, good. Because Service Level Agreements don't work, and something else is needed to meet the very real requirements that SLAs try to fulfil – clarity, completeness, standards, and quality of IT services in the business environment.

Finally my argument against SLAs is supported by the question: 'does any other internal department have an SLA with their business?'

12.3 Intentional tension – driving core-production

If the CIP function had their way, no-one would implement new systems into CIP's stable environment – and this is as it should be. Unfortunately new technologies and applications are figuratively 'left on their doorstep' as a matter of course in the day-to-day business of running and growing the business. I once worked with a dairy company which was very successful. As agricultural subsidies were cut, and farming costs rose, smaller dairies struggled to keep afloat. This dairy company would ride to the rescue, offer a buy-out package and would grow their own capacity by taking over the smaller company. Trouble was it took about 18 months to integrate the new dairy's computer systems into their systems, while the mother company was acquiring one new dairy per year. Clearly the IT function was losing the battle. I would like to report that they applied a few key strategies and resolved their problem, but I can't. The solution, in the end, was to rebuild the mother company's architecture from the ground up to encompass the strategic intent of constant acquisition. The tension to adopt new applications eventually won out as their legacy systems were replaced with systems that were as open as they could make them.

So to my mind, the core-production environment includes two key elements – keeping the current environment stable while adding new technologies and environments 'in flight.'

12.4 Running the CIP factory

The Core IT Production process can and should be run as a factory. This means that your CIP Manager should be familiar with two major subject areas: Information Technology and Operations Management. Operations Management includes operations design, including services, layout and flow, process technology and job design, and work organisation. Planning and control functions including capacity tracking and planning, supply chain planning and control, and quality planning and control. The area of factory operations gives us sophisticated operations improvement methods, and robust failure prevention and control mechanisms.

I am not going to go into much Operations Management detail. The purpose of this section is to prompt you to take up a text-book or two on Operations Management, and adapt and adopt their collected experience, wisdom and techniques.

The primary techniques I have found useful from the Operations Management discipline are their quality and failure management approaches.

There are five approaches you can take to quality, all of them of some validity[2]:

The transcendent approach, strives to make your quality incomparable with any other service. The manufacturing-based approach looks at the elements of the operation and makes each element as high quality as it can be. The user-based approach makes sure that the service exactly fits user requirements. The product-based approach views quality as a precise set of characteristics which must be met, and thus presumably meeting user requirements. Finally the value-based approach recognises that quality costs money, and users may accept lower quality outputs if the service costs very little. Hmm!

Statistical process control contributes various control charts which help us highlight variances in service which can lead to pre-emptive actions. Certainly normal curves can be used in terms of attributes such as response times, and moving averages plots track attributes over time pointing to degradation over time. Of course most network and system monitoring software tools should have their own built in control reporting tools and charts. The issue comes back to attitude again. Is the purpose of CIP to operate IT infrastructures and fix things when they break, or is its purpose loftier than that? Adopting a mindset which accepts the challenge of 'Providing stable IT capacity' from which to run business operations, is heading in the right direction. However, an externally focused strategically linked mindset such as 'Competitive edge through peerless operations' tends to get the blood flowing faster.

Failure tracking and correction are precise disciplines in operations management, and the CIP processes can benefit from numerous operations management tools and techniques. I have mentioned the Bathtub Curve, which tracks the history of a component or system over time. In the early stages of a systems life-cycle, the number of recorded problems is high, invariably due to programming or customisation faults, but also related to fit to user requirements. In the 'standard' life period the system meets the requirements of the user, but as time goes on, the number of problems may rise. Unlike the appliance and machinery context, in which 'late-life' failures are due to mechanical wearing out of parts, computer systems fail in later life because of loss of fit. The hardware and operating software on which the applications run lose fit with technological advances, and the number of problems increases as the old system interfaces with increasingly complex new technologies. There is also a loss of fit problem with business requirements. The commercial world has moved on, and patches need to be made to the application to accommodate

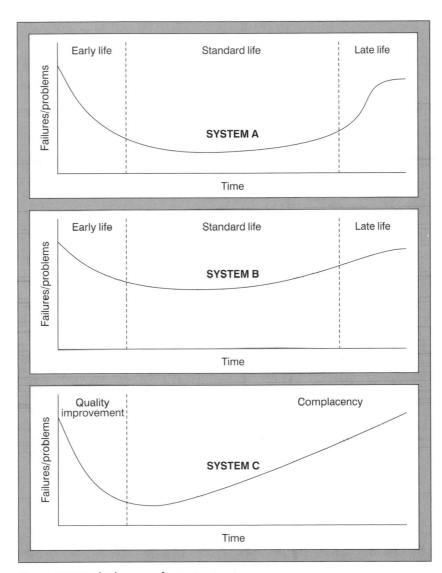

Figure 12.2 Bathtub curves for various systems

these business changes. Invariably the problem count will rise, even if the 'problem' is that the system cannot perform a function now required by the business.

System A follows the path I described, and it will be relatively easy to motivate for an upgrade or replacement. System B is more troublesome. It never really settled down. The system has always been difficult to maintain, and replacement will be either difficult or easy to motivate, depending on whether the CIP facility has tracked the total cost of ownership of the system. System C is another case altogether, and is sadly generally true of systems with a high people input. A period of high profile concentration on the system reduces the problems associated with it, but as time continues and boredom and complacency creeps in, or people's attention is diverted elsewhere, the problem count rises. The question I raise is how will you take pre-emptive action if you don't track the stability record of a system over time.

Other operations failure concepts worth examination include component reliability factoring, in which each component's reliability is tracked, and the multiplication of the reliability factors of all components in the system gives you an indication of the total reliability of the system. Concepts such as 'mean time between failure' (MTBF) which tracks how long the system is stable, and 'mean time to repair' (MTTR), the time taken to repair a problem give you an indication of availability. The equation is simple:

Availability = MTBF/(MTBF + MTTR)

In a system in which failures seldom occur, and repair time is quick, the availability will of course be high. But if the system often fails or takes a long time to restore, some attention will have to be given to the robustness of the system. A special case of 'system needs attention', and it is the chief headache of many CIP personnel: a system in which there are critical availability periods, usually month-end processing systems, can exhibit a high availability even though they fail every month. This of course is a definition problem, and the mid-month processing period probably needs to be separated from the month-end processing time. Such availability figures will probably be instructive.

Many CIP operations appear to skate from one crisis to another, seldom slowing down to analyse why they have to skate so fast. The problem seems to be created by two factors: staffing levels, and the culture and attitude of the CIP function. If CIP exists to 'make as few mistakes as possible' its response to problems will differ significantly from a culture of: 'sustain business superiority through operational advantage.' The former culture will fix a problem and move on, the latter will regard fixing a problem as the first stage in making sure that it never occurs again. Most of the latter's efforts will be relationship and preventative action-based.

Again, CIP can learn something about failure analysis from the Operations Management discipline. Failure mode and effect analysis identifies the causes of failure ahead of time and applying corrective action prior to failure. Other failure analysis tools include fault tree analysis, flowcharting, scatter diagrams, fish-bone diagrams, Pareto diagrams, and the 'five why' technique, in which the question 'Why?' is asked repeatedly until the cause of the problem (rather than various symptoms) is rooted out for preventative action.

Workflow analysis is a further operations management discipline which can add value to CIP services. This technique helps you design jobs around the IT component of the work. IT intensive jobs can be significantly eased if someone were to take the time to analyse the workflow and suggest improvements. And who is to do it? There is merit in CIP accepting the workflow, and indeed the ergonomic design mantle as part of their responsibility for installing new infrastructures and technologies.

Running CIP like a factory does not mean that it is a factory. It is an IT environment, but the learning that IT people can derive from tried and tested disciplines such as Operations Management will set them apart from the work hard, work late, fix it when it breaks, and feel unappreciated brigade of Facilities staff. Go the extra mile, look beyond IT for help and ideas.

12.5 In-house or out-house?

These days it seems that outsourcing defines the rule of the day for IT. It makes some sort of sense I suppose. Certainly the vendors of outsource services are very convincing. Their argument usually revolves around specialisation and economy of scale: if the core business of the outsource provider is IT service provision, and they have extensive capacity that they can leverage, then surely both the quality will go up and the costs will go down. However, researchers have found that the success of outsourcing is less than certain[3]: they found that in 15 companies that had outsourced more than 80% of their IT budget, only two considered the exercise a success. However, these researchers did find that partial outsourcing was much more successful.

Warren McFarlan, Professor of Business Administration at Harvard Business School outlined the drivers for outsourcing and the risks associated with outsourcing[4] (see Table 1).

It is apparent that there are significant pros (particularly in the mind of the vendor) to outsourcing as there are cons to the endeavour. The bottom line has to be: know why you are outsourcing and manage the risks.

The choice about outsourcing is a company one and there is no reason why an in-house IT function cannot provide the same value added services at cost competitive rates, as most outsourcers. The emphasis should be on value added rather than cost though. A CIP function with strong relationships with the business can add value in numerous ways. Firstly they can

Table 12.1
Drivers and
risks of
outsourcing

IT Outsourcing Drivers	Risks in IT Outsourcing
Frustration over IT costs and response time	Loss of control
Breakdown of IT performance	Cost savings not there
Intense vendor pressure	Vendor stability wavers
Simplify management agenda	Contract flexibility
Financial issues – Balance sheet and fixed variable costs	Conversion complexity
Unfreezing corporate culture	Interface to management poorly conceived
Access to quality staff in critical mass	Benefit timing mismatch

shortcut so much interaction that with a formal outsource arrangement they would have to go through more rigid and impersonal channels. Secondly their deep knowledge of the business means they can be on the lookout for business specific IT opportunities. There are many other value-add areas – they just need identifying and active promotion.

There are many sources of information on outsourcing, and the criteria that should guide your choice of what to outsource and to whom. Look them up long before the decision is taken. I can only offer my small addition to the debate: don't sell the farm Wilbur! Or at least don't sell the bits that matter. Don't try to 'in-source' either. Rather follow the internal value-add approach. Find the areas in which an internal function can add value over an external function and concentrate on those. Of course you have to get the nuts and bolts of CIP right as well.

It seems to me that one of the primary reasons why in-house IT functions don't manage to compete with outsource companies has nothing to do with specialisation and economies of scale, and everything to do with the need to conform to the mother company's personnel systems. Salaries must be banded according to some scientifically fair and levelling system. Career paths must conform to the Human Resources map. Well now. IT people don't fit into bands (unless it's a Dixie Band). The systems which cater for the masses hold back the exceptional workers, and in order to compete with outsourcers you need exceptional workers. (See 'Hourglass organisation', page 326.) If you must in-source then the negotiations should focus on value added benefits, capped costs, and in this case Service Level Agreements – because now the relationship moves to being contractual. *What is not up for negotiation is how your people will be paid, how you will organise or any 'how' questions.* The 'what' questions must be brought to the fore. If the business wants to dictate the how, break off the negotiation – it's not going to work.

The chances of in-sourcing success are limited. It would have to be an unusual company that allows a department to 'split off' and continue to provide services to itself. The effect on the culture of the mother company needs to be taken into account: 'did you hear that IT are paying their people twice as much as us?' is a very real concern for the mother company. And when IT start arriving in non-regulation dress/vehicles/mindsets the trouble is compounded. The organisation cannot generally afford to have such apparently incompatible behaviour within its ranks, because of their need to treat people 'fairly'. I worked with one such organisation that turned all its functions into cost centres. IT was no different and duly began pricing all its services. I was brought in to help them conceive a strategy to get their users to pay for IT 'attending user meetings, offering advice, researching IT and maintaining the user/IT relation-ship.' All of these were hidden costs of IT while they were an internal department. Their problem was of course that they hadn't factored in these indirect costs into the pricing of their tangible services. When they did, there was an uproar amongst their users. Finally agreement was reached on the cost issue, but still the in-sourcing exercise was in trouble. The problem was that IT remained on the mother company's payroll. And the mother company was (and still is), a mining group, which pays traditionally at the lower end of the scale. The problem was that IT wanted to attract top-quality people, and couldn't do so because of the pay-scale issue. They also ran into problems with many other bureaucracy factors. Eventually the mother com-pany sold off its IT to an industry outsource provider. It requires a brave company to in-source its IT because this former internal department will now cost more than they had anticipated, will become somewhat fixated on charging for everything and will need to have its own payroll, benefits packages and culture.

So if outsourcing everything is a mistake and in-sourcing is not destined for glory then what is the answer. True to all issues, the answer is a hybrid of both extremes. Some authors have called this the 'federal organisation', but it's less federal and more about dividing not only labour but interests. The functions which are in the interests of the organisation, are fit for purpose applications and the quality performance of the IT infra-structure. The fit for purpose element of the requirement calls for an effective translation of business needs into IT services, and effective use by the business of the IT capacity that is available. Into the quality equation go the cost, efficiency and conformance to requirements of the IT infrastructure. This translates into an in-house IT function which provides IT leadership to the business, identifies IT opportunities and translates these opportunities into a requirements document. They source providers of IT services, brief them and provide the business input. They monitor and manage what is delivered. If you want, they are the IT agents of the business. Now the question of outsourcing, or 'in-sourcing' becomes more viable. And you can afford to spin off your Development and Facilities Management functions, among others, allowing them not only to develop their own culture and style. But they can even find new clients if they want. But unless you have in-house IT people who act on behalf of the business in managing these outsourced functions, don't bother.

Over and above this new IT leadership and outsource management function, there is one function which should never be outsourced. Architecture. With its pivotal role in interpreting business and IT trends and matching them in a versatile framework it is an essential element of any organisation. I also think architecture plays a daily role within the organisation with its 30 second messages and its position papers. Finally, if IT is to provide leadership, it had better be architecturally-sound leadership. I worked with a company whose CIO practised 'magazine management'. The man was a technology freak of the first order. He travelled the world, researching new technologies, and bringing them home with nary a thought for architectural fit. He wasted millions, but because his company was technologically naïve and he had an eloquent way with words, his behaviour went unchecked. Eventually he made a technological purchase of such prodigious ineptitude that he was removed from his post. (I believe he has now set himself up as an IT consultant.) Architecture is a strategic force in IT and the organisation, is a unifying agency, and is a key information provider on a daily basis. Don't sell this part of the farm Wilbur!

12.6 Creating a self-organising core IT production facility

I have done some thinking around how to create a self-organising CIP facility. If one was to view the CIP function as a complex adaptive system, then we would have to answer the three questions:

- what is the driving purpose of CIP's existence?
- what few rules will CIP live or die by?
- what will the CIP environment look like?

In selecting a driving purpose, you will have to refer to some benchmark, whether it is to provide unsurpassed service or to stop making mistakes. You will need to choose a benchmark, examine what you will have to do to get there, look at the costs (both financial and personal) that must be borne, then go for it.

Some of the rules that you might choose include 'prevention rather than cure', or 'nobody rests when there's a problem' or 'CIP is a zero defect factory', or something like that. You are looking for fractal rules – these are rules that when multiplied by themselves create complex responses to environmental stimuli. I came across a simple rule the other day that was designed to help a CIP function tighten up on its internal processes, but ended up creating something significantly more. The rule is 'wasted time wastes everything'. They began to look upon anything that was not directed at production as time wasting. They started with small things like time spent messing with a stapler which had run out of staples. Time wasted on unnecessary bureaucracy. Time wasted filling out forms when things could be done online. They moved on to viewing problems as time wasters – both for themselves and for the business. And so on. It took a short while, but the time rule which was designed to focus people on niggling inefficiencies ended up creating a general efficiency culture, and then went beyond that to create a pre-emptive culture.

The final complex adaptive component is the environment in which CIP interactions take place. It seems that there is a two edged sword in the CIP function: the cobbler's children go unshod, but they don't like wearing shoes anyway. The people with access to so much technology, seem to use very little on themselves. Some CIP staff seem to revel in the 'arms buried up to the elbows in wiring' mindset. Unless they are working in the guts of the machine, they are not working. There is often an oversight with respect to what hardware and software is available to manage the CIP environment. But I have also seen CIP environments where it is a matter of pride that they have all the latest monitoring and testing gear, but are not using it to significantly improve the production environment. The trick is to enable the CIP environment with the necessary hardware and software, but then to insist on seeing direct links between these tools and CIP performance.

Another CIP environmental factor relates to a song in the movie 'Fame'. The song is called 'The Body Electric' and has nothing to do with IT. But 'The Body Electric' has everything to do with CIP. I talked earlier about the help-desk outsource facility that made the leap of insight by recognising that every piece of equipment connected to the network was connected to the network. This places enormous pre-emptive power in the hands of CIP if they choose to use it. Remote diagnostics, remote operations, remote fixes and problem resolution, and remote software management are among the few things that CIP can harness. They can move from a 'react to problems' mentality to a 'pre-empt' problems mentality. But it does require a mindset shift. I have seen numerous operators sitting behind their consoles, with error messages scrolling across the screen. When I ask what the problem is their answer is always something like: 'oh that always happens' or 'yes we know about that, we'll get someone to look at it'. The mindset shift required is that every error message is a signal from the connected electronic body that something needs action. Deal with error messages and warning notifications as if they are real, because they are.

So if the CIP function has a compelling purpose, a few fractal rules and an environment that enables proactive operations, you might be well positioned to create a CIP environment that reacts to its environment in surprising and adaptive ways.

Implementation ideas

1 Conduct a user survey to assess the organisation's perception of the quality of CIP service you provide. Enrol a few users to design it and use their words and perceptions of the CIP environment. Pilot the user survey first, and refine it if necessary.

2 Develop a set of metrics for stability: availability, integrity and durability. And metrics for capacity as well.

3 Look into hiring a capacity and performance specialist based on the ideas presented in this chapter.

4 Consider including workplace design and ergonomics in your installation team's set of skills.

5 Follow the approach to SLAs set out in this chapter.

6 Look for the value-add in CIP. Yes we know the role of CIP is to provide stable capacity. But what else? Because that's what differentiates an in-house CIP function from an outsourced function. If you can't find any value-added benefits to the business which are real, then outsource your CIP function.

References

1. Goldwyn, S. (1992) *The Oxford Dictionary of Quotations.* Oxford University Press, Oxford
2. Pycraft, M. et al. (1997) *Operations Management.* Pitman Publishing, London

3. Lacity, M.C., Willcocks, L.P. and Feeny, D.F. (1995) IT Outsourcing: maximise flexibility and control. *Harvard Business Review,* May/June
4. McFarlan, F.W. (1995) Strategic Outsourcing, the management agenda. In: *Index Review,* Fourth Quarter 1995, CSC Index, Cambridge, MA

13 Thinking ahead – new strategy processes

Why leave strategy until so late in the book? Normally the order of an IT book would include strategy right after the introduction. I have left strategy so late because of three things: firstly almost no-one will be reading this from a start-up situation. They have current realities that need to be dealt with. I remember a paper I read in the early 1980s that talked about what new managing directors and presidents do when they take over an organisation. I have tried to find the original reference but without success, so the following diagram (Figure 13.1) is based on my imperfect memory.

As you can see when a manager comes into a new position, their first change is invariably a small one based on putting out existing fires or dealing with pressing problems. But they then need a period of between 6 and 18 months to investigate the root drivers of the organisation, and only then do they make the radical strategic shift that everyone has been expecting from day one. Of course this is a vast generalisation, but I have seen it happen this way enough times to allow it to guide me. Strategy emerges from an increased understanding of the environment.

Secondly it is too easy to get into strategy and stay there. A very small percentage of the success of any organisation is based on having a good strategy. It is true that this percentage is an

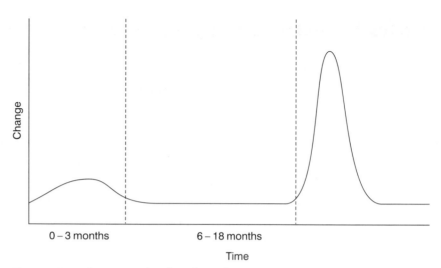

Figure 13.1 What CEOs do when they take over

essential percentage, without which few companies will survive, but the proof of a strategy is its execution. The clarity of thought, the commitment to spend time, money and energy on what is necessary, the courage to meet the difficulties and not withdraw to safe ground, and the resolve to continue when things look bleak. These are issues of discipline and execution and not of strategy formulation. As Michael Porter says[1]:

> Strategic planning in most companies has not contributed to strategic thinking. ... Few have transferred strategic planning into the vital management discipline it needs to be.
>
> (Porter, 1987)

Finally I place the strategy section so late in the book because strategy builds on knowledge. Perhaps all strategy sections should be placed at the end of books, otherwise how are readers going to include the thinking imparted in the book into their strategy?

13.1 Information management scenarios

My thoughts on strategy are guided by two linked concepts: Henry Mintzberg[2] introduced the world to the concept of emergent strategy or 'real' strategy, in which analysing the behaviour of the organisation gives you clear indicators about what to build on and what to stop. He points out that even in a perfect world there is a delay between the time the strategy is crafted, and the time that the strategy emerges. And in this delay we can find the real strategic drivers of the organisation. Peter Schwartz[3] describes the power of scenario-planning which allowed Royal Dutch/Shell to enter the energy crisis occasioned by the Yom Kippur war in 1973 as one of the weakest of the seven global oil companies, only to emerge in second place after the crisis. Finally, using scenario planning is an essential leadership role in a complex adaptive system. The strategic role of the leader in complex adaptive systems is to see the world as it really is (emergent strategy) and as it could be (scenario thinking) and to communicate that thinking clearly to the rest of the organisation. Finally Hamel and Prahalad[4] remind us that 40–50% of a leader's time should be spent looking forwards and outwards and discussing what they see in the organisational community. And the same has to be true of the Chief Information Officer. He or she should be looking outward and forward with the essential support of their architect, interpreting what may occur, communicating what he or she sees to the organisation, and readying the IT function to move in the right direction should it be useful or necessary.

Peter Schwartz describes scenario planning as:

> . . . a tool for ordering one's perceptions about alternative future environments in which one's decisions might be played out. Alternatively: a set of organized ways for us to dream effectively about our own future. . . . This approach

is more a disciplined way of thinking than a formal methodology.

(Schwartz, 1991)

I like Schwartz' thinking because it fits so well with my perception of the role of the leader. His or her job is to interpret the world in a disciplined way, and to tell stories about the future and the organisation's place in that future. But these are stories, designed to prepare people for possibilities which, had the story not been told, might leave people emotionally unprepared to meet the new challenge. Many tales can be told of companies that slipped when they refused to recognise the changing circumstances in the competitive environment. But as Schwartz says:

> Scenarios are not predictions. It is simply not possible to predict the future with certainty. An old Arab proverb says that: 'he who predicts the future lies even when he tells the truth.' Rather, scenarios are vehicles for helping us learn. . . . they present alternative images.
>
> (Schwartz, 1991)

Obviously there isn't space to give you all the thinking behind scenario planning, but here are the steps that Schwartz advises you to follow:

● the scenario building person – Schwartz suggests that some people will naturally take to building scenarios: people who can handle uncertainty, or people who have made mistakes will understand the idea of different realities more easily than those whose disciplines require accuracy and exactness like accountants and engineers (and IT people). These latter people focus on history and 'right and wrong', and so they should. Schwartz points out that they will need more practice in seeing possibilities without needing to know if they are real, or correct. Let them remain possibilities;

- what decisions await – look years into the future to see what major decisions loom in your future which will affect your performance, or investments or relationships. Then examine what questions you should be asking that will help in making these decisions. These decisions are usually buried in the subconscious and will require some teasing out. Not only that, but there is often discomfort in confronting the decisions so some assertive tact will be necessary if they are to be surfaced;

- information – scenarios will only work if they are based on real world observations. The scenario must 'ring true' to people, rather than be some dream sequence that may or may not have any grounding in reality. Therefore Schwartz proposes that you need to gather information from the following sources – science and technology, perception-shaping events, music (which expresses the feelings of people), fringe elements (tomorrow's leader may be today's edge-dwellers), and many other unexpected sources of information that can tell you about what's happening in the real world;

- the building blocks – identify the driving forces of your organisation, the things that move the plot of the scenario. Look in society, technology, economics, politics and the environment for the forces that shape them. Find out what you know. Look at past trends and see what they have unfailingly predicted, then base your scenarios on what these predetermine. Identify the critical uncertainties in your scenario. The assumptions that you will have to track to forecast the trends;

- tell a story – all good stories have a plot. You need to describe what you know, what the driving forces are and how they might behave and then sketch out alternative scenarios based on different behaviours. A story plot has characters propelled by motives which create a set of circumstances with a tension caused by this interaction. The motives are the driving forces. The tensions are the factors that will affect the future of your organisation.

Scenarios will only work if people listen. The aim of scenarios is not to predict the future, rather it is to enable better decisions. You need to capture people's attention, both while you are telling the story, and after. You need to create a tension that will inform decisions. You need the plot to be simple enough to follow, but real enough to resonate with the truth.

Schwartz writes a compelling book, in which he explains the brief sketch that I have attempted here in more detail and depth, and if you are serious about scenario thinking, you will read his work.

13.2 Compiling the IT strategy

We don't live in a world in which we can merely develop scenarios and wait for our strategy to emerge. We do need to have a plan. One that is visible, well considered and to which capital can be allocated with some confidence:

> . . . the strategic thinker has to be able to create a process that attracts support, leads to action and results in superior organisational performance[5].
>
> (Thurbin, 1998)

A strategy must be an animated narration – it must be energetic rather than dull if it is to attract support, and it must move as strategic factors change, and in line with scenario thinking it must have a plot and story-line. Therefore stay away from the thick bound volumes which only get put on the shelf anyway, and rather develop a strategy as a series of linked slides in a hypertext document which allows the reader to follow their own logic, but to get into supporting detail if necessary. With web authoring tools and data projection and intranet technology being where it is, there is no reason to have a static bland strategy document ever again. And if you have to present the strategy, try to be interesting about it. I have seen many strategies suffer 'death by overhead projection', as dull technologists exhaust their audience into numb acceptance merely so they can get out of the room alive.

Your strategy should start with a stakeholder analysis.[6] A stakeholder is someone who is involved in some way in the fortunes of the organisation. This includes the obvious stakeholders such as equity shareholders, banks and investors, employees and customers. But think beyond the usual. Your competitors are stakeholders as are your suppliers. Government, families of employees, professional bodies, alliance partners, unions, market analysts, and the environment represent stakeholders in your organisation. Stakeholders in IT are all or some of the above, but also there are internal stakeholders such as the board of directors, management, individual departments, IT vendors, outsource partners, contractors, power users, innovators, R&D, . . . the list can be long. But it's worth doing the stakeholder analysis, even if it's to identify those stakeholders who are important and those who are not. You needn't take action for each stakeholder group, but you will find that if your strategy is animated, you will be constantly referring to these groupings to think through how a particular event affects them.

A stakeholder analysis involves more than just listing groups of people, it requires that you analyse the tangible and intangible contributions of each stakeholder to the organisation. You also need to identify the values and beliefs of each group. And most importantly you need to identify how these stakeholders see and measure your performance.

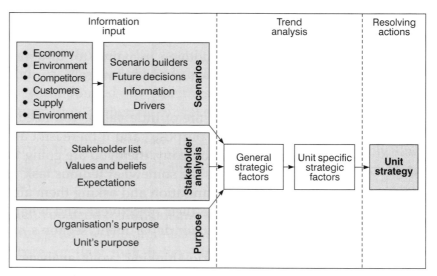

Figure 13.2 The IT strategy formulation process

the future . . . Strategy is made up of tough key decisions to make in the next six to 12 months that will cast a long shadow.

(Merton, 1994)

The levels of freedom in IT strategic planning depend very much on the strategic planning *modus operandi* of the mother company. It makes sense that an alignment factor for IT to consider relates to strategy formulation as much as anything else. I like the model developed by Gluck, Kaufmann and Walleck[10] which although it was developed in 1980, still helps us understand how the mode of strategy formulation fits the maturity of the organisation (Figure 13.3).

The strategy formulation mode that I've assumed in the 'gather information – extract trends – resolve actions' model probably fits well within the third stage of the Glick et al. model. But ideally scenario planning and complex adaptive systems move organisations towards the fourth stage of the model.

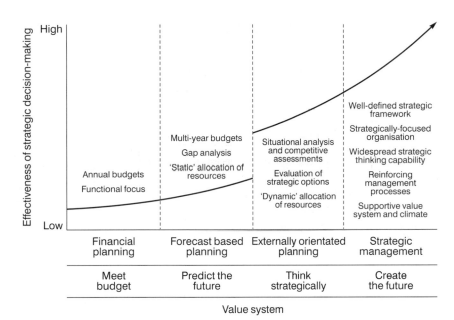

Figure 13.3 Gluck, Kaufmann and Walleck's model describing maturity of strategic planning in organisations

13.3 Strategy as a complex adaptive system

A complex adaptive system allows many interactions between factors or agents based on a few simple rules in order to create a system of advanced and intricate responsiveness. What then propels such a system? As usual it must be the vision, or driving purpose of the whole organisation. If the vision is clear and unambiguous, it informs every person working for the organisation what to do both now and in the future.

The fractal rules governing the strategic system must surely be based on the three strategic steps. Everyone gathers information, everyone interprets the gathered information, and everyone contributes to resolving what is to be done. Add to the information gathering environment the stories and plots derived from scenarios developed by the leadership and you're heading for a sophisticated strategic environment. In truly mature complex adaptive strategies, everyone just does the right strategically aligned thing based on the information available, the trends analysed and the scenarios identified and told.

This sounds chaotic and it is. But there is no reason why you can't set up the environment in which these rules can take force. Obviously you will need some form of knowledge management environment. There is a need to help employees act appropriately by filtering information and providing it to them at the right place, at the correct time and in the correct format. Further environmental actions in a strategic system require that leaders manage meaning and attention: 'what does the driving purpose mean? What does this or that trend mean for us?' And the management of attention requires that people in the business focus on strategically important activities, and stop focusing on strategically obsolete ideas and activities.

What is a complex adaptive strategic system aiming at? It seeks to provide a constant response to environmental and competitive forces. It seeks to move away from the concept that 'strategy' is an activity that is done by a group of senior people and which is communicated to the masses once the strategy is set. Everyone strategises. It seeks to remove the gap between strategy, tactics and operations by providing enough important information to everyone so that all their actions are strategically aligned.

Complex adaptive strategic systems are just that – complex, and constantly adjusting environments aligned with the strategic goals of the organisation.

13.4 Implementation

The final word on strategy must be on implementation. I have seen strategies developed and sit there like a loaded gun. And then nothing happens. Executive courage fails, or the cynical middle management of companies sabotage the strategy to serve their own purposes. But the most insidious underminer of strategy is what I call 'goal creep'. You've heard of scope creep, in which a goal is set and incremental additions to the work to be done result in the missing of the time and cost deadlines. Goal creep is a tad less obvious and is to do with compromise. The most successful leaders I know of set a target and do not compromise on the way to it. Invariably they make themselves unpopular in the process, but the results justify their attitude. Goal creep happens in organisations which are not culturally prepared to take the pain that comes with change. I read somewhere the statement: 'if you always do what you've always done, you're going to always get what you've always got'. The converse of this is more appropriate to make the goal creep argument: 'to get something different, you have to do something different.' And doing things differently in mature organisations is the old pushing the stone up the hill story. Change is painful. People don't like it. So to avoid the pain, we compromise on the strategy, saying something like: 'I know we said we'd have a PC on everyone's desk, but the outlay is too much. A PC on every second desk should suffice.' Similar goal creep statements like: 'putting every team leader through project management training is going to be impossible, so let's introduce a train-the-trainer process' or 'these improvement meetings are taking too long, let's schedule them for every second week.' On the surface there's not a lot wrong with these statements. But they are an example of interactions such as this that are happening throughout the organisation. What then happens is the goal becomes: 'a PC on every second desk', and a 'train-the-trainer' programme, and 'improvement meetings every second week'. Do you see what has happened? The goals have crept backwards towards the current situation. And in two years' time you look back at all these relapsed goals and wonder how you could have spent so much time and money for so little to have changed.

Avoiding goal creep requires that you have done your strategic thinking properly and that you then become unreasonable about attaining those strategic goals.

Implementation ideas

1 Read Peter Schwartz' book: *The Art of the Long View.*[11] Then go one step further – take action. Identify a team of scenario builders. Identify the big decisions that await both the organisation and IT. Gather information. Divine the driving forces. Build a plot or story. Tell the story.

2 Run a two-day strategy workshop:

I always use a divergence/convergence process when I strategise (see Figure 13.4). It forces two important things into the act of creating a strategy: the discipline to not jump to the answer (especially the first, obvious answer), and it allows you to move from the general to the specific.

This works best as a two-day workshop. Get some wise people together. Make sure that the first day is spent in the

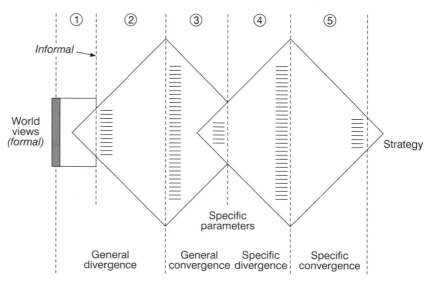

Figure 13.4 The divergence/convergence process for developing strategy

general, in the world and in the organisation, but not in IT. At the start the 'world view' is presented. This is all the information that you and others have gathered which relates to your understanding of the world and of your organisation. It is important that at this point there is no debate. This is exceptionally difficult. Everyone has an opinion (and if you're me, you have three opposing opinions all at the same time!). Brainstorming is a hugely difficult activity. Firstly everyone has to engage their brains, but is not allowed to use that brain for anything other than generation of ideas. The critical, judgemental facility that we have all been blessed/cursed with in our Western logical upbringing should be switched off. And this is where the discipline is required. The aim of this portion of the process is to have everyone get their view of the world onto the table *without* discussion.

Stage 2 of the process is to focus the thinking of Stage 1. Now debate is encouraged. You are looking for themes which relate to the general environment. Slowly you'll find that a pattern emerges. Document it – these are the overriding drivers of your strategy.

Now stop. At Stage 3 you need to start from a fresh base. And the best way to be fresh is to sleep on it. That's why I recommend that you do this in a two day workshop. Now is the time, once you have extracted the world and your organisation's strategic themes to put it all aside, think and talk about something else. On sessions I have facilitated, this now involves an evening of dinner, or some diversion. I have great belief in the power of the subconscious, and this is the time that the subconscious works for you.

In the morning with everyone fresh and rested, the themes distilled from yesterday are re-examined, and now a new divergence begins. Keeping in mind all the rules of divergence you now work around the question: 'knowing what we know, what is the possible IT treatment of the factors?' Again allow ideas to flow. Don't judge. There is a new rule however, which emphasises the role IT plays in the themes. Depending on the IT strength of the workshop group, I will often use a loosening up presentation on IT trends, before launching the brainstorming session.

Go through the divergence and convergence process again and distil the strategic themes for IT at the end of the day.

References

1. Porter, M.E. (1987) The state of strategic thinking. *The Economist*, 23 May
2. Mintzberg, H. (1994) *The Rise and Fall of Strategic Planning*. Prentice Hall
3. Schwartz, P. (1991) *The art of the long view: planning for the future in an uncertain world*: Currency & Doubleday, New York
4. Hamel, G. and Prahalad, C.K. (1994) *Competing for the Future*. Harvard Business School Press
5. Thurbin, P.J. (1998) *The influential strategist. Using the power of paradox in strategic thinking*. Financial Times, Pitman Publishing
6. Thurbin, P.J. (1998) *The Influential Strategist. Using the Power of Paradox in Strategic Thinking*. Financial Times/Pitman Publishing
7. Stewart, T.A. (1996) A refreshing change, vision statements that make sense. *Fortune Magazine* 30 September 1996
8. Stewart, T.A. (1996) A refreshing change, vision statements that make sense. *Fortune Magazine*, 30 September 1996
9. Merten, A. (1994) In: The myth of long term planning, Allen E. Alter. *Computerworld*. October 17, 1994; Vol. 28 No. 42
10. Gluck, F.W., Kaufmann, S.P. and Walleck, A.S. (1980) Strategic Management for Competitive Advantage. *Harvard Business Review*, July/August 1980
11. Schwartz, P. (1991) *The Art of the Long View: Planning for the Future in an Uncertain World*. Currency and Doubleday, New York

14 The new IT people

In Chapter 2, I asked the question: 'what if farmer Brown's cows were free to go where they would best be looked after?' And suggested that if workers had perfect knowledge of the employment market and could communicate freely with those offering the best work, then surely we should have to manage our people differently. Perhaps the comparison between IT workers and cattle is unfortunate, but possibly only from a worker's point of view. You might judge your organisation to be closer to farmer Brown than is comfortable after considering all the things you should be doing to manage your IT workers appropriately. Because your IT staff do have access to greener pastures. There is a vast industry directed specifically at enticing IT people to greener pastures. This industry has seen the web as their prime vehicle of enticement because IT people are all web-proficient. It is possible, in the space of a few hours of web-surfing to identify numerous job opportunities, compare packages and benefits and apply for the choice positions. There is a shift in power that most people haven't appreciated yet. The power is shifting rapidly from the employers into the hands of the worker. Gaining knowledge is easy for individuals, gaining access to jobs is easier, heralding the rise of the proletariat mercenaries – people who sell their labour, but know the value of what they are selling.

Business, with their confused meddling with people's security and self-worth, is not blameless in provoking this rise in individual power.

14.1 The new psychological contract

It is confusing and exasperating for people. While being told that 'people are our greatest asset' cost cutting, mergers, re-engineering, downsizing, and general belt-tightening are re-casting people as 'our most expendable asset'. And when the message differs from the actions, people respond to the actions[1]. And the apparent betrayal of employees in being told one thing while actions communicate quite the opposite, leave them feeling angry and helpless. Add to this milieu the paradoxical programmes to enlist the support and loyalty of employees into self-managed teams, quality improvement programmes, and customer focused perform-ance drives and you have a recipe for more than confusion and exasperation, you have a blueprint for depression and anger.

> The downsizing, delayering and other changes that have occurred in many work organizations have meant that the deal, or psychological contract, that many employees felt that they had with their organization has been broken. Some people feel a strong sense of injustice about this. To the extent that they can, they are likely to reduce their contribution to their organization both in terms of their own work performance and other 'good citizen' behaviours such as helping others and attending functions on behalf of their employer[2].
>
> (Arnold et al., 1998)

The psychological contract is the implicit agreement between employer and employee that each party has certain responsibili-ties: the organisation offers security of employment, career development, and training. The employee offers commitment and conformance and loyalty. But:

> The deal many employees thought they had with their employer has turned out to be worth less than the paper it wasn't written on.[3]
>
> (Arnold et al., 1998)

If loyalty and security and mutual respect are waning factors in the new work relationship, then there will be a new psychological contract based on a totally different set of criteria. These criteria will be shaped by expediency rather than trust, which is a pity. And employees will drive the conditions of the contract. However, I must stress that this holds true for the first-world in which competent and trained technical, management and service workers are in demand. In the third world the shoe is definitely on the other foot, and ruthless exploitation of hapless workers will continue.

An 'I will look after myself' attitude will dominate the relationship from now on. The employee-employer contract will also become more short-term focused, based on work assignments rather than jobs.

William Bridges, author of *Jobshift – How to prosper in a workplace without jobs*[4] has encapsulated the new rules of the employment contract as follows:

- ongoing employment will depend on the success of the employer (and the linkages will be obvious and direct);

- workers must continuously demonstrate value to their employer;

- workers must see themselves as outsource suppliers for their allocated assignments;

- employers will offer few, if any, 'benefits' like sick-leave, pensions, healthcare, training, etc.;

- workers will have to develop their own careers, and provide for themselves in sickness and retirement;

- the nature of work will switch from jobs and roles to assignment teams. Therefore workers must be able to quickly switch their focus;

- workers will also switch from organisation to organisation more readily. Long term employment is a thing of the past;

- workers will manage their own attitudes and behaviours. Employers will only measure results.

These new rules sound harsh and they are indeed. The traditional paternalistic relationship with employers is over, and workers will have to come of age, taking full responsibility for themselves. A number of employers have initiated programmes to help employees make this transition. In general these programmes are called 'employee resilience' programmes. The dictionary describes a resilient person as someone who readily recovers from shock, depression, etc. We're in for a rough ride.

14.2 What motivates IT people

Mahen Tampoe analysed what motivates knowledge workers[5] and found that personal growth (34%), operational autonomy (31%) and task achievement (28%) came in as the major motivators of knowledge workers. Money (7%) came in a poor fourth as a motivator. But we're talking about a class of employees who continue to be in demand worldwide and therefore their salaries are usually higher than other workers, so money probably enjoys its relatively lowly position as a motivator because it's not a problem.

Other researchers[6] find a similar order of motivators although their list is more extensive than Tampoe's:

Table 14.1
Motivators of IT
people

Motivation Factor	
The Work Itself	1
Opportunity for Achievement	2
Opportunity for Advancement	3
Pay and Benefits	4
Recognition	5
Increased Responsibility	6
Quality of Supervision	7
Interpersonal Relations with Peers	8
Job Security	9
Working Conditions	10
Company Policies	11

So the work and achievement ethic predominate amongst knowledge workers, while security and company conditions leave them cold. This bodes well for the new rules in the psychological contract, in that it is a performance focused 'adult to adult' relationship which assumes that the individual will look after him- or herself. The definition of the assignment to be performed, the clarification of the performance expected and the provision of the tools and environment to do the work is about all the average IT professional is looking for.

14.3 Remunerating IT people

Professor Erik Brynjolfsson of the Center for Coordination Science at the Massachusetts Institute of Technology did some interesting work[7] in 1994 in which he used an economic theory to predict where relationships between IT people and business would go in the future. The work is interesting in what he predicted from the model but the basis of the model itself is also worth examining, because it predicts the basis of pay and reward systems in the information economy. It also allows us to better understand the relationship dynamics between IT and businesses in general.

Brynjolfsson uses the work of Grossman, Hart, and Moore[8,9] in what he calls the GHM theory of incomplete contracts, to predict the role of IT people in future organisations, and the role of those organisations in co-ordinating and distributing information.

The GHM theory of incomplete contracts deals with the relationship between the principal (or owner of the business) and the agent (or someone hired by the owner to do some form of work). Standard principal-agent theory says that the principal must provide some incentive to the agent for his work. Normally this takes the form of a salary. But if the agent does more or different work in his allotted time, should he be able to claim more salary? The obvious answer is no. And the agent is often disgruntled by the amount of work he does that is not 'paid for.' Conversely, should the principal pay less salary to someone who doesn't work very hard at all? Again the answer is no, and the principal has every right to feel cheated. So the principal-agent theory suggests that fair payment is possible if it is based on outputs and outcomes, much like a salesman would receive a commission based on sales. But because the salesman must still do administrative work, and other non-sales related work associated with the company, he very often gets a salary and a commission. This is because there is no way that work is just sales, or marketing, or programming or anything. It is always a hybrid of activities. A pure contract of payment could only be negotiated if every element of work was known, measurable and accounted for. But it isn't. Suppose a principal employed managers to take decisions on his behalf (which is after all the job of management) and paid them only on turnover, or sales or profit? Where would marketing and research and maintenance be positioned on their list of priorities? So the pay package must be a hybrid and will still miss elements of work that must be done if the company is to succeed. Grossman, Hart, and Moore believe that knowledge about what work is necessary is always incomplete, and therefore the contract covering payment for that work must also be incomplete.

Which brings us to another form of incentive that used to be the preserve of senior management, but is growing as an incentive for IT people for reasons I'll explain in a moment. That form of incentive is 'ownership'. You are more likely to do all the myriad tasks necessary to make the venture a success if you have a stake in the venture yourself.

But the principal-agent theory gets complicated with information workers. The traditional principal-agent theory assumes that the principal owns all the capital in the company. But we know that information workers bring a significant amount of intellectual capital (ideas, methods, ingenuity, inspiration and inventiveness) to the party when they arrive. How are they to be rewarded for sharing this with what the company owns? With ownership of the enterprise in which they operate.

The following model encompasses the salary, output pay, and ownership element of incentives for information workers within the new psychological contract. Based on four criteria it is possible to think through what each party, employees and employers, provides to the relationship. The employer's role in the psychological contract is to provide a business vision. They need to expand that vision into a business model, and objectives, and need to define the assignments needed to be completed in order to attain that vision. They then need to provide the environment in which employees can enact the vision. This involves the tools and workplace environment. Importantly as a follow on from the assignment definition, feedback is an essential part of the employer's role. The obvious output for the employer is the supply of products and services to customers. Employees on the other hand bring their competence, experience, education, and time to the relation-ship. They apply these to the organisation's vision, objectives and assignments in an aligned way, conforming to operational norms and standards. They also apply their physical and mental energy to their activities. Employees deliver those objectives defined in the assignments definition, but IT employee-outputs will be systems, processes, documentation, IT stability and capacity, etc. However, the crunch, for IT employees comes from the outcomes produced as a result of their outputs, and these relate to business outcomes, and not IT outcomes.

I have one of the best Thesauruses that I have seen in years. But there is no way I can find sexy words for 'Input, Action, Delivery and Outcome' which will allow me to make a catchy acronym for this model. Accordingly I tried to write this section without naming the model, but also without success. Accordingly, I hereby name this model the 'IADO' model. Sorry but it's the best I can do.

As you can see from Table 14.2 there are a few critical omissions from the old psychological contract and significant changes in the remuneration philosophy. The obvious ones are that the employee arrives skilled, experienced, competent, and educated to begin their assignments. The employer will play no role in this. Neither is loyalty mentioned by either party. Which brings us to the new remuneration with the new psychological contract. Traditionalists may look at this and see that the old

Table 14.2
The
psychological
contract in IT,
linked to
remuneration

	Inputs	Actions	Delivery	Outcome
Employer's duty	Vision	Business model	Products and services	Profit
	Objectives	Environment		Growth
	Assignment definition	Feedback		Perpetuation
Employee's duty	Competence	Alignment	Code	Business results
	Experience	Energy	Systems	Changed behaviours
	Education	Teamwork	Processes	
	Time		Documentation	Customer satisfaction
			Training	(Defined by the business)
			Stability	
Employee remuneration medium	Salary	Salary	Delivery linked payment	Ownership

'salary' has now been divided into three areas – salary, delivery payment and ownership. Salary is paid for employee input and activity, a delivery linked payment is made when outputs are produced, and some form of ownership in the organisation is handed over based on outcomes. The old salary has not been divided into three – the salary paid for input and activity will probably remain exactly the same as old salaries. An *extra* payment will be made for delivery of outputs, and shares or options will be accrued to the employee's account based on some business outcome or outcomes.

Why will employers put up with paying the same salaries, *and* paying some fee on delivery of output, *and* surrendering some form of ownership based on outcomes? The power is shifting to employees. Employers cannot offer security so there will be a premium asked by employees. Neither will employers be obliged to train or develop employees. Therefore employers can put their training, development and general career management budget into the delivery payment. There will also be fewer benefits provided by employers – pension, health insurance and the like. As the power shifts to the workers they will not accept salaries without some form of 'training and benefits stipend', which they will probably take from their delivery payment. Finally, I'm with Brynjolfsson in his prediction that information workers will expect some form of ownership of the organisation for which they work. And from the employer's side, some form of loyalty can be expected from people who have an ownership stake in the organisation.

14.4 Treating employees as people

Notwithstanding the move towards a more delivery-based psychological contract, with loyalty, benefits, training and career growth factored out, those organisations that see their employees as complex and individual people, rather than an amorphous mass of workers without personality, will become employers of preference. Treating workers as people sounds almost as a trivial distinction, but I don't believe it is.

So what would happen if we treated employees as people?

Firstly, we would have to acknowledge their individuality. The problem with people is that they are not all the same. And IT people are probably less 'the same' than most. This means that a different approach must be used in our dealings between the organisation and each individual – each employment contract would have to be particular, each assignment would be unique. This would strain most Human Resource department's current concepts of how people can be organised, but a little bit of intelligence applied to the situation coupled with the power of information technology could considerably ease the strain. It is a mindset problem not an execution problem. If we want to treat each person in the organisation as an individual, we can.

We would also have to accept that employees have feelings. This means that we would have to tap in to a whole new set of management competencies – mentoring, caring, concern and counselling would become new arrows in the manager's quiver. Leaders will have to get in touch with themselves and the 'deep development' needs of their people. They have to develop their self-knowledge, and access their feelings and intuition. 'Soft skills' will define the leader of the future. Words like caring, love, and kindness would creep into the organisational vocabulary.

The personnel manual, currently as thick as a brick and about as useful, needs to be given the heave-ho. Personnel manuals enshrine the lowest common denominator – the mediocre. (Ask any manager who has been constrained to giving increases according to a normal curve.) Ricardo Semler[10], CEO of Brazilian company Semco, banned the personnel manual and replaced it with a small booklet – on each page is a cartoon and a sentence about how people in the company currently feel about things. For example one page says:

> Semco doesn't use a formal organisation chart. Only the respect of the led creates a leader. When it is absolutely necessary to sketch a structure of some part of the company, we always do it in pencil, and dispense with it as soon as possible.
>
> (Semler, 1994)

This doesn't mean they don't have an organisational structure, just that they don't enshrine it. Sentiments I totally agree with. If you started treating your organisation as a complex adaptive system you would have to treat your organisation structure as being fluid. In order to achieve their goals, people set up their own structures in spite of the formal organisation structure. The trick is to go with the flow, and allow these informal and fluid structures to take over, and to bin the organisation charts.

If employees were treated as people, their security would be important. And with the transformation of the psychological contract, no company can offer its employees job security. There is another option though – security can be offered by increasing a person's employability. So the new security equation will involve training and development but at a distance – allowing people time and giving them delivery-based payments to complete the training they want – rather than promises of continued employment. This would bring new pressures to the CIO: they would have to operate as if people could leave tomorrow (because they can). The paradox is that in order to keep people, you have to make them more employable elsewhere.

There are downsides to treating employees as people: firstly you will have to learn to live with ambiguity – people won't be predictable, nor will they be controllable. Secondly, managers will have to become leaders – and some might not make the cut. Also, things will become more complex and appear to be more chaotic. Finally, the more feminine side of human nature will gain ascendancy, which will be tough on the masculine management class.

What is the new reality in people-centre management?

● be very strong on vision, culture and buy-in. New leaders must set up the social mores and values that will guide each individual in every decision. Then allow people to take those decisions;

- believe in and act on people's potential. Help people to become everything they can be. Set up the support structure that will allow people to thrive;

- give people the tools to serve their customers. People know what they need to do their jobs;

- set up performance measures that are in-built and self-evident to every person. Peer pressure will manage performance. Be open with all information;

- have only a few rules which when carried out create complex and elegant adaptations to continually changing environments and pressures.

Treating employees as people is not a Utopian dream. It is hard work, fraught with complexity, ambiguity and difficulty. You can't control it or predict it. But you can guide it, give it boundaries and order.

The trick is to generate a 'highly creative zone'[11], in which there is a balance between stability and anarchy. This complex state is where the good stuff happens.

14.5 The job of managers

Whenever one of my managers was having difficulty with my expectations of his or her performance, I used to draw this little mental model for them (see Figure 14.1).

This model is very crude and has no basis in research, but it has helped me and others to understand how roles differ. The horizontal axis represents the passage of time, and the vertical one can be labelled quality, production, competitiveness or whatever measure of work you wish to apply. Entropy rules in the case of work, and line 'A' represents what will happen to work over time if a team or department is left without supervision, or no natural leader steps forward. Line 'B'

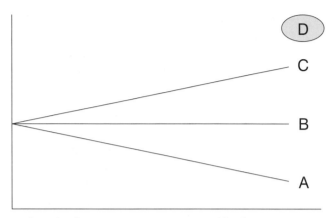

Figure 14.1 The role of supervisors, managers and leaders

represents the role of a supervisor: to make sure that policies and guidelines are enacted and that quality does not deteriorate over time. To preserve the status quo. It is the role of a manager to improve things over time, and this is represented by line 'C'. More importantly, in his or her role as a manager, he or she changes things and should be seen as an agent of change (rather than a resister of change). Finally, it is the role of a leader to stand at 'D', a discontinuous point in progress, lighting the way to a new unrealised development. The role of a leader is encompassed in the AMTS acronym that I discussed in Chapter 2. A leader points people in the right direction, and captures their *attention*. He or she explores the *meaning* of following that direction. He or she manages *trust*, by being constant and by rewarding appropriate behaviour and not rewarding inappropriate behaviour. Finally, he or she leads the way with his or her actions or *self*.

14.6 The hourglass organisation

Conventional organisation structures are triangular in shape. This structure has its origins in military organisation with a general at its head, various officers and aides in the 'management team', and of course the troops out on the battlefield. The idea behind traditional military organisation is to have all the strategy and thinking done by the general, the monitoring and management done by the officers, and the actual dying done by the soldiers. The last thing you wanted was to have your soldiers thinking, because the first thing they were likely to think would be, 'let the generals go and die, I'm staying right here'. Therefore, much of a soldier's training was aimed at driving free-thought out of the troops and unquestioning obedience into them. It may even be an effective way to run an army, but it is no longer effective to apply this structure to business organisations. In the past businesses have built their intelligence into their organisation, in the same way Henry Ford built the intelligence of his manufacturing process into his production line. But now we want our 'front-line' people to think. Customers demand it, technology demands it, the speed of business developments demands it.

The problem is that you will never get people to think while the old organisation structures remain in place. New organisational structures cannot be triangular – globular or amoebic would be more like it. People need to gather round specific assignments in line with their ability to add value to the assignment, irrespective of their organisational position or place in the hierarchy.

There are many types of organisation structure available to you: there is the triangle which gets narrower towards the top. Such structures 'flattened' or 'delayered' to take out layers between workers and management are the usual results of re-engineering efforts. But the General is still the General and the troops are still the troops. Project team structures are often found in engineering companies and organisations that deal with discrete units of work. Networked structures take advantage of IT to spread people geographically letting them work in small teams in different locations. The more advanced networks include customers and suppliers in the network. Matrix structures usually have a dimension which relates to products and a dimension relating to functional area. Some matrices have a further dimension of skill or expertise. Elegant on paper, these structures are fiendishly difficult to manage and even more difficult to be managed in – individuals have two or three bosses, and that requires a mature disposition in everyone. If you want to explore organisational forms in more detail, read a book called *Images of Organisation* by Gareth Morgan[12].

If there has to be an organisational hierarchy in IT, don't have a triangular organisation, or even a diamond-shaped structure. Rather go for what I call the 'hourglass' structure. Picture an hourglass with its two bulbs and constriction in the middle – that's how IT could look. In the top 'bulb' would be the experts. They are the 'best-of-class' staff who are at the forefront of their particular technical area. They are highly skilled, responsible, trusted and aligned with the organisation's aims. They have exceptional productivity, and they receive exceptional pay. The upper bulb operates as a collegiate environment in which everyone is recognised for their area of expertise and recognises everyone else for theirs. That's all very well for these wonder kids, but how does someone get there? Well they start in the bottom bulb of this organisational hourglass. This is the learning environment. High potential people are paid normal salaries for their energetic learning, and gaining of experience. They are eager and ambitious to advance, but humble enough to know they have a lot to learn. The constriction in the hourglass is the 'testing ground' where high potentials who believe they are ready can try out for the big stakes game. The conditions are stringent, perform well or don't move into the upper 'glass'. There is no reason why mentoring and guidance can't happen, but the assignment undertaken by the high potential must be real and measurable, and must be seen as a 'rites of passage' assignment.

Before I move on from a discussion of organisational structures I must describe the structure I find in most organisations, even though everyone tends not to acknowledge it. It is what I call the 'executive club' structure and it is the difference between form and function. The company can have any organisational form described above (usually it's triangular), but functionally it operates like a boy's club (even if there are girls involved). They meet in their tree-house to discuss secret things. They stick together and have secret codes and stuff. There is usually a bully, and a weed in the team. Each member of the gang has his or her henchmen, although they are not part of the team. Very often there is so much plotting within the 'team' that their energy is largely directed away from business, in fact business is the vehicle they use to gain advantage over each other in the gang. But most importantly, the boundaries of the club are impermeable. Work done outside the club is always outside the club. No-one crosses the boundary without permission, and very often there is an initiation ceremony. Outsiders remain outsiders (often even though they may be part of the executive team, they are not part of the club). Woody Allen describes similar circumstances in an essay he wrote entitled: 'a brief, yet helpful guide to civil disobedience[13].'

> . . . the oppressors . . . are easily recognised as they seem to be the ones having all the fun. The 'oppressors' generally get to wear suits, own land, and play their radios late at night without being yelled at. Their job is to maintain the 'status quo' . . . It should be noted that the oppressors never revolt and attempt to become the oppressed.
>
> (Allen, 1972)

This cynical view of organisations serves two purposes: firstly examine your management team to see if it is a boy's club. If so then know that those outside resent it, and that information is not flowing across the club boundary, and that significant time is being wasted within the club rather than looking outside towards the organisation and more importantly to the customers, and finally if you are the senior person in this team, know that your behaviours reinforce club behaviours. Examine all the privilege forms around the club (parking, offices, dining room, etc.) to see where club behaviours emerge. Secondly, if you are not part of the club, you are going to have to play the game the way the club plays it. So look at the club and pick up the underlying rules to see how the game is played. Then examine yourself to see whether you can or want to play the game.

14.7 Work in IT

Workflow systems have as much, if not a greater role to play in IT, as they do in the rest of organisations. A workflow system automates the flow of work (surprise, surprise) in such a way that it is visible, and that it is tracked and escalated if it gets stuck. That's what I wanted when I ran an IT function, a way of seeing where work is getting stuck, and moving it on. But thinking about workflow in IT opens up new possibilities for all IT work.

The definition of work in IT needs to be clarified, firstly from its broadest meaning (what work is actually done here?) down to a form of user requirement specification. Goals and targets need to be defined, and tracked, which fits well with the ABR and Formative Evaluation concepts described in Chapter 11 on IT Solutions Provision.

Workflow systems will assist the hourglass organisation, with IT practitioners moving work between work 'stations' when complete. More importantly workflow systems allow you to adopt an IADO (Input, Actions, Delivery, Outcomes) remuneration model, and take it one step further. Work could be 'auctioned' to IT staff, based on their inputs, and the assignment definition. The need to pay for boring or difficult work would have to be balanced against the anticipated outcome. In this way we might move closer to getting essential work done and leaving non-essential work on the shelf. The obvious benefits of tracking progress on work and managing bottlenecks and difficulties is also evident in a workflow system.

The purpose of workflow systems in problem and incident management in the CIP environment is clear. However, it's surely how you choose to implement such a system that is the important factor here. Will you use workflow as a way of managing problems when they occur, or as a way of making sure problems don't occur in the first place?

Of course, workflow allows you to bring users into the loop. And you should use this opportunity to shorten linkages and cross boundaries in your company. It will also allow you to become more visible to your company, as the list of tasks is in progress or awaiting assignment to individuals or stalled and not going anywhere should be available to all who use the system. Also, getting users to do their bit becomes easier.

But why stop at users? A workflow system allows IT to work on the same assignments from anywhere, either as a telecommuting set-up, or as regional units working from anywhere in the world.

One thing is clear – your workflow system must help individuals do their jobs or it will definitely fail. Allow this to be the credo when examining and designing your workflow in IT. Also pay great attention to defining and allocating work – it should be a voluntary process on behalf of the receiver, and that means that the receiver of work should know what he or she is taking on.

The benefits of workflow systems in IT are obvious to me, but must be woven into the approach and vision of the IT function. You need to test these workflow ideas against your chosen direction and see where the fit lies.

Finally I recommend that you encourage 'communities of practice' in your IT function. Allow these communities to cluster around specific areas of expertise or of work, give them the resources to improve their practice, then get out of the way.

People know what they need to get the job done well. Give it to them. Don't set conditions other than getting the work done efficiently and effectively. If you have set the driving purpose of your IT function properly, people in communities of practice will allow that purpose to drive a continuos questioning on how to improve their practice. And don't constrain these communities to the lofty experts only, allow everyone in the organisation to form a community if they are so driven, from secretaries to leaders and everyone in between.

14.8 Self-managed teams

There is something perverse about most people – they like to be told what to do, and they hate to be told what to do. Well they do if they're anything like me. It depends on how we get told what needs to be done that dictates how we react to the task. Certainly the 'do this and don't ask questions' approach will create at best a response of doing exactly what we're told and no more, and at worst a resentment that sabotages the task at every turn. So the allocation of work to people needs some finesse. If you have succeeded in creating a driving purpose which focuses everyone's efforts at every turn, then the allocation of work is significantly simplified. If you follow the workstream approach, a posting of assignments on some common 'bulletin board' should ensure that a team forms to get the task done. This leaves room for people to decide what work they want to do, how they are going to do it, and how they are going to ensure that the outputs and outcomes are delivered. An idealistic aspiration perhaps, but it is attainable by putting into place the right environment and conditions.

14.8.1 Structure

If we are to believe the 'new-age' advisors (and I am one) then you merely set up the environment, the driving purpose and a few simple rules and the appropriate structure for the job will emerge. However, perhaps a nudge in the right direction may be useful. In the beginning, it is probably a good idea to link people directly to work. This may be done in a gradation from allocating individuals to explicit teams and assignments, all the way through to allowing people to choose what assignments (and what teams) they want to work on. Some organisations collect a group of people together, put them in a room and tell them they are a team:

> The problem with creating teams in this way is that teams are imposed onto people, which makes it no different from traditional work groups with a single leader and set agenda, except that these groups are, at least, honestly autocratic.[14]
>
> (Lewin and Regine, 1999)

But let's for the moment assume we have a group of people who have reached a point at which they are all allocated to an assignment. They will need to structure who does what in the group. There are many useful team role models that you can help the group with.

However, if you have set up a workflow system for IT work, and have a voluntary selection of work, you will be heading for a self-structuring environment in which teams emerge to work on a collective goal. They self-select, self-organise, and self-manage around a goal which contributes to the driving purpose. This is indeed a dramatic approach to teams and it requires courage and energy to implement. But those who have, have been surprised and pleased by the results.

14.8.2 Who does what?

So now we have the team and the work to be done, all that remains is how the work gets done. Within the framework of

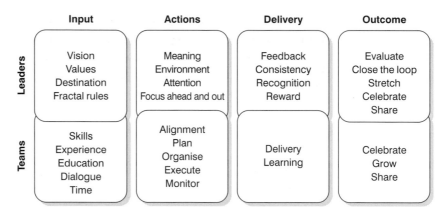

	Input	Actions	Delivery	Outcome
Leaders	Vision Values Destination Fractal rules	Meaning Environment Attention Focus ahead and out	Feedback Consistency Recognition Reward	Evaluate Close the loop Stretch Celebrate Share
Teams	Skills Experience Education Dialogue Time	Alignment Plan Organise Execute Monitor	Delivery Learning	Celebrate Grow Share

Figure 14.2 Roles and activities in self-managed teams

self-organising work in complex adaptive systems the framework for activity within the IADO model in Figure 14.2 might prove useful.

You will see that I have placed activities on 'cards.' During the input and outcome elements of the model, the Leader's cards are above those of the team, and the team's cards prevail during the activity and delivery stages in the model. This means that leaders concentrate on inputs and outcomes, and allow teams to get on with delivering the goods. Micro management is no longer appropriate. In fact you will see that the team card during the action stage of the model, contains the POEM (Plan, organise, execute, monitor) activities. Because this used to be the role of management, but in a self-managed environment, it becomes a team role. What, after all is 'self-management' if there is no management action for the team?

The role of leaders during the input stage is multi-leveled. The vision, values, destination and fractal rules apply to the entire organisation, but certainly in the early stages of applying this model, leaders need to provide a vision, destination and fractal rules for every task assigned to a team. This is the assignment definition part of a leader's job. As time goes on, it will be possible to lift the focus from micro-definition of tasks, but this will remain a critical early activity for leaders.

Leaders play an important but less prominent role during the action stage. They manage attention and meaning in the organisation. The management of attention requires that they reinforce the vision, not only in directing people's attention to work and activities which support the attainment of the vision, but also stopping people from paying attention to unimportant stuff. I once heard, and am cynical enough to believe, that in a mature organisation probably upwards of 60% of work done is unnecessary, in terms of reaching the strategic objectives of the company. It almost doesn't matter what the percentage actually is, the leader's job is to eradicate unnecessary work. Managing meaning is an important dialogue issue. I am not necessarily talking about semantics or etymological studies, although the words an organisation chooses to use are an important part of its culture. Rather I use the term 'meaning' in the sense of implications and consequences. For instance, the leader would say something like: 'if we're going to improve our turn-around time by 25% what does that mean?' or 'this team has committed to delivering "X" goal in "Y" time, what does that mean?' Or on a larger scale the leader might say something like 'our company has committed itself to delivering high quality customer service, what does that mean?' But the role of the leader is not just to ask questions (that's far too easy), but to lead. And to do that they have to manage meaning. This involves revealing your thinking on the topic, and guiding errant thinking where you find it. Management of meaning is not a ruthless secret police activity of controlling thought, it is more about making sure that the deep questions are asked and answered and continue to be so. Many mature organisations get into trouble because they stop allowing the deep questions to be asked.

The role of the leader during the delivery and outcome elements of the IADO model involve a completion and building activity. They are responsible for closing the loop, celebrating the successes, extracting and sharing the learning and yes, sharing the rewards from the work done by everyone in the organisation. This is probably the most neglected part of a leader's job in indifferently performing organisations, and one of the key differentiators of leaders in flourishing companies.

Leadership is a role. There is no reason why leaders are not team members for some of the time and leaders for the rest.

The roles of teams throughout these activities is to contribute positively and in an aligned way to the driving purpose of the organisation. Most of the items in the model are self-evident but I need to explain a few things. In the input element of the model, teams must engage in the dialogue. This means they need to make the up-front time available to discuss with the leadership of the organisation, the driving purpose and their contribution to it. For this is the way that leaders shape their thinking. Teams must also be aware of the gravity of defining the assignment. Here I am guilty. Whenever I start a new task, and someone is trying to tell me about the detail, I find myself saying 'yeah, yeah, we'll sort out the particulars later.' This always comes back to haunt me. So I confess here to preaching what I don't practice – but then some of the world's great sports coaches could never do what they tell their charges to do. (That sounds like a weak defence even to my ears.)

During the action element of the IADO model, guess what? The team does stuff. But, and this is a critical but, it plans, organises, executes and monitors *in an aligned way*. This is so important that I need to stress it. It's really weird to me that people will take the money of an employer and yet undermine them continuously. I'm not calling for unquestioning conformance to 'Big Brother's' will. Lively dialogue and debate must be encouraged. But to me it's critically important that during the 'input' stage of the process, people assess whether their personal vision harmonises with the organisation's. If it doesn't, there's going to be trouble.

And the individual will invariably suffer. To work in an organisation in which your vision and values clash with those of the organisation is nothing short of toxic. Get out while you can.

There is a role to be played by teams during the output and outcome stages of the IADO model, which is no less important than that of the leadership. Deliver the goods. But also join in the celebration. Learn from the experience, and more importantly, grow, get better, improve, because of the experience. This means that teams must consciously change after every assignment – ask the question 'what are we going to do differently as a result of what we have learned?' and then do it differently.

14.8.3 Information

Self-management requires information. In organisations trying to enlist the brains of their people, but in an informationally bankrupt environment, this enlistment will be stillborn.

According to Margaret Wheatley in *Leadership and The New Science*[15] we cannot manage information, much less control it. And neither should we try. She and many business thinkers have adopted a new attitude to information in organisations: we should encourage it. We should flood the organisation with as much information as is available. We should give everyone the tools to interpret information and then let the principle of self-organising systems takes over.

With information, people can act. Max Du Preez, author of *Leadership Is an Art,*[16] agrees:

People find more ways to use information constructively than the leaders dispensing it would ever imagine.

(Du Preez, 1990)

Knowledge is power, and so the power of teams must be fed with information. In organisations I have dealt with, the universal cry is usually, 'yes but what about confidentiality and security?' Keith Merron[17] answers:

> Which is more important: withholding information for fear of competitors, or the trust which releases creativity, knowledge and commitment?
>
> (Merron, 1995)

Many companies tell the world what they are doing, why they are doing it, and how they are performing. They do not fear that their competitors will use this information, because they know that while information might be the life-blood of the organisation, it is just that – blood. If you don't have the body to house this life-blood, you can't use it.

But you will need to do four things that will allow information nourish self-managed teams:

- pay vigorous attention to your vision, your driving purpose. Constantly reinforce the vision, discuss its meaning, promote a constant conversation about what your company is doing, why you are doing it, and how you can do it better. Allow questions, debate, dissent and dialogue;

- constantly try to unleash new potential in your people. Take their competencies seriously, and be equally serious about allowing people to perform. Try not to have the rules, job descriptions, and procedures which undermine creativity, productivity and intuition;

- give people the tools to do their jobs. Expect your people to know what they need to perform their assignments better, and give it to them. Allow your people to think, and to act on those thoughts;

● be very strong on the four areas for which you are prepared to pay: inputs (knowledge and expertise), *aligned* action, outputs or deliverables and very importantly, pay attention to outcomes. Be seen to be attending to each of these elements – it is no secret what you want from your self-managed teams – tell them and everyone else. Clarity, openness and peer pressure work wonders.

And into this system, they pump information. About everything.

14.8.4 Caveats

People choose the easiest path.

I once had a team whose team-leader was transferring elsewhere so I proposed some 'self-management' to the team. As the first step, the team was to choose their next team-leader. There were two candidates. They interviewed the applicants and made their choice. (Both applicants told me that this was the toughest interview they had ever had in their lives.)

However, the team chose someone who would be nice to them. To go easy on them when things were tough. And the team started to miss deadlines. But they were happy. It is an unfortunate part of work that there will be tough times, and people will need discipline – often externally applied. This didn't happen.

I didn't pay enough attention to the four elements of work – and the team concentrated on the inputs and action side only. After I while I spoke to the team, and they all agreed (including the chosen team leader) that they should have elected the less-liked and stricter candidate as team-leader.

Self-managed teams should concentrate on all elements of performance if they are to be successful.

Implementation ideas

1 Read *The Soul at Work* by Lewin and Regine[18]. It is the most practical look at Complex Adaptive Systems that I have come across and it presents a large section on practical applications of New Science thinking to real situations. Then start applying some New Science to your IT organisation.

2 Examine the Psychological Contract that your organisation has with its employees. Look at how this is, or will have to change. Pre-empt these changes.

3 Fill in the following table for your organisation:

	Inputs	Actions	Delivery	Outcome
Employer's duty				
Employee's duty				
Employee remuneration medium				

4 How could you treat employees as people in IT? How would you accommodate their individuality, feelings, need for security, need to be trained and developed – all within the new psychological contract?

5 Structure an hourglass organisation for your department. This organisation still fits well with Handy's 'Shamrock

Organisation' with the hourglass fitting entirely into the 'core'. But test the practicalities for your specific situation.

References

1. Stewart, D.W., Hecker, S. and Graham, J.L. (1987) It's more than what you say: Assessing the influence of non-verbal communication in marketing. *Psychology and Marketing*, Vol. 4
2. Arnold, J., Cooper, C.L. and Robertson, I.T. (1998) *Work Psychology – Understanding Human Behaviour in the Workplace*. Financial Times, Pitman, London
3. Arnold, J., Cooper, C.L. and Robertson, I.T. (1998) *Work Psychology – Understanding Human Behaviour in the Workplace*. Financial Times/Pitman, London
4. Bridges, W. (1995) *Jobshift – How to prosper in a workplace without jobs*. Nicholas Brealey Publishing Limited
5. Tampoe, M. (1993) Motivating knowledge workers – the challenge for the 1990s. *Long Range Planning*, Vol. 26, No 3
6. Young, R. and Mould, K. (1994) *Managing Information Systems Professionals*. Butterworths
7. Brynjolfsson, E. (1994) *Incomplete Contracts Theory of Information, Technology and Organisation*. Center for Coordination Science, MIT
8. Grossman, S. and Hart, O. (1986) The costs and benefits of ownership: a theory of vertical and lateral integration. *Journal of Political Economy*, 24(4)
9. Hart, O. and Moore, J. (1990) Property Rights and the Nature of the Firm. *Journal of Political Economy*, 98(4) pp. 1119–1158.
10. Semler, R. (1994) *Maverick – The success story behind the world's most unusual workplace*. Arrow Books, London
11. Lewin, R. and Regine, B. (1999) *The Soul at Work – Unleashing the Power of Complexity Science for Business Success*. Orion Business Publishers

12. Morgan, G. (1997) *Images of Organisation*. Sage Publications, CA

13. Allen, W. (1972) A brief, yet helpful guide to civil disobedience. In: *Without Feathers*. First Sphere Books, London

14. Lewin, R. and Regine, B. (1999) *The Soul at Work – Unleashing the Power of Complexity Science for Business Success*. Orion Business Publishers

15. Wheatley, M. (1993) *Leadership and The New Science*. Berrett-Koehler, San Francisco, CA

16. Du Preez, M. (1990) *Leadership Is an Art*. Berrett-Koehler

17. Merron, K. (1995) *Riding the Wave: Designing your Organisation's Architecture for Enduring Success*. Van Nostrand Reinhold, NY

18. Lewin, R. and Regine, B. (1999) *The Soul at Work – Unleashing the Power of Complexity Science for Business Success*. Orion Business Publishers

15 Last round please – final observations

15.1 There is another way of doing this

In the final analysis everything is just words. Unless actions back up the words, this will have been an interesting read for you, which you can either ignore, or allow to inform some areas of your thinking, or you could implement wholesale all of the suggestions outlined in the book. The choice is yours. But I changed my life's path one September in 1993 when I read a book called *Stewardship* by Peter Block[1]. I thought that this was interesting and exciting stuff, but not significantly different from the many other management books I had read over the years. But the book sat on my bookshelf and filled my office with whispers. Eventually I presented some of the ideas from the book to my management team. They lit up. We tried empowering people. We failed, but we went back to it again and again and finally changed the face of the IT department in our organisation. All because that book kept whispering to me, 'there is another way to do this'.

There is another way to do In-house IT. The choice is yours.

15.2 So you want to be on the board?

About 50% of IT managers are represented on the executive team of their organisation. The way to get onto the board is to be

relevant and to add value. The way to stay in a support role is
. . . to believe your job is a support role.

Barry Oshry[2] is fascinated by systems and offers this advice to
would-be leaders:

> I am concocting a witches brew for the power move. The
> necessary ingredients:
>
> ● the ability to see the system as a whole – what is IT's
>   condition, what does IT need?
>
> ● seeing one's centrality in the system, the belief that you
>   could make a difference
>
> ● experiencing one's responsibility for the system, not
>   only that you could make a difference but that you
>   should;
>
> ● treating anxiety not as something to be narcotised but
>   as a potentially productive clue that something is
>   wrong with the system and your relationship to it.
>
> Conversely, if you want to sleep well at night, the formula
> is quite simple: see yourself as a sideline player in life and
> believe that others, not you, are responsible for your
> systems.
>
> (Oshry, 1999)

Oshry isn't talking about computer systems here of course, and
I would suggest that he is talking about a wider worldview of
the environment and your company, and appealing to you to see
yourself as a central player in that system.

CIO Magazine[3] analysed what it takes to be an IT leader in an
organisation and came up with the following:

● CIOs Must Become Vendor Managers;

● Focus on Strategy, Not Tactics;

- Make Outsourcing the First Option;

- Lure New Staff with Unique Offerings;

- Work With the Business – not Against It – to Manage IT;

- Make a Name for Yourself.

There's no rocket science here. You've read it all before. So the question must be, 'why aren't you doing this stuff?'

Let me add my two cents' worth to the above list:

- focus on outcomes – don't be bound by IT. Think much wider than IT. See yourself as a provider of business solutions from an IT perspective;

- look after the hygiene. The relationship between IT and the business is based on delivery. Trust is formed when you keep your word. And your 'word' in IT is to deliver what the business wants and when they want it. Build your business 'bill of rights' and see to it that you deliver on those 'rights.' Later in this chapter I review these rights and my approach to each of them presented in this book.

- use complexity science. Business and IT is a complex adaptive system whether we like it or not. Wouldn't it be a good idea if you knew the rules of the game?

15.3 Complex adaptive systems and IT

Throughout this book I refer to complex adaptive systems and at the end of many chapters I make an attempt to apply complexity science thinking to the specific area in IT. It is never as simple as a few paragraphs in a book, and it certainly cannot be as simple as the following table, but I have attempted to summarise my thinking on complex adaptive systems as applied to IT in the following table. Use this as a 'thought provoker.' But you'll need to develop your own approach.

IT Domain	Informer of Driving Purpose	Fractal Rules	Environmental Actions	Emergent Behaviour
Architecture	Business purpose Technological trends Economic trends Social trends	30 second message Models Position papers	Feeding the gut Delivery conditions	Flexible informed architecture Open doors to future Stable present
New Technology	Go with the flow	Say yes Preempt Guide and mentor	Relationships Architecture	Seamless innovation and integration
Solutions from IT	Outcome space	Active Benefit Realisation and Formative Evaluation Stakeholders = team	Not a project – an environment Habitat definition	Business outcomes Benefit streams

IT Domain	Informer of Driving Purpose	Fractal Rules	Environmental Actions	Emergent Behaviour
Production	Benchmark	Prevention Pre-emptive action Factory rules	The cobbler's shoes The electronic body	Invisible launching pad Swan
Strategy	Scenarios Business purpose	Everybody is a strategist Information gathering Trends Action	Knowledge management Meaning Attention	Emergent adaptive strategy
People	Common purpose People are important		Trust Bowl Self	Self-elected task teams Amoeba teams

15.4 The business bill of rights and the new IT function

In this section we'll take another look at the business bill of rights and I'll include my thinking on how you address these rights:

15.4.1 Stable platform

Give the business a stable platform from which to run its computing applications. Business people have a right to expect stability from their existing systems. Use factory and operations management to strengthen your approach and base of IT operations. Treat each application as an environment with its own measures and resources. Adopt a pre-emptive approach to problems. Make sure they can't happen and you won't have to fix anything. See the IT infrastructure as an electronic body and listen to all the messages it sends you, then act on the messages.

15.4.2 Flexible future

This same stable platform should be flexible enough to accommodate as yet unforeseen systems. Build an architecture and live by it. Make 30 second messages, IT models and position papers, a way of life and communication in the business.

15.4.3 The same time-frame

Provide IT solutions to business problems or opportunities in the same business time-frame. Use Active Benefits Realisation and Formative Evaluation to manage changing goalposts within equally volatile timeframes. Focus on business outcomes and relate everything that happens in a business environment to the desired outcome. Build an environment stakeholder list and use it to manage your relationships.

15.4.4 Technological leadership

Identify technologies which provide business opportunities, and lead the business in exploiting these technologies. Use your architecture and communicate in a user friendly way. Use Intranet sites, in-house magazines and any method you can find to attract and keep attention. Use scenario planning in IT to tell compelling stories to your organisation.

15.4.5 IT education

Improve general IT competence and understanding at all levels in the organisation. Build your relationships. Have marketing and communication plans that you take seriously. See IT education as something you need to attract business people to, rather than something you push onto people.

15.4.6 Strategic IT leadership

Provide guidance and leadership to business within the strategic intent of the organisation. Use scenario planning and stakeholder analyses to find out what's important to the business. Then apply an IT perspective. Make your strategy more than accessible – make it attractive, something that business people refer to because they want to. Use position papers to generate interest in future technologies.

15.4.7 Alignment

Align systems processes with the organisation's vision, mission, strategic intent, values and culture. See IT's role as a business role, with an IT perspective.

15.4.8 Relationship

Manage the relationships. Actively and purposely. Build your stakeholder analyses and use it and keep it updated. Draw relationship maps and use them to act.

15.4.9 Changing requirements

Allow business to change their minds after they have specified a system. Use Active Benefits Realisation and Formative Evaluation. But discuss and negotiate these concepts with business people first. You cannot apply ABR and Formative Evaluation from one side of the relationship.

15.4.10 Meet the need

Above all give business people what they need; both information and functionality. Conduct user surveys regularly and work hard to meet the required needs. If you can't meet specified needs, then it's back to relationships and negotiation.

15.5 Endroduction

This is a weird word, but it's the opposite of 'introduction' and I just made it up.

At the end of the book I suppose the question must be asked: 'will this just be another book you once read, or will it change the way you think and work?' It's up to you.

I believe that in many instances IT has become a follower rather than a leader. Leadership is difficult. Think of leaders who you admire. Does this person have their own world-view? Do they follow other people's rules or do they have their own set of rules that fit their world-view? Do these people have integrity? Are they good communicators? Do they compromise on their chosen path?

If you wish to become an IT leader then these are the areas you must develop. I hope this book helps you on your chosen path. Good luck.

References

1. Block, P. (1993) *Stewardship*. Berrett-Keohler, CA
2. Field, T. (2000) IS at the Crossroads. In: *CIO Magazine*, June 15
3. Oshry, B. (1999) *Leading Systems*: *Lessons from the Power Lab*. Berrett-Koehler, San Francisco CA

Index

Ability, 14, 21, 34–5, 56, 62, 64, 88, 111, 155, 157, 170, 181, 327, 344
Above and below the line thinking, 120, 144, *see also* Momentum Line
Account management and marketing IT, 130
Accuracy of role perception, 14
Acquired competence, 65
Active and passive thinking, 163
Active Benefits Realization, 254–5, 261, 265, 348, 349
Agricultural revolution, 95
Alignment of purpose, 101
Amazon.com, 31
Ambiguity in thinking, 154–5, 171, 324, 325
American Airlines, 31–2
American Hospital Supplies, 31
Architecture, 201
   as a shopping list, 205
   communicating an, 206, 212, 217
   and crowd control, 210
   definition of, 203–4
   managing the architect, 212
   objectives of, 207–10
   position paper, 211, 214–6, 219, 224, 227–8, 292, 348–9
   reasons for having an, 206–7
   reasons for not having an, 202
   shared meaning, 214
   the bottom line of architecture, 212
   the role of the architect, 211–12
   the thirty second message, 211, 212, 213–15, 219, 292

Assets, 29, 33, 54, 58, 62, 86, 109, 168
Automating, 6, 7
Availability, definition of, 268

Back to basics, 33, 36–7
Balanced Scorecard, 58
Barter, removing cash from the system, 47, 53, 74
Bathtub Curve, 27, 284
Benchmarking, 12, 130, 270
Bill of Responsibilities, 113
Bill of Rights for business, 110, 113
Blackmail, 22, 70
Boiled frogs, 46
Boundaries, 54, 72–4, 80, 124, 138, 142, 158, 175, 189, 204, 252, 261, 262, 325, 329, 331
Brightsizing, 19
Budget, 6, 22, 49, 132, 136, 142, 159–60, 182, 222, 288, 322
   project, 260–2
Builder's quote syndrome, 277
Business cycles, 4, 210

Canute, 221–2, 234
Capacity planning, 276
Capital expenditure, 15, 258
Change control, 21, 110
Change management, 18, 26, 39, 154
Chaos, 50, 89, 99, 101, 120, 173
   chaos theory, 50, 89
   chaotic system, 50

City-state, 64
Cleopatra, 39
Club of Rome, 51
Co-evolution, 254
Collegiate environment, 78–9, 328
Command and control management, 60
Communicating in the dark, 131
Communities of practice, 331
Community, The IT community, 130, 180
Compatiblity, forward compatible
    applications, 207
Complex Adaptive Systems, 96–104, 340, 345
    complexity modelling, 100
Compression, 25, 34, 61–2, 75
Consistency, 85, 241, 270
Consultant, 37, 103–4, 114, 145, 223, 253, 258,
    292
Consulting, 15, 104, 154
Control, guidance versus control, 172
Core IT Production, 144, 268–9, 283
    the body electric, 294
    self-organising, 292
Cows, If c. could fly, 80–1, 313
Crossing the chasm, 135, 214
Customer capital, 86
Customer, definition of, 187
Customer-focused culture, 187–8
Customer power, growth of, 77

de Bono, Edward, 38, 155, 158–9
Decision making in organisations, 81
Democracy in organisations, 76, 88
Determinism, 171
Digitised Cash, 73
Disaster recovery plan, 274
Disintermediation, 63
Distributed control in complex systems, 100
Documentation, 21, 237–8, 247, 262, 273, 278,
    320
Domain management, 138
Domains in IT, 129, 140
Downsize, 17, 53, 164
Dumbsizing, 19
Dual-economy, 47, 53, 74

Durability, 268, 270, 275, 296
    definition of, 268

Economies of scale to economy of scope of
    network, 87
Education, 75, 321
Emergence, 18, 57, 101, 104–5, 299
Empathy, computers and, 68
Empowerment, 65, 70
Encryption, 73
Environment, 52, 262–3, 269, 293–4, 308
    definition of a business environment, 262
External customer, 32, 185, 188, 199

Facilities Manager, 61, 138, 267, 270, 274
Facilities, and factory operations
    management techniques, 283
Factory, IT, 135, 283, *see also* Core IT
    Production
Federal Express, 31
Federal IT organisation, supply and demand,
    132
FIFO, Fit in or ..., 109
Filters of new technology, 225
Finance and administration in IT, 142
Flow of money, 49
Foreign commerce, 48
Foreign investment, 48
Formative evaluation, 57, 254–7, 261–62
Forward compatible applications, 207
Fractal rules, 103–5, 234–5, 293–4, 307, 334
Frameworks, 71, 129, 134–6, 140, 148, 173
    cost justification, 136
    future, 135
    list of frameworks, 134
FUTURE operational versus strategic work,
    117

Games people play, 184–5
GIGO, 272
Goal-posts changing, 263
Governance, 26, 78

Grievance, 8
Growth, 51, 321
Gutenberg, 63–4, 108

Handy, Charles, 8, 19, 38, 46, 58, 145, 167
Head Office, 239
Help-desk, 268, 271–2, 294
Here be dragons, 39
Hourglass organisation, 326
Humanity, loss of, 51, 66, 104
Hygiene in IT, 6, 9, 12, 113, 120, 345

Ignoring, 15, 18, 32, 246
Inclusion, 280
Incremental change, 5, 46–7, 91
Industrial revolution, 59, 82, 95–6, 105, 136
Infomediaries, 63
Informating, 5–7
Information exhaust, 74
Information flows, 50, 69
Information in self-managed teams, 338
Information overload, 71, 74
Information revolution, 82, 95–8, 107–8, 172
In-source, 15, 16, 18, 290–2
Integrity, definition of IT integrity, 268
Intellectual capital, 29, 319
Internal customers, 112, 185–6, 188
Internal versus external perspective, 118
International trade, 48
Internet, 1, 34, 69, 70, 80
Internet based backup, 75
IT costs, 289
IT factory, 128, *see also* Core IT Production
IT function failure, 132
IT people:
    hourglass organisation, 326
    motivators, 316
    people-centred management, 324
    remuneration, 318
    remuneration - the IADO model, 319
    theory of incomplete contracts, 318
    treating employees as people, 322, 325

IT strategy:
    and executive courage, 309
    and vision, 304
    as a complex adaptive system, 307
    compilation, 302
    levels of freedom, 306
    stakeholder analysis, 90, 105, 124, 129, 148,
        199, 303
IT vision, 140

Jobshift, 315

Knowledge assets, 29
Knowledge economy, 59
Knowledge management, 160, 190, 246, 308,
    347

Learning, 7, 9–11, 57, 66, 71, 86, 99, 103–4,
    108, 229, 232, 257, 267, 287, 328, 336
Legacy systems, 16, 144, 282
Limits of growth, 51

Magazine management, 122–3, 292
Maintenance, 27, 31, 87, 143, 177, 230, 237,
    260, 267, 273–4, 319
    conflict between maintenance and
        development, 273
Management:
    AMTS, attention, meaning, trust and self,
        84, 327
    command and control management, 60
    magazine management, 122–3, 292
    management of attention, 83
    management of meaning, 83, 335
    management of trust, 84
    management styles, POEM to AMTS, 83
    line-of-sight management, 60, 67, 82, 105
    moving to leadership, 102
    of distributed workers, 68
    paternalistic, 78–80, 316
Manhattan Island, 31
Miniaturization, 60–1

Mission, 21, 59, 71, 79, 85, 102–3, 111, 138, 140, 148, 173, 217, 259, 271, 272, 349
Misunderstood, 10, 263
Mitroff and Linstone, thinking styles, 152–4
Momentum line, 120, 143–4, 269
Money flows, 50, 69
Motivation, 14, 79, 115
Motivators of IT workers, 142, 316

Newton, Isaac, 160, 168
Non-financial measures, 58
Nucor Steel, 62
Nuts and bolts in IT, 124

Object-oriented development, 123
Operations, IT operations as background activity, 137
Organisations:
   decision making in organisations, 81
   democracy in organisations, 76, 88
   four-leafed clover organisations, Charles Handy, 145
   organisational forms, the executive club, 329
   supply and demand, federal IT organisation, 132
Otis Elevators, 31
Outcomes:
   outcome space, 57, 253–6, 261, 264–5
   difference between an output and an outcome, 252
   the need for visible, 253
   defining, 253
Output, 17, 52, 59, 108, 228, 252, 320, 322, 337
Outsourcing, 15, 17–19, 62, 257, 268, 288–9, 291–2
   fit with payroll systems, 290
   what to outsource, 292
   why businesses outsource IT, 137

Package, 11, 17, 25, 31, 41, 66, 189, 234, 280, 282, 319
Paradox, 28, 158, 239, 324

Participation, forces driving participation in organisations, 76, 231
Partnership, 85, 181, 259
   exploitation in, 132
   IT/Business, 132
   people as partners, 191
Past-focus in IT, 127
Pay, 67, 318–9, 321–2
   pay for play, 118
   for attendance, 67
PC – portable computing, 66, 69
People:
   people are important, 119, 347
   people environment, changes in, 77
   as work-capable units, 169
Perspective, a newcomer's, 267
Peruvian Indians, 46
Peter Principle, 267
POEM, Plan, organise, execute, monitor, 83, 102, 138, 259, 333
Pollution, 53
Power:
   coercive, 197
   expert, 197
   invested, 196–7
   organisational, 196
   positional, 196
   relational, 197
   respect, 197
   results, 197
Printing press, 64, 108
Proactive IT, 132
Profit centre, 16
Project, definition, 260
Project, environments and domains, 262
Protection of territory, 223
Prototype, 11, 21, 227, 234
Psychological contract, 314
Punters not investors, 56

Quality:
   five approaches you can take to quality, 283
   and Service Level Agreements, 280–1

Rapid Application Development, 20, 265
Re-engineering, 127, 314
Reframing your thinking, 9, 13, 151
Relationship management, 26
   definition, 130
   successful, 131
Relationships:
   changing relationship between employers
     and employees, 87
   mapping of, 193
   organisational, 178
   and stress, 178
Resistance to change, 13, 19, 231
Return on information investment, 15, 109
Revolution within a revolution, 95
Reward, *see* Pay
   Rewarding the self-managed team, 334
Reward system, behaviour consistent with,
   141

Satisficing, 171, 172
Scenario planning, 299–300, 306, 348–9
Scope-creep and goal-creep, 309–10
SDLC, 20, 24, 27
See it when you believe it, 115
Self-managed teams, 332, 339
Self-organisation, and information, 71, 190,
   234
Service Level Agreements:
   form versus function, 279
   waste of time, 278
   relationship based, 281
   why an SLA is necessary, 279
Seven IT domains, 129
Shamrock organisation, 145
Shareholder, 55–6, 84, 187, 304
   as punters, 56
Short-termism, 88
Sign-off, 4, 22, *see also* Blackmail
Silver bullet, 11, 221
Six hat thinking, 38
Socio-psycho contract, 35
Solutions:
   solutions providers, 15, 16, 251, 258–60, 263
   solutions provision, 132, 263

and projects, 260
from an IT perspective, 251
over the wall solutions, 251
providing solutions when the goal-posts
   change, 263
Russian dolls, 257
the new role of in-house solutions
   providers, 258
why vendors cannot provide complete
   solutions, 252
Specification, 4, 21–2, 24–6, 237, 253, 330
Stability, 28, 35, 85, 110, 124, 135, 206, 230,
   234, 268–74, 286, 289, 296, 320, 325, 348
Standards:
   abolishing standards, 238
   advice on using, 237
   and boredom, 247
   dealing with those who ignore them, 248
   definition, 238
   dismantling old standards, 244
   implementing, 247
   reasons for imposing, 239
   removal of old standards, 244
   setting, applying and monitoring, 242
   the need to sell standards, 245
   why have standards, 240
   why people ignore them, 237
Stewardship, 76, 343
Strategic intent, 57, 111, 282, 349
Strategic IT, Three elements of, 139
Strategy, 29, 138–9, 297, 306–7, 344, 347
   analysis paralysis, 297
   communicating the strategy, 302–3
   scenario thinking, 140, 299, 302, 305
Sub-optimise projects, 201
Success, business, 114
Sugar-coated information, 81
Supply and demand, federal IT organisation,
   132
Systems development, 4, 239
Systems development life cycle, 20, 27
Systems thinking, 170

Tangible production to intangible outcomes,
   86

Team, 163–4, 185, 186, 258–9, 262, 264, 275, 278, 309, 310, 325, 327, 329, 332–6, 339
  composition of new implementations, 231
Technology:
  adoption processes pages, 226
  issues and problems in implementing new, 230
  keeping up with, 234
  filters of new technology, 225
  self-organization and, 234
  triggering the technology adoption process, 226
  undercover technology, 222, 224
  why do technology?, 60
Technophobia, 9
Telecommuting, 82, 241
Theory of business, 111
Thinking:
  active and passive voiced thinking, 163, 166
  five ways to be wrong, 155–6
  four ways to be right, 159–62
  renegade, 174
  systems thinking, 170
  the new IT mindset, 165
  thinking styles, 152–4
Threats to IT, 14–30
Transformating, 5, 6, 7

Transformation, 1, 9, 13, 26, 60, 135, 324
Triggers of new technology adoption, 226
Trigger point, 4

Unintended consequences, 63, 64
University of IT, 136
Unrealistic expectations, 10–11
User acceptance, 25

Value for money, 3
Value of human capital, 169
Velocity of a business, 100, 143
Vicious cycle, 6, 7

Ways to be right, 159
Ways to be wrong, 156
When users ask for the best, 275
Why businesses exist, 55
Withdrawal strategies, 23
Work:
  measuring the value of, 67
  specialised knowledge work, 77
  people as work capable units, 58
Workflow systems in IT, 330
World economy, 48